Library of Congress Control Number: 2006907664

ISBN: 1-893618-79-X

David Bull Publishing, logo, and colophon are
trademarks of David Bull Publishing, Inc.

This product is officially licensed by Dorna SL,
owners of the MotoGP trademark (© Dorna 2006)

Printed in England

10   9   8   7   6   5   4   3   2   1

David Bull Publishing
4250 East Camelback Road
Suite K150
Phoenix, AZ 85018

602-852-9500
602-852-9503 (fax)

www.bullpublishing.com

Book and cover design Lee Parsons

Photography All photographs copyright Neil Spalding
unless otherwise indicated

DAVID BULL PUBLISHING

MotoGP
Technology

Neil Spalding

CONTENTS

Look at the regular blotches in Rossi's tyre mark. What do you think is going on?

© MARK WERNHAM

INTRODUCTION

Since I decided to earn a crust writing about MotoGP the learning curve has been almost vertical. When I came to the MotoGP paddock I thought I was fairly well trained, but I never expected to see the lengths the teams and factories go to to make their bikes competitive.

It's one thing to see teams moving the forks and changing the adjusters to make a bike work for a rider, but here were teams building swingarms, or for that matter entire frames, and then simply throwing them away in the search for just a few parts of a second every lap.

To arrive just as the top class experienced its biggest changes for 30 years was even better. Moving from years of 500cc two-strokes to 990cc four-strokes meant that the whole of the pit lane was experimenting, looking for answers to their new problems. Whether the problem be engine braking into corners, throttle sensitivity at the apex or grip on the way out, the arrival of the big four-strokes had seriously changed the game.

Following those changes has not always been easy, but even in the notoriously secretive world of a racing paddock enough information can be gleaned to understand the magnitude of the tasks, and the way in which workable practical solutions evolve.

This is written as the era of the 990cc bike draws to a close, but the move to 800s will start the battle again. In the meantime, the development that we have seen has already changed the face of sport motorcycling, and over the next few years the technologies born in the heat of the battles on track will mature onto all road bikes.

In particular, electronic throttles represent a major advance in the fight against emissions. At first they were there to try and control the power, but the drop in the permissible fuel capacity from 24 to 22 litres really increased the speed of their development. Then, once the problems were understood, the fuel consumption came down and, in Yamaha's case, power outputs increased by up to eight per cent as well, and all in the course one single year.

If we could get similar improvements out of our normal road bikes, MotoGP would pay for itself in weeks. And we will get those improvements because that's the way the world in which we live is going.

This then is my record of the changes we have seen in the pit lane in the last five years, the stories of the bikes and their factories as they stood to meet the challenges set by the MotoGP rule book. It is also an explanation of some of the major technologies that have matured in the same period. It's not exhaustive, way too much has been happening for that, but I hope it gives you an insight into the machinery that makes MotoGP one of the greatest sports on the planet.

THE HISTORY

So how did we get here?

Moto Guzzi's outrageous V8 500 was the peak of technology in the late '50s.

Motorcycle racing has a long and honourable history, and one of the first major events to be organised was the 1907 Isle of Man TT. The First World War intervened between 1914 and 1918, and it wasn't until the early 1920s that classic Grands Prix started. By the mid-1920s, races were being organised in half-a-dozen different European countries, but no championship existed to draw all these races together until 1938 when the FICM (Federation Internationale des Clubs Motorcyclists), the predecessor to the current FIM, announced a European championship. That series was to last less than two years, the second year being brought to an abrupt end after only seven of the planned nine rounds, because of the start of the Second World War.

The technical rules then were very different from today – each classic race catered for bikes with capacities of 500cc, 350cc and 250cc, reflecting the common road-going engine classes of the time. All the machines were usually on track at the same time. Supercharging was allowed, and the 500 class was won in the first year by BMW with Georg Meier on a supercharged 500 twin, and in the second year by Serafini on a supercharged Gilera four. DKW, using a supercharged 250 two-stroke, won the small class on both occasions, and to show that the classic single-cylinder design still had its place,

the 350 class was won by Ted Mellors on a British Velocette. As war broke out, there were many supercharged bikes being prepared, from the Benelli 250cc in-line four to the Velocette Roarer with its contra-rotating crankshafts.

After the war it was some time before a truly international series started. It wasn't easy, and poor quality fuel was an issue. Indeed, for a while, the availability of any fuel at all was a serious problem. Nevertheless, in 1946 the FCIM met to try to set the rules to allow world championship motorcycling to begin. New technical rules were put together that suited the more austere environment of the time. Supercharging was to be banned, as was high-octane fuel, but the classic engine sizes remained the same at 500cc, 350cc and 250cc with a new 125cc class joining in.

The ban on supercharging meant that a good number of the pre-war singles remained competitive, albeit with lower compression ratios and less power, but many pre-war two-strokes relied upon some form of supercharging, so they were out. Race machine production took time to restart, but once it did it wasn't long before technology started to move forward again. AJS brought out a very tidy twin-cylinder 500, nicknamed the Porcupine, and then Gilera arrived with an air-cooled across-the-frame four-cylinder machine. Both, however, had their roots in pre-war designs intended for supercharging. By 1949 the economies of the world were on the mend, and the FCIM linked the six or so races that had restarted into a formal world championship. Even then, Germany was unable to take part, only being allowed back into international competition in 1951.

The singles initially struggled, as more and more multi-cylinder bikes appeared, but the wider availability of better fuels proved to be their saving, and the battle between the light and narrow singles and the increasingly complex multis was on. It was a battle that was to last until the late 1950s, and it showed beautifully the manner in which light and easy-to-ride motorcycles can hold their own against much more powerful but cumbersome opposition. Over time the number of classes expanded, with the classes being joined by 50s.

In the 1950s the smaller classes were dominated by the Italians; a burgeoning utilitarian motorcycle industry needed somewhere to showcase its skills, and the Grands Prix were perfect for that. Virtually the whole of the Italian industry withdrew from Grand Prix racing for cost reasons in the late '50s, however, because the arrival of cheap cars had simply destroyed their day-to-day markets. It hadn't been all Italian, though. Factories from other countries came into racing, proved their technology and left during the same period – NSU and DKW being particular examples. Advances in the understanding of exhaust harmonics, predominantly by Walter Kaaden in the late '50s, brought two-strokes back onto the scene too.

As most of the Italians left, the Japanese industry was just kicking itself into high gear and, as ever, racing motorcycles offered the perfect way to demonstrate technical prowess. The first Japanese bikes arrived at the Isle of Man TT in 1959, and over the next decade they went from simple single- and twin-cylinder machines all the way up to 20,000rpm 250cc sixes. The technology race exploded as engines were persuaded to develop ever-higher power outputs with more and more cylinders. As a result, bigger gearboxes containing more and more gears were added, allowing the riders to make the most of ever-smaller power bands. Faced with increased costs and the pressing need to use R&D facilities for production-bike purposes, the Japanese slowly withdrew until only Yamaha were left in 1968. The Japanese made race bikes for sale, but these were typically simpler in design than the works machines. Faced with clear evidence that the costs had got out of control, the FIM (the FCIM renamed) brought in rules that limited racing machines to a single cylinder for 50s, two cylinders for 125s and 250s, and four cylinders for 350s and 500s. Gearboxes could contain no more than six gears. These rules reflected quite closely the 'customer' bikes available from some factories. Economy racing was back in vogue.

For the next few years, GP racing was supported by production racers made predominantly by Yamaha, and it wasn't until the mid-'70s that the factories came back in force. Both Yamaha and Suzuki had only ever produced small capacity motorcycles, but, as they started to expand their ranges, they decided that taking on MV Agusta, the current leaders in the 500 class, would be a way to change their image. Yamaha arrived with a 500cc across-the-frame four based on a pair of 250 TZ twins in 1973, and a year later Suzuki presented a square-four; both were two-stroke. All of a sudden the factories were racing again. MV Agusta had dominated the 500 class for years and, after a series of battles with Honda in the mid-'60s, no one had seriously challenged them for several years. But MV Agusta was a small privately-owned team making its own motorcycles, and the occasional road bike; it was a four-stroke factory. MV fought the new two-strokes as hard as they could, but scored their last win in 1976. After that, all GP racing was essentially two-stroke, except for one particular bike.

Honda re-entered racing in the late 1970s. By that time their car business was up and running and they had learned enough about emissions to keep their bikes within the rules for a while. Honda had always been known as a four-stroke racing factory – the foundations of their business are four-stroke. So their strategy was to return and race in the premier class with a four-stroke. But Honda are also quite adventurously managed, and those managers knew they had to develop a racing culture again. Having been virtually 12 years out of racing meant the core of the racing department had gone. They launched the NR500 project in 1979, an ultimately unsuccessful oval-piston eight valves-per-cylinder V4. The bike contained many technical innovations (some successful, others not) and while it was not a success on the track it succeeded brilliantly in educating a new group of engineers into the world of racing.

After three years of effort, and with Yamaha and Suzuki slugging it out at the front of the 500 class, Honda got practical and built the V3 500 two-stroke, known as the NS500. Still unconventional, the V3 was smaller and lighter than the V and square fours of the opposition. Freddie Spencer seized the championship in 1983 and, from that point on, the 500 Grand Prix class became a three-way fight, and all two-stroke again.

The quality of racing in the '80s and '90s was, at times, absolutely superb – the light and difficult to master 500s providing a wonderful spectacle. But, from a technical point of view, little real progress was being made. At the same time that emissions fears brought legislation against the two-strokes, Grand Prix motorcycles were losing the all-important link with their road-going cousins. The costs of Grand Prix racing need justification. Technology can be developed without going near a racetrack, but you learn an awful lot very quickly when you are in a racing environment. Re-establishing the link to their day-to-day products became a top priority for the factories.

Towards the late 1990s, Honda and Yamaha got together and proposed that the 500 class should be changed. It should be replaced by something that allowed them to develop new technologies that would be useful on the road, and that would keep the spectacle on track. In 2000 it was announced that the top class of motorcycle racing would change from being a 500cc (by default a two-stroke class) into a four-stroke only 990cc class.

As this book is written, that 990cc class is coming to an end – the bikes have proved to be just too powerful. Significant technical milestones have been achieved, both in making the power and learning to use and manage it. MotoGP racing has a worldwide audience much larger than it was just five years ago. In an acknowledgement of the staggering levels of power now routinely seen, the class is being replaced by one using 800cc engines. The five years of 990cc MotoGP have been another golden age of technical development and superb racing, and a great promotion for the sport of motorcycling.

THE RULES

Pushing the limits within the boundaries

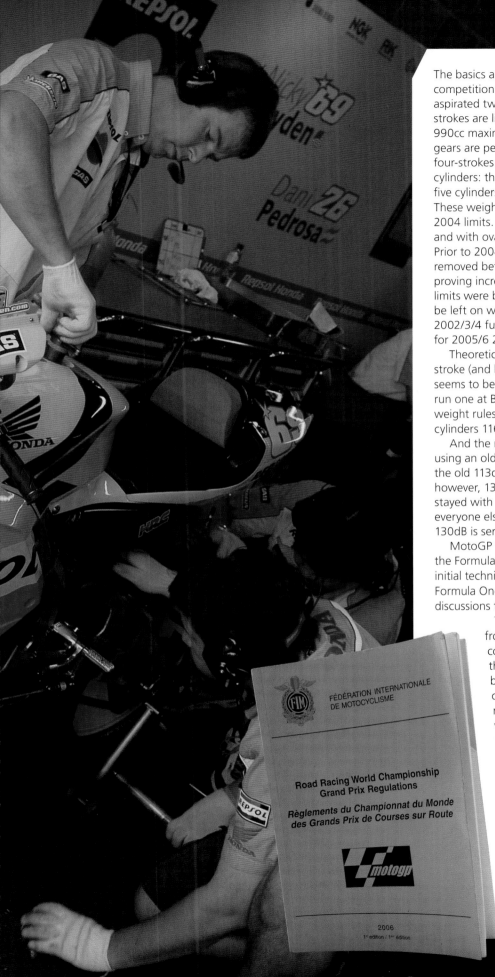

The basics are quite simple. MotoGP is a competition open to motorcycles with normally-aspirated two- or four-stroke engines. Two-strokes are limited to 500cc and four-strokes to a 990cc maximum capacity. No more than six gears are permitted, and minimum weights for four-strokes are based on the number of cylinders: three cylinders or less 138kg; four or five cylinders 148kg; six cylinders or more 158kg. These weights reflect a 3kg increase over the 2004 limits. Engines with five cylinders or less, and with oval pistons, suffer a 10kg penalty. Prior to 2004, the rules required fuel tanks to be removed before weighing, but, as this was proving increasingly difficult, the higher weight limits were brought in, and the tanks can now be left on when the bike is weighed. The 2002/3/4 fuel load maximum was 24 litres, and for 2005/6 22 litres.

Theoretically, you could still use a 500cc two-stroke (and have up to 32 litres of fuel!) but that seems to be discouraged. WCM were the last to run one at Brno in 2003. They have their own weight rules: two cylinders or less 101kg; three cylinders 116kg; four cylinders 131kg.

And the noise – yes, the noise. If you are using an old 500 two-stroke you are down at the old 113dB, if you have a four-stroke, however, 130dB is the limit. Only Yamaha have stayed with any form of muffling (silencer); everyone else is running fully open pipes – and 130dB is seriously loud.

MotoGP was quite deliberately shaped to be the Formula One of motorcycling. Indeed, the initial technical rules owed a lot to those used by Formula One at the time the initial MotoGP discussions took place.

The rules carefully distance the bikes from production models. Whether for contractual reasons, or just to maintain the purity of the field, the initial rule book specified that the engine cases, cylinders and cylinder heads 'should not be from industrial production'; which, despite the clumsy English, was supposed to mean no volume production parts (if we were writing legal documents we should still be asking for a definition of 'volume'). WCM, in particular, fell foul of this rule and were kept off track waiting for their own heads, cylinders and cases to be cast.

The desire to keep some distance between street and GP bikes has now become even more difficult to define, with the latest

FÉDÉRATION INTERNATIONALE DE MOTOCYCLISME

Road Racing World Championship Grand Prix Regulations

Règlements du Championnat du Monde des Grands Prix de Courses sur Route

motogp

2006
1ère édition / 1er édition

iteration of the rule book insisting that four-stroke machines not entered by a member of the MSMA (the Motorcycle Sport Manufacturers Association is an organisation currently made up of Aprilia, Ducati, Honda, Kawasaki, Suzuki and Yamaha) must be approved for participation by the Grands Prix Commission (which is a committee comprising representatives of rights-holders Dorna, IRTA (the Teams) the FIM and the MSMA). Suffice to say, the bikes cannot be road bikes.

LET'S CONSIDER THE ENGINE SIDE OF THINGS FIRST

'Normally-aspirated two- or four-stroke engines'? So, no forced induction, except for the 2% to 3% available from having the airbox inlets in the centre of pressure on the front of the nose.

Power comes from the efficient use of fuel, and the fuel capacity restrictions are deliberately designed to make fuel consumption part of the challenge. As mentioned, the rules at the start of the series specified 24 litres, and this was reduced to 22 litres for the 2005 season onwards. There are also restrictions on the make-up of the fuel. Although exhaustively specified, the broad intent of the rules is to make the fuel consumed similar to that allowed on public roads. That doesn't stop everyone having special fuels made, but this is as much about consistency of supply as for any particular power advantage.

Then there are the materials you can build your bike out of. The MotoGP restrictions on materials limit themselves to a requirement that 'the basic structure of the crankshaft and the camshaft must be made from steel or cast iron. Pistons, cylinder heads and cylinder blocks may not be composite structures which use carbon or aramid fibre reinforcing materials'. In addition, 'no parts of the motorcycle or engine may be made from metallic materials which have a specific modulus of elasticity greater than 50 Gpa/g/cm^3'.

PRACTICALITIES

During the first years of MotoGP several technologies had to be understood. On the engine side, this included controlling the effects of engine braking and the development of sophisticated throttle systems that accurately follow precisely the smallest possible rider input so that he can make the best possible use of the very small traction area available.

We haven't seen many bikes run out of fuel during a race, but fuel consumption is certainly an issue. In MotoGP we seem to have quite low peak power outputs by comparison to something like Formula One, where engines operate at about 320bhp per litre. MotoGP is still around 250bhp per litre; indeed they seem to be struggling to increase the peak power levels. But, since more

revs means more fuel usage, it is unlikely, with the current fuel restrictions, that riders will be able to rev their engines much more and expect to finish the race. Also, the right type of power, with a very sensitive throttle response, still seems easier to achieve with longer stroke, relatively slow-revving engine types. It is certainly far more important to the bike's performance.

Theoretically, the generous rules within MotoGP leave the path open for some very exotic materials. One such is a metal matrix composite (MMC) piston – lighter and stiffer than aluminium. However, advances in machining and design techniques in recent years, along with the fairly conservative rev limits, means it is far more likely that most pistons in the MotoGP pit lane will be forged in the classic WW2 aero piston material RR58, or its equivalent, rather than anything more exotic. In the same way, the current MotoGP rules appear to allow MMC cylinder liners to be used, but the construction of the engines makes it simpler to merely use plated aluminium instead.

So, although MotoGP has very open regulations, current competitors do not push the envelope very far, with the limiting factors on machine development so far being control electronics, fuel consumption and chassis design.

CHASSIS AND AERODYNAMICS

The main aim of both chassis and aerodynamic research in MotoGP is to provide the best possible handling and the best aerodynamics for all situations. There are no real restrictions on chassis design, but the material restrictions included in the engine section apply equally here. There is the standard ban on the use of titanium in anything structural, and some safety-related rules, such as the requirement for a bladder in any fuel tank made of composite materials. Beyond that, designers can do whatever they want.

Aerodynamically, the rulebook specifies what must be 'on show', and how big the fairing and seat can be. No moving aerodynamic aids are allowed, but there can be wings, as long as they are within the permitted width. There has been a slight relaxation in the limitations on fairing design in the last few years, but the rules are basically the same as those brought in at the end of 1957, when the FIM banned the then new full enclosure fairings. These fairings covered the front wheel and were responsible for a dramatic increase in top speeds, especially in the hands of the works Moto Guzzi team. Although the Moto Guzzis didn't appear to have any particular side-wind sensitivities, the cheap copies of their fairings used by some of their competitors most certainly did, and the FIM reacted to a few accidents by enshrining the exposed front and rear wheel look of the motorcycle into the regulations.

On construction, the 'normal' rules apply – from minimum diameters for the pointy ends of anything that sticks out, to the use of the bottom of the fairing as an undertray to collect oil and coolant should the engine spring a leak.

Wheel and rim sizes remain unchanged from the old 500 class. At the front the maximum rim is a 4.00 and at the rear it is a 6.25. Diameters are not restricted.

PRACTICALITIES

Initial MotoGP fairing designs included a Honda that was deliberately ineffective, aerodynamically, in a straight line but which theoretically allowed better cornering. That soon changed when Ducati turned up with an Alan Jenkins perfected fairing that ensured they set the highest top speed at most of the circuits they appeared on. Most MotoGP fairings are now at least tested in a wind tunnel. One major area of work has been perfecting radiator exhaust ducts that allow air to move easily through the radiators, removing the not inconsiderable heat the engines make, and the drag that goes with a radiator that cannot pass air easily.

Even though the rules allow aerodynamic work on the forks, the front end of the motorcycle is typically very untidy. The exposed front wheel and discs are bad enough, but the circular section front forks are an aerodynamic disaster. Some improvements can be made with a mudguard designed to help reduce the worst effects but, until it is worked out how to make the forks more aerodynamic, the front end of a MotoGP bike isn't going to be very slippery at all.

We are seeing engine design changes that allow better use of space, the latest being Suzuki's new 75° V4 and Kawasaki's new forward-leaning block. What we haven't seen are any particularly adventurous chassis designs. Although the dramatic increases in power and torque have led to a much better understanding of the physics of chassis design, from controlled flex to improved tyre grip and weight distribution, we simply have not seen the carbon monocoque chassis or the wishbone front suspension that you might have expected.

Although the limits of motorcycle performance have been pushed in the last few years, the MotoGP rule book is still one of the least restrictive in motorsport. Perhaps the reason for that is simply that none of the competitors can currently see a way to gain any further great advantage out of taking things further. However, with the 800cc formula to come, that situation may be about to change.

MATERIALS RULES – YOUNG'S MODULUS

So, what is this modulus that you are not allowed to exceed? It's a measure of the rigidity of a material, and the more rigid it is (as long as it's not also brittle), the lighter you can make things like pistons and brake calipers. The modulus of elasticity is a measure of how much force is required to elongate or stretch a material – it defines the stiffness of a material. The higher the number the more stiff the material is.

Both cars and bikes allow brake calipers to be made of aluminium with a maximum measure of 80Gpa. Normal aluminium has a Young's Gpa of 68.3, so the rulebook allows slightly stiffer material for this important part.

There is another basis of measurement that can be used. In MotoGP, materials in your engine must not exceed a specific modulus of 50Gpa/g/cm³. This is the old limit from Formula One a few years ago. This longer definition is the 'Specific Young's Modulus', rather than simply the 'Young's Modulus', i.e. it takes into account the density of the material as well as the stiffness (units are GPa/(g/cm³) rather than just GPa) so you are allowed stiff materials as long as they have a high density.

On this basis, aluminium with a modulus of 68.3 and a density of 2.83 will give a specific modulus of 68.3/2.83 = 24.1, way below the limit. This means that it is possible to use specially-made materials called metal matrix composites (MMC). Amongst other things, these materials allow the design of very light yet stiff pistons, permitting higher piston speeds and shorter strokes. In Formula One, these materials have now been banned, so alternative technologies using better machining techniques and CAD design are used instead.

Brake calipers can be made of materials slightly stiffer than aluminium.

THE MOTORCYCLE

The end product of
technology and ideas

It is not often that an entirely new racing class is launched, and extremely rare at this level of motorsport. Despite being given the opportunity to 'start again', the desire of the various race departments to carry forward existing concepts that they knew worked was very marked in the first few years. Suzuki and Yamaha built their 990 fours based on the chassis dimensions of their 500s. Kawasaki started with a big-bore version of their superbike, and Honda have admitted that the internals of their RC211V started off very similar to their RC45 superbike. But, as the class developed so did the various machines. Having learned a lot from their initial year, Suzuki built a completely new bike for the second year, as did Kawasaki. Yamaha opted for the fast development route and used several different chassis and engine combinations during the first year. Honda, on the other hand, had a very good package in their first chassis (that they allowed us to see, anyway!) and, despite trying several different variants, the original chassis design with an uprated engine, electronics and suspension, was still competitive in the final year of the class.

All this means that all the bikes are still using aluminium (or steel tube lattice in Ducati's case) beam chassis; standard type 'upside-down' forks and, with the exception of Honda, conventional engine layouts. While the basic layouts have changed over the last five years, as controlled flex of the steering head and swing-arm has been better understood, it does mean that the basic design of the bikes is currently pretty mature. That's not to say that someone isn't going to try to turn the form book upside down with a carbon-fibre monocoque chassis using hub-centre suspension in the near future, but it does mean that the level they have to reach to get it on track and be successful is very high indeed.

So, if the design of the bikes seems pretty mature, why was there a lot of excitement at a new racing class? It was mainly because, for the first time in years, there were new problems to face. The 990cc formula was designed to ensure that the class would be all about controlling an excess of power rather than an all-out horsepower race. What actually happened was that, never mind the intentions, we had a horsepower race; but instead of it being for peak horsepower, it's been for rider feel and mid-range grunt. During the same period, each of the factories has had at least one set of circumstances that has shown where the limits are in our understanding of the physics that affect the motorcycle.

Motorcycle racing hasn't seen this amount of effort put into the development of new technologies for a long time. The legacy of this return to prototype four-stroke racing will be seen in our street bikes for years – a better understanding of electronic controls, more efficient engines and better-handling bikes being just the headlines.

DUCATI

Development of the Desmosedici

ENGINE: Liquid-cooled 90° V4 four-stroke, desmodromic DOHC, four valves per cylinder

CAPACITY: 989cc

POWER: Over 250bhp

TOP SPEED: Over 216mph (347km/h)

TRANSMISSION: Six-speed cassette-type gearbox with alternative ratios available

IGNITION: Magneti Marelli programmable CDI with adjustable mapping

CHASSIS: Tubular steel trellis-style chassis, pressed aluminium swingarm

SUSPENSION: Ohlins upside-down 42mm front forks and Ohlins rear shock

WHEELS: Marchesini

TYRES: Bridgestone 16.5in front and rear

BRAKES: Brembo, two 320mm carbon front discs, two four-piston calipers, single stainless steel rear disc, twin-piston caliper.

WEIGHT: 148kg

BELOW: Early PR shots of the 2003 bike. Even though the picture is ghosted you can see there are no radiator exhausts. The open pipes are for the screamer engine used in 2003.

RIGHT: Ducati built a proper clean room environment specially for their MotoGP programme. All the engines are built here and that is where all the bikes are initially built.

Ducati came onto the scene in 2003, the second year of the MotoGP formula, with a quite spectacularly high-revving V4 engine. The Desmosedici uses Ducati's favourite desmodromic valve actuation system. This system dispenses with valve springs, relying on rockers to mechanically open and close each valve. From the start, Ducati revved the engine to 16,000rpm plus, sufficient to ensure that they were the fastest bikes in a straight line at most of the initial GPs of 2003.

Cooling was always going to be an issue, and a high-pressure cooling system was fitted from the start. Higher pressure raises the coolant's boiling point, which means that the whole engine can run hotter, and a slightly smaller radiator can be used. As Ducati discovered, though, it only works if the bike is designed to deal with the side effects.

The initial fairing design had very small radiator exhaust ducts and, with the engine giving off a lot of heat, the bike gained a reputation for 'cooking' its riders. The fairings were modified over the first few races, and a revised design – featuring larger exhaust ducts and rider cooling vents – was fitted from Brno onwards. However, these modifications were less aerodynamically efficient, and the consequent increase in drag brought a temporary end to Ducati's domination of the top-speed listings.

ABOVE: You can see that this fairing has the larger radiator exhausts and upper fairing airscoops, introduced at Brno in 2003, to cool both the bike and the rider more efficiently.

BELOW: Capirossi was suffering badly from the heat given off by the engine during the races. These cooling holes were drilled to try and cool him.

After the weight distribution of the 2004 bike proved to be difficult to handle, two 2003 bikes were built from spares for a back-to-back test at Le Mans after the race. GP3 is on the left and GP4 on the right.

The 2004 bodywork was cosmetically similar, but under the surface the ducting delivering air to the radiator and routing it out past the rider was completely revised. It was at this point, though, that Ducati tripped themselves up; testing involved revised weight distribution which theoretically would help traction but which appeared to be giving the riders some problems. Then, at the final test of the year, Ducati introduced an uprated engine. Simultaneously, Michelin changed from 17in to 16.5in front tyres, and the conbination was enough to cause serious problems for the riders. A disastrous first GP of the year was followed by an announcement of a major retrenchment at Jerez. The first few GPs of the year would be testing different weight distributions. A couple of back-to-back tests (the old bike against the new bike) would be arranged, and a couple of major revisions to the engine would occur that would make it more rideable.

Ducati have always tried to leapfrog the other teams – not for them to simply follow along and be beaten – and they had to do something major to jump ahead. The trouble was, the second-year engine was substantially more powerful and the bike responded too quickly to throttle inputs. As a result it was almost unrideable. Just as the rest of pit lane had recognised that Yamaha's big bang had changed perceptions of grip, Ducati addressed their very quick but flawed new engine with a major redesign, resulting in an irregular-firing crankshaft being fitted and tested immediately after the Catalunya race. Most irregular-firing engines seem to produce less peak power than their screamer versions. There are several theories as to the advantages of these engines, and one is that the slightly softer power that they produce is simply easier for the rider to come to terms with. It took Ducati most of 2004 to get their bike competitive again, and it wasn't until the last race of the series that Bayliss managed to get to the podium.

The Ducati engine is a 90° V4 and, as such, has perfect primary balance; even with its irregular firing order it is a very smooth engine in vibration terms. Like the other factories, Ducati will not release their engine specs, but we believe the engine has an 86mm bore and a 42.6mm stroke. This makes the Desmosedici one of the most over-

The final part of sorting out the 2004 bike was the adoption of a 'Twin Pulse' motor. This required separate pipes. This is the new engine's first outing which also involved the use of a large gyroscope mounted on the tail for datalogging purposes.

The early swingarms were fabricated from several pieces of aluminium.

The screamer engine introduced at the start of 2004 used two 2-into-1 pipes. It proved to be too brutal for the rider to handle.

A shift light was considered a necessity.

DESMODROMIC VALVE ACTUATION

Desmodromic valve actuation, in its current form, uses a simple conventional opening rocker and an L-shaped closing rocker moved by a reverse-form cam lobe. One tip of the L-shaped closer runs on the cam, the other hooks under a top-hat-shaped closing shim secured to the valve by collets. One supposed benefit of this arrangement is the high rate of 'jerk' (the rate of acceleration applied to the valve) that can be applied to open and shut the valves. Ducati is known to have spent some time dealing with the issues that came from much higher revs than they had previously dealt with, and the way those forces make the 90° rocker flex in use. This is technology that is directly applicable to future road bike developments at Ducati. Initial Ducati PR enthused about the reduction in internal friction this arrangement delivered, mainly as a result of the minimal effort used in compressing the very light valve springs used in this design. Other commentators point out, though, that while other valve systems require more effort to compress a valve spring and open the valve they then 'give back' that energy as the valve shuts and the spring acts against the closing side of the cam lobe.

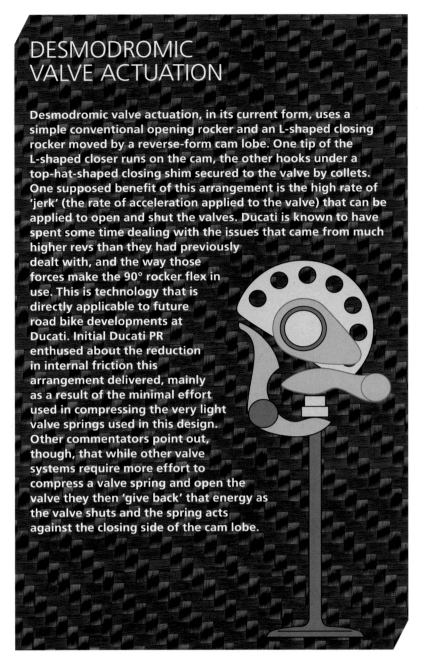

square motorcycle engines ever produced, with a bore/stroke ratio of 2.02. The genesis of the engine was a joint collaboration between Ducati and Piero Ferrari's High Performance Engineering concern. Ducati needed to understand much higher-revving engines than they had previously dealt with, and Piero Ferrari's organisation had a lot of experience of current Formula 1 technology. Formula 1 rules had changed just a few years previously, with all engines required to be V10s and the basic 249cc cylinder design of the 1995 044/1 3.0-litre V12 was available. While the engine was undoubtedly designed specifically for the Desmosedici a large chunk of the know-how came from F1. HPE failed to persuade Ducati to

use the pneumatic valve actuation that came with the original Ferrari, Ducati preferring to remain with the Desmodromic valve control that is the unique selling point of their street bike range.

Another new development for Ducati was the design of a vertically-stacked gearbox that allowed the use of a longer swingarm.

Just like all the other manufacturers, Ducati sought to control the hopping effects, which a high-compression four-stroke has on the rear suspension and rear tyre grip, by fitting a slipper clutch. Looking very similar to their superbike unit, the clutch used four springs to clamp the pack together, and plain ramps. It was felt that the ball mechanism, usually built into slipper clutches for smooth operation, would suffer under 250bhp and so instead the clutch is taken off and serviced after every track outing. Ducati first used a motor that looked very similar to a Yamaha EXUP power valve actuator, to act as a throttle kicker, but by mid-2004 they too were using uprated Weber Marelli electronics to help out with traction control. While the 90° V provided plenty of space between the cylinder heads for throttle bodies and efficient inlet tract porting, it made the engine long. This forced the bike to be very long with all the side-effects you would expect on the handling. Since the start, the engine has always revved very high. Indeed, we know that it's been fuelled up to nearly 18,000 revs, and while it has undoubtedly been tested at these revs it's unlikely they would be used on the racetrack except under excessive downshifting. The engine, however, has proved to be extremely reliable, typically being used for two Grands Prix before being removed for servicing.

After the start of 2004, the engine and the chassis needed substantial development to get them balanced enough to actually win races. Ducati's wins in mid-2005 were undoubtedly down to the tyres being particularly well suited to individual circuits, but the tyres would not have helped if the bike had not also been ready. It is a testament to Ducati's development skills that the bike that had been almost unrideable in early 2004 was winning races in 2005. But there were clear signs that some parts of the bike were on their limit to achieve this. By the time the bike was winning races, it was quite common to see tyre marks on the front cylinder head and on the bottom of the radiator immediately above. If they keep the same basic architecture, and all the signs are that they will, Ducati could be one of the main beneficiaries of the new 800cc capacity, for no other reason than a shorter stroke engine will itself not be as long and will allow a little more leeway in the chassis setup.

The Ducati chassis is unique in not having the support outside the end of the swingarm. Ducati's

1 The engine acts as part of the chassis with the frame being mounted onto the cylinder heads.

2 The carbon fibre airbox needs to be strong to act as a resonant chamber for more power.

3 The swingarm pivots directly in the crankcase.

4 A Ducati standard four-spring slipper clutch is fitted. The additional two holes are to allow the clutch to be pinned solid for starting through the rear tyre with a slave motor.

design uses high-quality bearings built into the crankcase immediately inside of the swingarm pivot, and their engineers are quite certain that this is as strong, if not stronger, than any of the other designs in the pit lane. Capirossi, however, was certain that he had handling difficulties because of the lack of additional support outboard of the pivot. Ducati addressed this by providing two additional spars on a chassis during a test after the Phillip Island Grand Prix in October 2004. The modification was quite convoluted, as the strut had to travel between both front and rear engine mounts, necessitating modified catch tanks and alternator, both of which were in the way. Capirossi declared himself satisfied with the result and ran the modified chassis all the way

1 The swingarm was designed to rely on the bearings in the crankcases.

2 Capirossi believed the lack of outboard support for the swingarm allowed the bike to weave in a straight line so special outriggers were fitted to his bike. These are the alloy ones used from Mugello onwards in 2005.

through to Mugello in 2005. At that time, supposedly in a quest to reduce weight, the additional strut was redesigned in aluminium. The chassis was only then changed after Capirossi's successful ride at Brno. Although the Ducati swingarm design was extremely strong, one of the downsides of mounting the pivot directly on the crankcase was the lack of adjustment. Immediately after the MotoGP, however, when it was obvious that Bridgestone had found a way to develop more grip, the swingarm pivot position on Capirossi's bike was changed so that, under power, the tyre was forced more firmly into the tarmac. Moving the swingarm position meant that the outrigger struts couldn't be used and, once Capirossi had won a couple of Grands Prix without them, they never returned.

2005 brought new pressures for Ducati. The reduction in fuel tank capacity from 24 litres to 22 litres set a difficult target for all the factories, but particularly so for Ducati because their engine is such a high-revving unit. If the engine is turning at 16,000rpm and displaces 990cc, then very close to 8000 litres of air is being put through the engine every minute, containing the appropriate amount of fuel for the correct mixture for burning. Ducati sought to address the situation several different ways. The engine was made as efficient as possible, the fuel tanks were filled as far as they could (with any fuel that might escape because of heat expansion being held in the bike with the use of clips and pliers on the breather pipes) and Ducati attempted to build an automatic clutch. The logic of the clutch design was fearsomely simple – if the engine management computer, throttle systems and slipper clutches were all working overtime to kill off engine-braking, it would allow the engine to take over on the entry to each corner. This would have the effect of dramatically reducing engine revs on the approach to corners, and the sum total of fuel saved would allow Ducati to run at maximum power during the rest of the Grand Prix. The major issue was the clutch disengaging smoothly and, most important, re-engaging smoothly. The system was tested during the winter of 2004 and was given its first public airing at Catalunya immediately prior to the start of the season. Unfortunately, although Ducati had a very successful winter's testing, with the riders looking forward to the new season kicking off, suddenly, just before the first race, they were asked to ride a machine with a completely new system on it. There were several small crashes at Catalunya but the system was retained and used at Jerez both in testing and in practice for the Grand Prix.

Capirossi set a competitive time, well inside the top ten, but in the final two laps of practising he crashed heavily, injuring his ankle. It appeared the system was particularly difficult to set up for qualifying tyres. There's uncertainty as to whether this was because more time was needed to find the right settings or whether the violent way the machine had to be used on qualifying tyres gave the system problems. Whatever was the case, after practice the decision was made to remove the clutch systems, and on Sunday morning both bikes came out with conventional slipper clutches fitted. The system was tried again at the end of the year at Valencia, where the opportunity was taken to do a back-to-back test against the figures from the conventional slipper clutch during the Grand Prix. However, the technical difficulties in making the system smooth and easy to control have ruled it out for the time being. That's a shame, if for no other reason than the way it sounded. When the bike was on track and one was standing in the Jerez pit lane you'd be suddenly aware of a red motorcycle whistling past emitting virtually no noise, then, as it pitched into the first corner, suddenly exploding into life as the rider opened the throttle and simultaneously the engine revved up and the clutch engaged – quite spectacular.

After the problems at the start of 2004, you'd have thought that Ducati would have chosen not to experiment on the bikes immediately before

ABOVE: The GP05 kept the electronic clutch switch gear on the top triple clamp all year. The rev counter for 2005 was also uprated, the dash allowing revs of up to 19,000rpm to be displayed!

BELOW: Even with the bikes on track, Capirossi's manager Carlo Pernat keeps briefing the press. Note that Bridgestone have a very close relationship.

© DUCATI CORSE

The dyno room at Ducati Corse is a state-of-the-art facility with motors being required to run reliability tests lasting several hours.

the start of the season, but they did it again with the clutch. It took Capirossi several races to return to fitness and Checa also took his time in declaring himself fully race ready. The elimination of the automatic clutch meant that Ducati had to revert to plan B – running the bike deliberately lean wherever fuel was an issue. With a lean mixture the bike did not have access to full power as often as Ducati would have liked. This is not such an issue at circuits like Sachsenring, where the race distance is shorter and the circuit type does not encourage plenty of full-throttle use, but at places like Mugello it is most certainly an issue.

For 2005 Ducati decided to set themselves apart from Honda and Yamaha and use Bridgestones. Although their tyres were already being used by Kawasaki and Suzuki, Bridgestone had only won races with Honda, and Ducati looked as if they could give them more opportunities to win. It was certainly the first time any team had walked away from the opportunity to use Michelins. For Bridgestone it mattered that they had a team with a pair of full-power bikes – 260bhp, just like the Hondas. What Ducati wanted, more than anything else, was differentiation from the Michelin dominance via both Yamaha and Honda. The logic was that if Yamaha and Honda are on the same tyres, then whenever they had a 'bad tyre weekend' Ducati

would also suffer. The rest of the time Ducati would have to try to beat them. If, however, Ducati was on a different but increasingly competitive tyre, then, whenever Honda and Yamaha were in any form of tyre difficulty, Ducati would have a chance of being on competitive tyres against an emasculated opposition.

It was a gamble, as it was quite possible that Bridgestone wouldn't have very good tyres at more than half the circuits – they certainly didn't when Ducati signed up. Despite disappointing early runs while Bridgestone experimented with tyre profile, construction and compound, the strategy appears to have worked. Bridgestone have always been strong at Motegi, and have shown well at Kuala Lumpur. Other circuits where Bridgestone have been good include Jerez, Mugello and, before it was dropped from the calendar, Brazil.

At first, progress seemed painfully slow, the Ducatis suffering particularly badly in China and France, where it seemed the tyres just did not work. After a promising ride at Brno, all was forgiven at the Japanese Grand Prix event where Capirossi set the fastest lap, took pole position and won the race. He did the same a week later in Malaysia on the Kuala Lumpur track. An injury in testing for the Australian Grand Prix kept Capirossi out of the remaining races of the year,

An official CAD
rendering of the
2006 Desmosedici

RIGHT: After four
years of measuring
rear ride height off
the seat unit, Ducati
finally built a ride
height tool for the
Desmosedici in 2006.

BELOW RIGHT: Major
internal cooling system
changes on the GP06
meant that the bikes
had to be very carefully
bled and purged of air
every morning.

but it was quite apparent that Bridgestone had
turned a corner in their development.

Ducati ended 2005 with a motorcycle that
handled well, on tyres that worked well with it
and which, even with a lean condition engine,
produced enough power to match the best
around. For 2006 this constant fiddling at the
edges paid off. During winter testing they
concentrated on reducing friction in the engines
to improve fuel consumption, and thereby
develop the power they've always had within the
engine for the whole race. At the same time they
worked on the chassis and, without compromising
the feel and handling of the bike, improved
rigidity so that the forks did not allow the front
wheel to move back and hit the radiator. This also
allowed the team more set-up latitude as they
could drop the bike further down the fork legs if
the rider wanted, increasing weight on the front
wheel, without the danger of the wheel
contacting the bike.

Other changes were also made for 2006.
Ducati admitted that the cooling system within
the cylinder block had been changed, helping
cooling and improving overall efficiency. Grafted
on to a now five-year-old engine design, this
clearly needed careful preparation as the
mechanics could be seen bleeding the system
extremely carefully each morning. The mornings

The GP06 used a more sophisticated Birdcage chassis designed to continue to allow the sideways flex when leaned over in corners but to stop the forks bending back into the radiator under heavy braking.

were also quieter – this is the time when all the MotoGP bikes are brought out of the garages and warmed up before first practice at 10 o'clock. Ducatis have always been blipped mercilessly while they warmed up, but in 2006 they could be left on a fast idle just like the Yamahas. Ducati had already admitted that they were using a fully-computerised throttle system, but the quality of its mapping had clearly been improved over the winter. Although it had not featured on all the race bikes by the second race of the year, the test bike ridden by Guareschi had a different twist grip assembly. Rather than the complex cable and potentiometer system used on the team bikes, the

twistgrip was modified so that the potentiometer – the device that tells the computer how much throttle is required – was actually mounted in the twistgrip itself. This saves weight and ultimately reduces complexity.

The new chassis had additional tubes running between the downtubes and the steering head, clearly improving support to that area. In addition, for the first time both riders were using carbon-fibre outer tube forks, not because they were lighter but because they were stiffer, enabling the mechanics to get the right set-up without the front tyre trying to wear through the cylinder head. Ducati also talked about a seat unit that

RIGHT: Ducati routes its throttle cables to a potentiometer on the left of the bike. The butterflies are all moved by high speed stepper motors mounted on the throttle units inside the airbox.

FAR RIGHT: Guareschi's test bike used a fully electronic throttle with the only cables coming off it being electrical ones. Note the Ohlins steering damper alongside the fork leg; a change brought in in mid-2005 for smoother operation.

allowed the different stiffnesses to be dialled in, giving the rider additional feel.

As part of an overall tidy-up, the bike's electronics were relocated onto a redesigned carbon-fibre subframe around the nose, and the switches that controlled the quick shift and level of anti-skip were moved from the top of the triple clamp to above the dashboard. The new tank design, first seen at Brno in 2005, allowed the riders to tuck in slightly better, yet still have the right level of support on the inside of their thighs while cornering.

At the first race of the year at Jerez, Capirossi stormed to the front with another fastest lap, pole position and race win. However, his new team-mate, Sete Gibernau, had to retire early in the race because of a failure of the gear position sensor, which robbed his engine management system of any knowledge of what gear the bike was in, therefore making it impossible for the electronic throttles to know what fuel map and throttle position they should use. This was the first mechanical retirement for Ducati since they had come to MotoGP.

The rest of the year certainly had its ups and downs. Several podiums followed in the early part of the year, notably at Le Mans where Capirossi's Bridgestones stayed on the pace better than the competition's Michelins, and he snatched second place in the last few laps. At Mugello, both bikes put in an inspired performance with only Rossi, at the top of his game, stopping a Capirossi win. The bike did not change much, but a large part of the middle of the year was lost following Sete Gibernau's crash into Capirossi at the first corner at Catalunya.

After four years of constant effort and development, Ducati had got the bike to the point where any major performance improvements during the last few races were down to Bridgestone getting the tyres right for the circuits. Capirossi's Brno win showed the bike's capabilities when the tyres were right.

Ducati's strategy of differentiation from its

opponents meant that wins were typically unchallenged romps, with tyres, bike and rider in harmony. As the Bridgestones got competitive at more circuits, those occasions were seen more often. But Grands Prix are not easy to win, and the importance of those wins to Ducati, and the effort that went into them, should not be underestimated.

AFTER FOUR YEARS OF CONSTANT EFFORT AND DEVELOPMENT, DUCATI HAD GOT THE BIKE TO THE POINT WHERE ANY MAJOR PERFORMANCE IMPROVEMENTS DURING THE LAST FEW RACES WERE DOWN TO BRIDGESTONE GETTING THE TYRES RIGHT FOR THE CIRCUITS

BELOW LEFT: Gibernau joined Capirossi in using stiffer and lighter Carbon Fibre Outer Upper tube Forks. This meant more extreme chassis set-ups were possible without the front tyre contacting the radiator under braking.

BELOW: The GP06 had a new carbon subframe to tidy up the electronics. You can also see some of the camera gear each bike is required to carry for the on-bike camera coverage.

© DUCATI CORSE

HONDA

The V5 masterpiece reveals its secrets

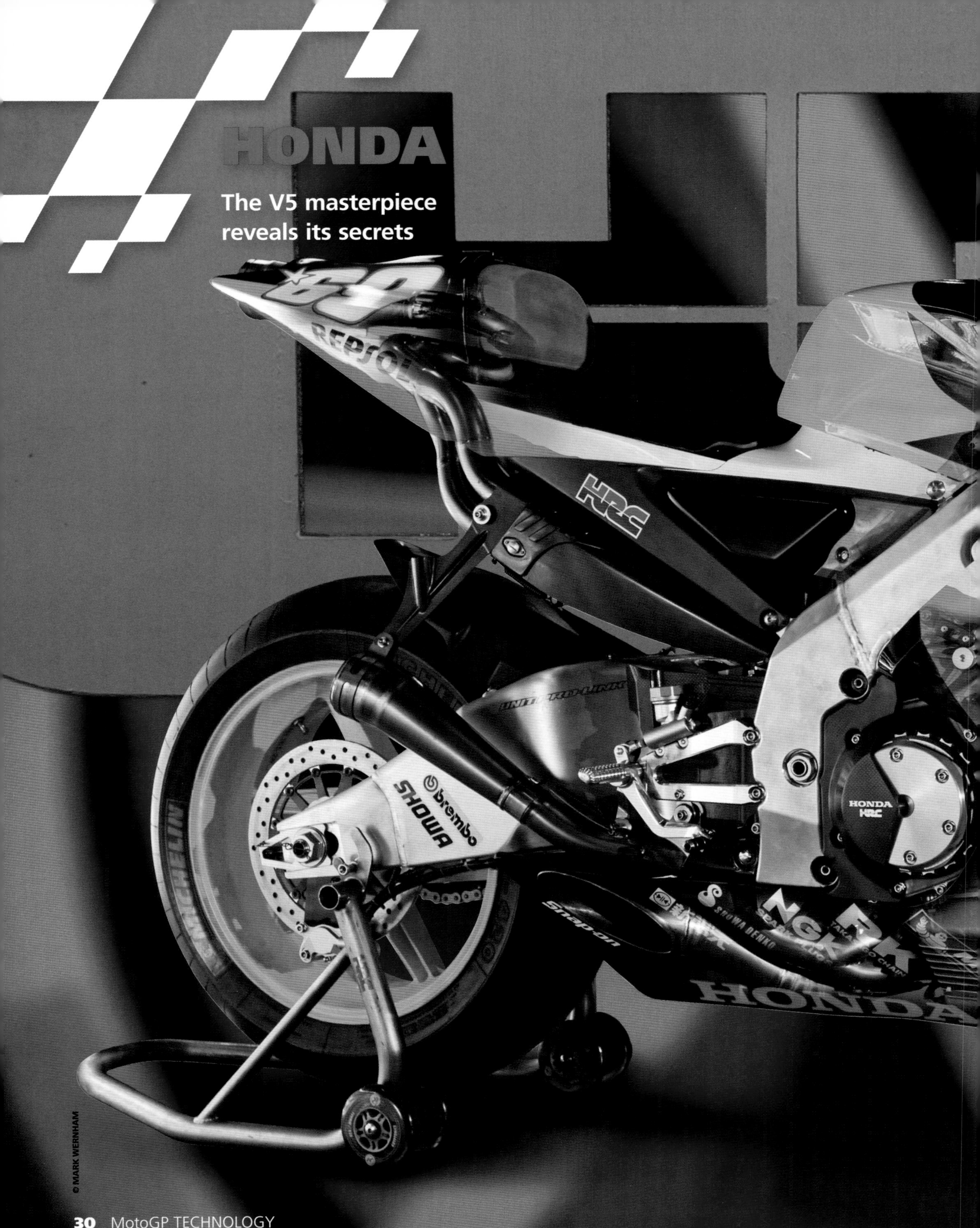

© MARK WERNHAM

ENGINE: Liquid-cooled 75.5° four-stroke V5, 3 cylinders front, 2 rear

CAPACITY: 990cc

POWER: Over 260bhp

TOP SPEED: Over 216mph (347km/h)

TRANSMISSION: Six-speed extractable

IGNITION: Electronic programmable CDI

CHASSIS: Aluminium twin tube

SUSPENSION: Showa telescopic front fork, Unit Pro-link with Showa monoshock at rear

WHEELS: Magnesium

TYRES: Michelin 16.5in front and rear

BRAKES: Brembo, two carbon front discs, two monoblock calipers. Single HRC rear disc with Brembo caliper

WEIGHT: over 148kg

From the start, the Honda RC211V V5 was designed as a complete piece. Honda have a long history of racing V-format engines, and they clearly decided that their engineers should have the additional challenge of building an engine in a unique configuration. Project leader Heijiro Yoshimura (now Senior Chief Engineer at Asaka R&D) led a team drawn from HRC and Honda's R&D department at Asaka made up of Honda's 'minority elite'. After considering all the options allowed under the new rule book, they laid out a V5 across the frame design with three cylinders at the front and two at the back. It is wide where it doesn't matter so much (in front of the rider's shins and in front of the main frame spar) and narrow where it matters a lot (between the rider's legs and that same main frame spar). Honda has confirmed that the basic specifications of the engine were similar to the RC45 race bike. An RC45 and additional front cylinder would displace 936cc, and its power output would be more than enough as a starting point for a 990cc MotoGP engine – somewhere in excess of 200bhp. It would be relatively simple

to stroke the engine slightly to attain the maximum 990cc capacity.

Several things were apparent. The chassis was different from the two-strokes then in use, featuring a much longer swingarm and a correspondingly longer wheelbase. The aerodynamics were very different, using almost vestigial main fairing designs to minimise the effect of crosswinds, for high manoeuvrability and providing fairly minor protection for the rider at high speeds. These fairings gave minimal aerodynamic assistance for top speed – not that that was much of an issue with an initial power output of around 220hp. The aluminium beam frame was the first to use the 'flexible steering head design' with a front engine mount low down on the cylinder block, and long individual struts stretching up to the steering head.

From the beginning the Honda looked right. And, from the very first pictures through to its first Grand Prix win and, to be honest, until the end of this class, the overall look didn't change that much. Rossi's first ride was at a test at Suzuka on 7 August 2001 along with Colin Edwards. The two had won the Suzuka 8-Hour race the weekend before. Before that the bike had been ridden by Tohru Ukawa, Shinichi Itoh and Makoto Tamada. The first major

Rossi on the 2002 bike. Note the large lump of plastic on the end of the crankcases to protect them in the case of a crash.

© GOLD AND GOOSE

INSIDE THE HONDA V5

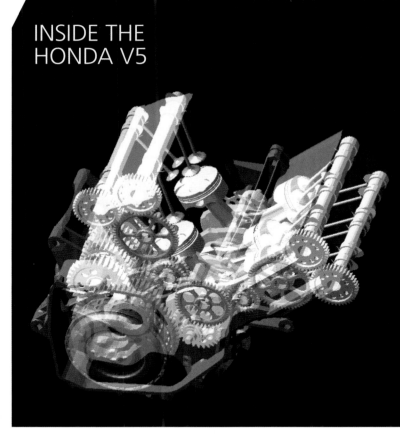

The Honda V5 has proved to be a fascinatingly simple engine in execution, but brilliant in terms of design. Designed to take maximum advantage from a set of rules that allows the same weight for either four- or five-cylinder engines, the V5 is configured to fit extremely well into an aluminium beam chassis. With three cylinders on the front bank, the widest part of the engine is in front of the rider's legs, the two cylinders on the rear bank fitting easily between the rider's boots. These rear cylinders are actually slightly smaller than the rear two cylinders of an equivalent-capacity V4. The choice of the 75.5°V angle was quite curious to start with, as was the absence of any form of balance shaft to keep the engine smoother. Indeed, with the six-speed gearbox and diaphragm slipper clutch system, the whole engine was devastatingly simple.

Initial pictures clearly showed both over-the-butterfly and under-the-butterfly injectors, and the mountings for a gear cam-drive system. There was also a six-speed gearbox (the maximum allowed under the rules). Other than its unique layout, the engine didn't appear to be particularly special. But that initial view of a very simple design completely underestimates the sheer brilliance of the decisions made in the initial design stages. This engine has features that some of the other factories only understood after the second or third year of the competition.

At about the same time that Ducati was driving off corners faster than the rest of the World Superbikes, Honda produced a big bang two-stroke in Grands Prix. That design was equally effective at generating more drive than the opposition screamer engine types. These irregular-firing engines appeared to make life easier for the tyres, although even now there is a substantial argument as to why this should be the case – most tyre companies deny that they see any difference in the condition of their tyres from the screamer types. Nevertheless, Honda's choice of a V, the angle they set their cylinders and the way they incorporated the fifth cylinder – first to minimise vibration and second to maximise tyre grip – remains one of the most elegantly simple solutions to a whole raft of problems ever seen in motorsport.

modification was an extended seat to accommodate the lanky Valentino Rossi and, more important, his riding style of using his height to vary the weight over each wheel and to change traction as and when required.

The whole big bang theory is so complex that we have given over an entire chapter to the subject, so suffice it to say here that Honda had it from the start. The choice of V-angle at 75.5° meant that the front cylinders could be held sufficiently clear of the front tyre to allow the engineers to look for optimum weight distribution without the front tyre hitting the radiator or the front cylinder bank. That same V-angle was not so narrow as to get in the way of a very power-efficient intake system and intake port design. The 75.5° V meant the rear cylinder exhaust ports came out sufficiently above the gearbox not to cause problems. It also kept the intake system low enough for a good-sized airbox to slot in above, without getting in the rider's way, and it allowed (using a new Honda patent) for the fifth cylinder to provide the balancing function necessary to avoid the use of a power-sapping balancer shaft. Add that to the advantages of fitting it into the chassis mentioned above and you have an engine that is sheer brilliance.

For the first four years the engine changed little externally – there were a few small

The guts of the Honda V5. four valves per cylinder, gear driven cams and a crank that works like a V4 with an independent centre cylinder set, we think, 104.5° out.

Gibernau's 2003 bike at Mugello. Note the muffled exhaust system and the repositioned swingarm pivot position.

modifications, a 'turbine' cover for the slipper clutch that cooled it down a little, and the works engines appeared to have additional surface machining. With the basic specifications closely related to the original RC45 that had a 72mm bore and a 46mm stroke, simply adding a fifth cylinder would get a 936cc engine, and stretching the stroke 2.5mm would take us to 987cc. There have been many rumours, but it seems likely that at several times over the last five years the engine has been progressively short stroked – a 74mm bore and a 46.1mm stroke would seem the most logical initially, followed by a 76mm bore and 43.7mm stroke. All of these bore stroke ratios are very conservative, though. The first has a bore/stroke ratio of 1.548, the second 1.6 and the third 1.74; these numbers are only slightly more radical than top-line street bikes – indeed, Ducati's top of the line 999R twin is the same 1.74 ratio. All of these modifications would allow the factory to keep the piston speed down as they increased revs in the search for more power.

Fuelling is controlled by a Honda PGIM injection computer, and by 2003 this was backed up by a computerised air and fuel bleed to provide very accurate control of the corner entry fuelling. The bike also had a traction-control system that compares front and rear wheel spin and changes the ignition timing to reduce power

as necessary. In an unusual admission, Shogo Kanaumi, then HRC RC211V team leader, confirmed, 'We use a traction-control system, we compare front and rear wheel speeds and adjust the ignition system to soften the power if the spin becomes too much.' Although Honda did not say it at the time, they had moved away from a simple cable throttle system at the end of 2002, and some elements of the system were electronic from that point on. It seems likely that the bike Barros rode at Motegi in 2002 was one of the first to use a modified throttle, as it was much more stable into corners than Rossi's similar bike. Photos taken at the time when Barros crashed in practice showed an additional mechanism in front of the handlebars that could well have been a prototype throttle system.

2003 brought in the era of the 130db exhaust. Honda had initially fitted the bike with muffled exhausts, a 3-into-1 on the front and a 2-into-1 on the rear. The rear pipe needed a signature curly pig's tail design to get the right primary pipe length to match the front pairing. The search for more power brought an open megaphone system from Estoril onwards; this used a single pipe for the centre cylinder of the front bank and two 2-into-1 pipes from each of the outer two cylinders of the front bank and the rear bank. The single pipe was a long taper, beautifully welded from

ABOVE: Rossi's early bikes had muffled exhaust systems; Honda wanted to move to open pipes for more power, but Rossi doesn't like noise so they built him this 'muffled megga' to try and have the best of both worlds. This pipe was only used on the Friday of the Estoril GP in 2003; after that he used open pipes.

BELOW: Rossi's Honda at the 2004 Portuguese GP. Note the carbon fuel tank, the first use of the very loud megaphone exhausts and the turbine cover plate covering the slipper clutch. Note also the excellent packaging of the 75.5° motor in the chassis.

'WE USE A TRACTION-CONTROL SYSTEM, WE COMPARE FRONT AND REAR WHEEL SPEEDS AND ADJUST THE IGNITION SYSTEM TO SOFTEN THE POWER IF THE SPIN BECOMES TOO MUCH.'
SHOGO KANAUMI

many sections; the 2-into-1 pipes used relatively small pipes but with short megaphones, reflecting the fact that they worked at twice the frequency of the single pipe. Rossi didn't like the noise, so he stayed with the old pipes for a couple more races, even experimentally using a 'muffled megaphone' at Estoril to try to get the best of both worlds. Rossi also got a bigger fairing for the last few GPs, worth 2kph or 3kph on the top end, and this was a start towards attacking Ducati's dominance of the top speed charts.

2004 saw additional sophistication. Suddenly the RCVs had a speed limiter for the pit lane that made the bikes sound like a small war in motion. The throttle system was described in detail in a briefing given at Motegi in autumn 2004. The throttle system described was based on a differential – using variable gearing for each gear, 50% in first, 60% in second and so on. The initial system had all the butterflies operated on this basis but only in the first three gears. The latest systems are slightly different with only the rear pair of cylinders operated in this way, but the effect is now available in all gears. This allows the computer's changes to be coarser without upsetting the feel of the bike. It also allows the rear two cylinders to be used to limit power more aggressively than with the old system. As computer speeds increase it is more likely that we

Honda's latest throttle system uses only partial assistance from a computer. To maintain the sensitivity required, three font butterflies are now operated directly by the rider. The two rear cylinders' throttles are under the control of the ECU, which makes the Honda throttle system similar to the Marelli systems used by Yamaha and Kawasaki.

Honda's differential throttle control allows different ratios between twistgrip and throttle butterfly. Initial versions were fixed, but later ones allowed different ratios to be programmed in according to rider preference in all gears.

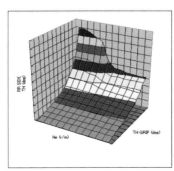
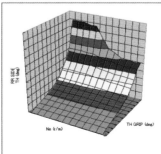
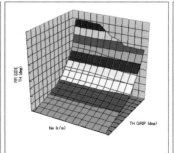
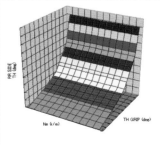

1st **2nd** **3rd** **4-5-6th**

would revert to a system where all the throttles are under the control of the ECU. A new swingarm also appeared in 2004, with a new, deeper aluminium structure placing the shock absorber further up in the chassis. The new swingarm was machined from solid and welded together like most of the other bikes, except the WCM and Ducati. The works team tested the new swingarms from the start of 2004, but the customer teams didn't get the new chassis until just before the Catalunya test, and there was immediate criticism, with some riders claiming it caused chatter. The entire linkage assembly was effectively an inverted version of the 2002/2003 set-up, and it seemed to move the shock absorber up closer to the centre of the bike. Honda claimed that the design changed the way the forces from the suspension affected the chassis – but, with the benefit of hindsight, this redesign wasn't a success. The basic 2004 customer bikes also benefited from the 'Rossi only' fairing from the previous year. Additional changes were made to the nose fairings of the works bikes during the year, tidying up the airflow to the radiator and up over the nose and over the rider. Some of the bikes were fitted with Honda's unique HPEC electronically controlled steering damper; although not all Honda riders were fans, with one or two retaining the older parts.

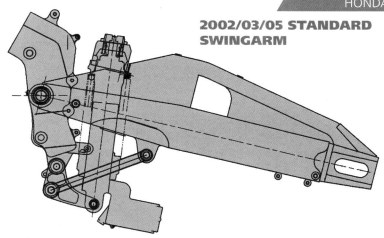

2002/03/05 STANDARD SWINGARM

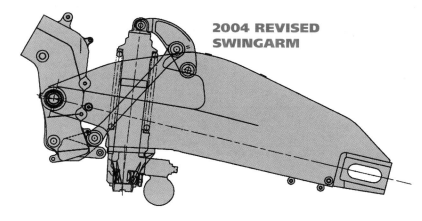

2004 REVISED SWINGARM

Nicky Hayden's 2004 bike. This had the upside down linkage that didn't ultimately work satisfactorily. For 2005 the factory team reverted to the 2002/03 design.

© HONDA PRO IMAGES

Barros got a new engine and these independent rear pipes for Sachsenring in 2004. Honda said it gave more torque and was easier to control.

At Sachsenring several of the top Honda riders' chassis showed up with revised swingarm pivot mounts, changing the bike's reaction to inputs from the chain. Most of the MotoGP bikes in the paddock routed electronics externally to the foot controls – quickshifter, brake pressure sensors – but the RCVs had very tidy electronics. Until 2005 very little was visible, and when things did get added they were unusual, the most intriguing being a clutch lever travel monitor. The most notable thing about the controls was the disappointing section of inner tube doing double duty as a rear brake return spring.

2004 saw some other experiments. Until Sachsenring, all the 2004 RC211Vs had an open megaphone exhaust system, the front cylinder bank had a titanium exhaust system with both a 2-into-1 pipe and a single pipe with a shallow taper on it for the independent fifth cylinder. This pipe from the centre cylinder of the front bank was made of many individual components, allowing it snake around the bike until it exited under the rider's right foot. Usually the rear two cylinders also had a 2-into-1 system with a small megaphone, but at Sachsenring Barros's bike had a dramatic-looking new 2-into-2 system that looked very similar in design to the single pipe off the front

centre cylinder. Honda won't confirm that something fundamental had changed, but this sort of thing was normally only done when the firing order was revised, as the exhaust pipes could no longer equally share the scavenging duties. A new front system linking the centre and left cylinders, and the use of independent rear pipes certainly gave the impression that there was a change in the crankshaft set-up. When the new pipes were fitted for the first time to Barros's bike on the Thursday evening, a new engine had also been flown in from Japan. Honda continued to claim that this engine had different, and improved, engine characteristics, more torque and was easier to control. Equally, their competitors were sure it had a different combustion sequence, certainly the exhaust rearrangement suggests that something different was being tried.

While it appears Honda initially used a longish stroke engine for its improved 'rider feel', the same longer stroke would make it difficult to rev in the search for more power. Initial engines peaked around 15,000rpm – for a long time the radical Desmosedici revved higher, despite only having four cylinders – but in 2005 Honda boosted their peak revs in the search for Rossi-beating power. At the start of the season 16,000rpm was the limit, but during the year it crept up to 16,500rpm. After engine failures at Motegi, the limit was temporarily reduced back to 16,000rpm but, by the end of the season, 16,500rpm was again the norm. These revs might not seem much by comparison to the world of Formula 1, but because of the length of the stroke, the piston speed, a notable limiting factor in engine design, is the same in a 16,500rpm 74mm bore 990cc five and a 19,200rpm 3000cc 98mm Formula 1 engine at 25.5m/sec.

In 2005 it was obvious that Honda needed to do something to try to attack the Yamaha and Rossi takeover of MotoGP. Their answer was to appoint extra riders to the HRC programme, in addition to the Repsol works team of Hayden and Biaggi. Gibernau was the rider that had been taking the fight to Rossi most of the time, and he was added as an additional HRC rider, but operating out of the Gresini Team garage. The choice of Hayden and Biaggi was quite unusual, Hayden having a set of riding preferences influenced by his earlier career in US dirt track riding, and Biaggi being the arch 250 rider. The chassis went back to the original 2002/2003 design, the swingarms looked identical, but the main chassis had adjustable steering-head bearing housings. These were

Gibernau got Honda works bikes for 2005. You can see that Honda had reverted to the early chassis and swingarm layout. At Le Mans Yamaha decided they were interested in some of its design features.

big enough to allow head angle changes and some small repositioning of the steering head, front or back. The customer bikes continued with the bigger section swingarms and the inverted shock and linkage. Additional details of Honda's sophisticated injection system also came out during 2005, Sete Gibernau was dicing with Rossi for the lead in the Czech Republic and ran out of fuel just a few hundred metres from the end of the race. Honda were measuring the fuel usage during the course of the race on active basis, and if the rate of consumption showed that the bike was likely to run out of fuel the mixture was

leaned off in areas of the fuel map where such a change would cause the least possible damage to the bike's performance. That system failed on Gibernau's bike. The next GP was in Japan and, under the guidance of Honda engineers, the fuel was measured very carefully, and extremely publicly into all the other customer Hondas in the pit lane. Honda won't comment as to why they did this, but it did demonstrate the precise capacity of the fuel tanks. For the record, they held 21.85 litres, just under the maximum allowed of 22 litres. An unkind observer might point out that if they had displaced the full 22 litres,

BELOW LEFT: Hayden's bike being stripped in 2005. The throttle system uses overhead injectors firing through wire grilles placed on top of the velocity stacks to increase intake charge turbulence.

BELOW: The engine sidecover is off here and you can see the primary drive, the crankshaft position rotor and the start of the cam gear drive. Note also the stick coils and the close fit of the frame around the rear cylinders.

Gibernau's bike would have still been running at the end of the Czech Grand Prix.

Biaggi had a disastrous year, being unable to get the kind of feel that was crucial to his riding style. It did mean, however, that the bike was developed more in line with a 250.

As soon as the 2006 customer bikes became available, it was apparent that the welds that we had thought were merely relocated swingarm pivots on the Repsol bikes were, in fact, the engine being raised by 5mm at the front, and a small change having to be made to the swingarm position to accommodate this at the rear. The slightly higher centre of gravity this brought about made the initial reaction to a rider's command to turn slightly slower, but because the weight was held higher the bike would then 'fall over' into the corner more quickly. It proved to be a modification that suited people who had not ridden the 2002/2003 chassis more than it suited those who were used to the older design.

During 2005, several special chassis were used. Gibernau and Biaggi had revised headstock frames with what looked like a more vertical headstock angle for the German GP at Sachsenring. This circuit is particularly tight and twisty and such a modification would help the bike turn in the tight corners. Biaggi continued to use the chassis all the way through to Motegi,

although Gibernau dumped it immediately after that race. Melandri, who by this time was showing an ability to chase Rossi, was also helped with a special chassis. The chassis was identical to the 2002/2003 chassis, in having the old-style swingarm but, unlike the works riders, it did not have an adjustable steering head. This was tested at Brno, and Melandri used it for his late season charge against Rossi.

Honda were determined to beat Rossi in the final year of the 990cc competition. The 2005 Brno test showed just how serious Honda were. They debuted a new long swingarm version of the RCV, known universally as the 'Brno bike' since its launch. Honda called it the 'new generation' machine. This bike has a different engine externally, shorter overall because of careful repackaging and a semi-stacked gearbox, and the clutch has been lowered 5 or 6mm, allowing the swingarm to be lengthened by something like 15mm, but maintaining the same wheelbase. The bike had a very contentious development period, appearing at Brno but not being able to be tested because of some unspecified mechanical malady hitting the Japanese test bike the morning before the test was supposed to occur. As a result Biaggi and Gibernau only did a few laps on the bikes that had been flown in specially for them. These bikes were not used for the rest of the year, but

At Brno in 2005, Max Biaggi tested the 'Brno bike' just for one afternoon of testing. The bike had a shorter engine and longer swingarm for better stability under the brakes. A development of this bike was used by Hayden in 2006. Note the slight differences in the swingarm section between this bike and the Hayden 2006 bike on page 42.

© HONDA PRO IMAGES

photos of Tohru Ukawa testing the bike in Japan kept popping up.

The bike did not appear again in public in 2005, not even at the Sepang test in early December 2005 where the rest of the factories showed their 2006 bikes, or at least their prototypes. In early February, back at Sepang, Tady Okada was pulled out of retirement to retry the bike, only now there were a lot of other changes. The chassis was modified, and the engine looked far more dramatic, with the sump and the front of the engine having developed fins over the winter. In addition, the familiar turbine covered diaphragm spring clutch had been redesigned using coil springs.

For 2006 the new 'standard issue' bikes used the 5mm-higher-in-the-frame design developed with Biaggi. They were fitted with a swingarm that adopted the deeper section of the 2004 inverted shock swingarms, but used a variation on the 2002/2003 version of the linkage. This was seen very briefly during the test at Brno in 2005, but neither Gibernau nor Biaggi, who tested it, seemed to want to continue with it.

The 2006 test programme kicked off with all the riders using the previous year's chassis, and the new number one rider in the HRC pit, Hayden, testing all the items tried and disposed of during 2005 by both Biaggi and Gibernau. At the same time, Dani Pedrosa was getting used to the RC211V, which had a different fuel tank and seat assembly to help him get closer to the handlebars, and the ground. During the last two tests, Honda clearly decided they needed to push forward the development of the Brno bike, and Hayden was required to use the bike for at least the first five Grands Prix. In the lead up to this change of direction, Tohru Ukawa was replaced by Tady Okada as test rider, with Ukawa moving on as an engineer elsewhere within Honda.

The initial testing showed a bike that had clearly met its design brief of being quicker and more effective into corners. Satoru Horiike, the Managing Director of HRC, even confirmed that the brief had been to match the Yamaha into corners, and acknowledged that the swingarm section used on the bike was very close to that

Hayden's New Generation bike being stripped. Note the differences between this and his 2005 bike on page 39. The clutch is the special works coil spring clutch used only by Hayden and Pedrosa.

THE 2006 TEST PROGRAMME KICKED OFF WITH ALL THE RIDERS USING THE PREVIOUS YEAR'S CHASSIS, AND THE NEW NUMBER ONE RIDER IN THE HRC PIT, HAYDEN, TESTING ALL THE ITEMS TRIED AND DISPOSED OF DURING 2005 BY BOTH BIAGGI AND GIBERNAU.

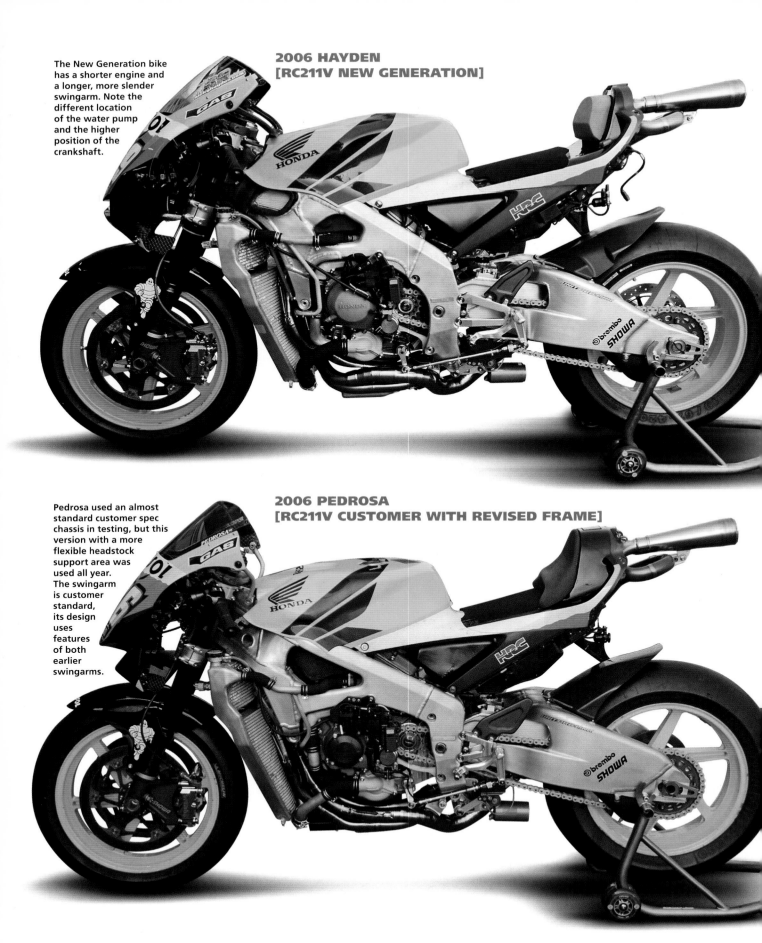

The New Generation bike has a shorter engine and a longer, more slender swingarm. Note the different location of the water pump and the higher position of the crankshaft.

**2006 HAYDEN
[RC211V NEW GENERATION]**

Pedrosa used an almost standard customer spec chassis in testing, but this version with a more flexible headstock support area was used all year. The swingarm is customer standard, its design uses features of both earlier swingarms.

**2006 PEDROSA
[RC211V CUSTOMER WITH REVISED FRAME]**

1. **Marco Melandri's 2006 customer-spec engine. Front block has three cylinders and DOHC.**

2. **Cams are gear driven with conventional 'stick coils' being used for sparks.**

3. **Gearbox is a cassette type. Here it has been removed.**

4. **Flywheel cover contains a small easily removeable flywheel so that the engines response characteristics can be easily adjusted.**

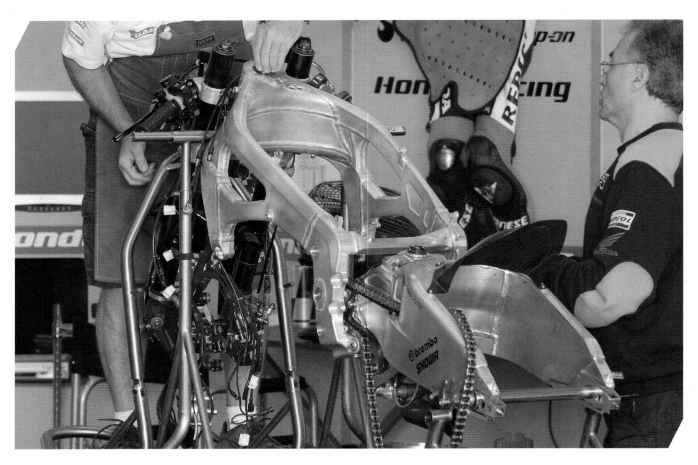

Pedrosa's bike being stripped at Jerez after the race. Nothing is left to chance.

used by Yamaha. He also acknowledged that the coil-spring slipper clutch adopted on both of the Repsol bikes had partially been developed with the same thought in mind. The initial difficulty was that, while it was quicker into the corners, it appeared to have sacrificed everything else. It is possible that some aspects of Hayden's riding style didn't help. He uses a much larger rear brake than is normal, and he goes into corners without loading up the front tyre as much as other MotoGP riders.

Once the season started, however, the pressure to develop competitive settings was much higher. At the test after the Jerez race (where Hayden had snatched third), the front fork offset and the frame

bearing housings were changed, after which he promptly set a time half-a-second quicker than anybody else at the test. At the following Qatar GP he was able to run right at the front, and had only just been beaten by Rossi, determined to re-establish his Alpha male credentials.

While this development was carrying on, Honda was simultaneously working with Pedrosa to upgrade his chassis. From halfway through testing he had a bike with a different series of welds around the steering head, most possibly for additional flexibility. After Pedrosa's second place at Jerez, the same chassis was given to Melandri to test. Melandri was having severe trouble with the

RIGHT: Melandri also had the use of the Pedrosa style chassis after the first race at Jerez. As a test rider and not a works rider, he did not have the use of the coil-spring clutch; you can see he has the old style clutch seen here with its face plate off.

FAR RIGHT: Project leader Yoshii flags off Hayden in one of many dummy starts in the test at Motegi while Honda tries to replicate the starting problem.

2006 customer chassis, and had been given back his 2005 chassis by Honda for the Jerez race, but Honda didn't want to continue this arrangement, choosing instead to sign up Melandri to a testing contract, allowing him access to the latest HRC bits immediately after the Repsol team.

Hayden continued with the New Generation machine, and regular testing slowly moved it to a setup that he could use. The bike's longer swingarm was designed to provide a more stable corner entry, something that was at odds with Hayden's usual style. But that more stable corner entry allowed Hayden to counter the Yamaha's perceived edge on the brakes – something that Rossi excels at using to his advantage.

During the year HRC made the 'Pedrosa style' chassis available first to Melandri and then to Stoner. This had a slightly more flexible steering head area that helped the bike into corners.

At Donington they introduced a revamp for Hayden's New Generation chassis too. Honda wanted a chassis that allowed the tyres to last longer. They also wanted to tidy up the design of the Evo chassis so they prepared a new frame and swingarm with none of the complex cuts and welds that had characterised the prototypes. This was used in the first day's practice sessions, and it rapidly became apparent that the new chassis required a different setup to the old one and that

the middle of a GP wasn't the time to try and find it. The chassis itself had a more 'repeatable' look to it. The major structural change was a revised shock absorber position, slightly offset to the right and set slightly lower, although Honda insist this did not change the linkage ratio; the new shock position required Honda to route the 'fifth' cylinder's single exhaust pipe to the left of the bike rather than to the right. The chassis wasn't seen again until the test days after the Czech GP at Brno, and new settings were found that gave Hayden the confidence to use it again.

Hayden struggled for power all through the year. Although the bike made more power that the 2005 bikes, something about the Evo bike's intake or exhaust plumbing cost the bike a little power compared to the normal chassis 2006 bikes, such is the nature of the compromises forced onto bike designers. Several new exhaust parts were tried at Brno in the search for more power and Hayden swapped clutches around too.

It's not certain if it was the mental pressure or a genuine clutch problem, but Hayden suffered from clutch problems in the last few races. After roasting the clutch on the start at Brno, Hayden had all sorts of problems, being too nice to it in Malaysia. Then the setup allowed slip all the way to the first corner in Philip Island. Honda reacted with new parts and lots of testing, but a lot of damage had been done.

THE SECRETS OF THE V5

Honda finally disclosed the secrets of the RC211V at a presentation in Motegi in September 2006. No details of the materials used were given but the overpowering impression was of complex design simply executed. The crankshaft was a lightweight high inertia design featuring almost full circle crank webs. Honda confirmed that the 5th cylinder's crank pin was offset by 104.5 degrees and that gave a firing order of 0–75.5–104.5–180–75.5–284.5. This provided the power impulses to the rear tyre in the long bang sequence that has the best effect for traction. As far as the 2006 bike used by Hayden was concerned, Honda claimed that the engine's mass was centralised and its weight reduced.

Honda had also redesigned their electronic throttle arrangement to allow the rider direct 100% control over the three butterflies serving the front bank of the motor, and the ECU to control the other two. This system allowed more precise control over the small throttle corrections the ECU was required to make. The computer-controlled butterflies use the same electronic differential system seen on the previous generation of bikes.

It became apparent in the last seven or so races of the season that Hayden was having trouble with his clutch. He could try and get his normal hard start, after which the plates would warp and then he would have inconsistent clutch behaviour for the rest of the race, or he could baby the clutch off the line and get blitzed on the way to the first corner. Hayden and his crew swapped from a coil spring to a diaphragm clutch and back again during this period, but both suffered problems. The clutch was clearly overheating on the starts and at some races it slipped all the way to the first corner. And this was a clutch that now benefitted from more cooling air due to its lower position in the New Generation engine. Extensive testing at Motegi after the race found some

Nicky Hayden's 2006 RC211V New Generation engine in parts. Of particular note are: the crankcases (above) showing Honda's 'semi wet sump' design; the very short pistons, with their substantial valve cutaways, are very light and use one compression ring and a three-part oil control ring; the Steel valve springs and the titanium small stem, large diameter valves; the titanium conrods with their 'filled in' I-beam section; and the lightweight but high inertia crankshaft with its separate flywheel to enable the engine throttle reactions to be tuned to rider preferences. This one is marked NV5H.

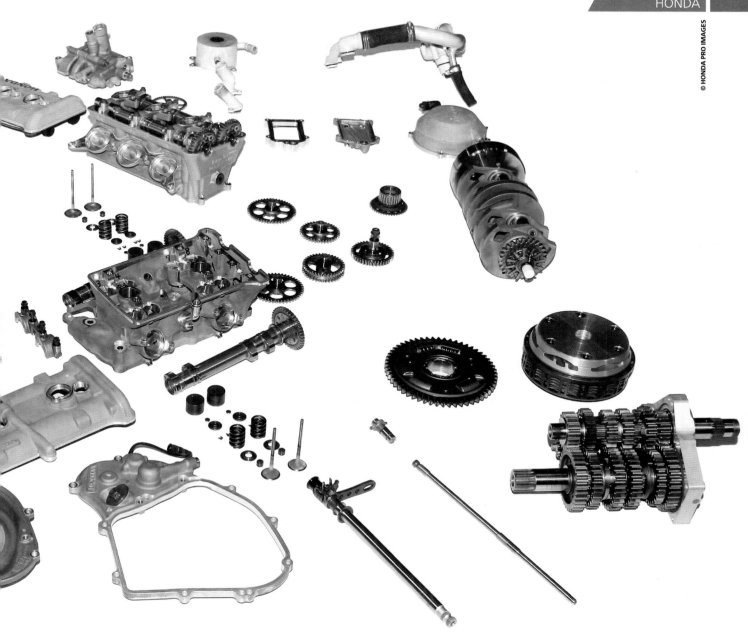

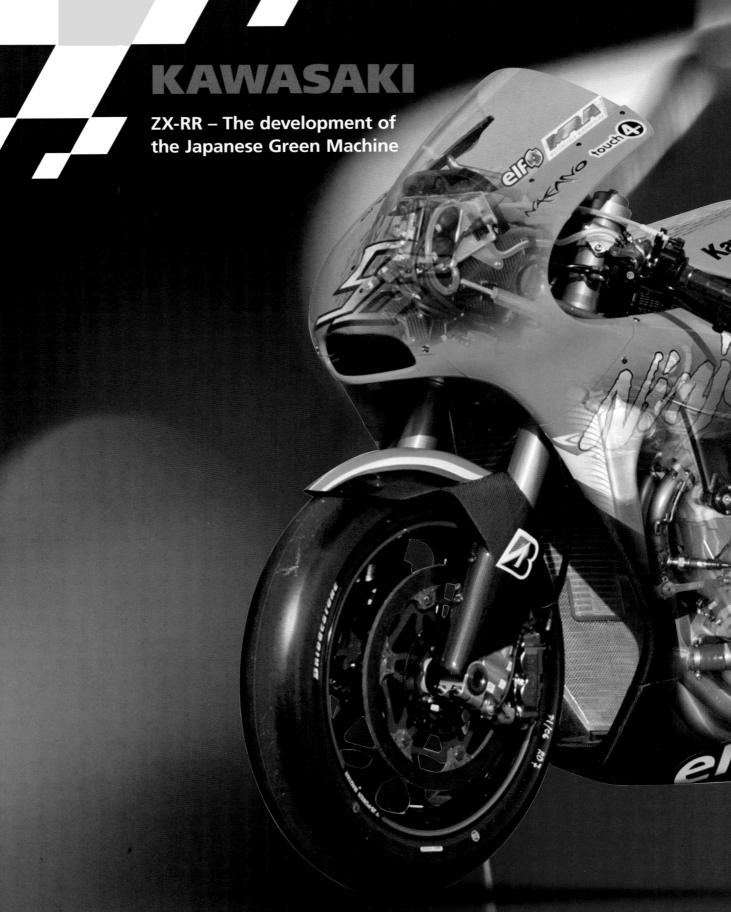

KAWASAKI

**ZX-RR – The development of
the Japanese Green Machine**

ENGINE: In-line four cylinder, four-stroke, DOHC four-valve

CAPACITY: 990cc

POWER: Over 230bhp at 15,000rpm

TOP SPEED: Over 200mph (320km/h)

TRANSMISSION: Six-speed extractable cassette

IGNITION: Electronic programmable CDI

CHASSIS: Aluminium twin-spar

SUSPENSION: Ohlins, inverted telescopic front forks, rear monoshock

WHEELS: JB-Power Magtan

TYRES: Bridgestone 16.5in front and rear

BRAKES: Brembo, two carbon front discs, single steel rear disc

WEIGHT: over 148kg

Kawasaki motorcycles are part of the consumer products group of the massive Kawasaki Heavy Industries company and, as much as anything, they exist as the public face of this vast industrial empire. Kawasaki's decision to go MotoGP racing was, therefore, more about KHI's company image than just selling a few extra motorcycles. This is not the first time Kawasaki has raced in Grands Prix, though. Over the last 40 years it has had several notable successes, ranging from one-off 500 wins, and a 125 World Championship with British privateer Dave Simmonds in the 1960s, to a chain of 250 and 350 championships in the late '70s and early '80s. In recent years, though, their presence on the track has been about racing what they sell in the World Superbike Championship.

The initial decision to leave their official involvement in WSB and move to MotoGP was taken in January 2002, and that meant that Kawasaki would have to face competition which already had almost a year's experience under their belts. Within a month an early development bike was being tested. This first prototype was a 'super superbike' using mostly standard superbike race parts and a big bore kit. Emboldened by the success of the design, Kawasaki made a new engine, displacing a full 990cc, and a new frame.

A very short time later (just seven months) saw a completely new bike on track being tested by

Akira Yanegawa, recently retired from World Superbike competition. Called the ZX-RR, it was styled in a very futuristic, edgy way. We were told it had been wind-tunnel tested, and the shape was certainly quite unusual. Kawasaki then put it in the last four races as a wildcard entry. The first MotoGP race was at the Japanese GP at Motegi in 2002. This initial outing was badly marred, as Yanegawa crashed halfway through the race on a motorcycle that never looked even slightly stable on the brakes. Kawasaki rapidly moved forward with a full team entry for 2003.

The 2003 bikes were developments of the Motegi bike with, unusually, large sections of the frame sandcast for rigidity. The engines were conventional across-the-frame, double-overhead-cam, four-valves-per-cylinder, four-cylinder engines. The cylinders were almost completely vertical, with a standard, non-stacked layout, together with a Suter-designed slipper clutch. The crankcases were exquisitely machined from solid, no wall thickness more than 5mm and many quite a lot thinner. If one ignored the exotic machining of the crankcases, though, it was still a super superbike. To try to reduce some of the rear wheel hop problems that were so obvious on the bike's debut at Motegi the year before, a small servo motor was fitted to one of the flat-slide injector bodies. Depending on the gear selected,

Akira Yanagawa gives the brand new Kawasaki ZX-RR absolutely everything at its debut race at Motegi 2002.

the throttle position and the engine's revs, this stepper motor would hold open the throttle ever so slightly and reduce the engine-braking on the run in to corners.

The bike's overall layout included an air intake through the nose and around the headstock. The chassis looked extremely rigid with the headstock, in particular, a massive cast-aluminium piece. The first few races were a little chaotic, as parts were changed in an attempt to find an acceptable set-up. Kawasaki realised the size of the problem, and employed ex-Red Bull crew chief, Hamish Jamieson, as a technical advisor to help out. He introduced a strict programme of testing, and brought some order to the chaos.

One of the major areas where MotoGP has changed motorcycling is in chassis design. The mantra until the the last few years of the last century was that rigidity was everything, but it is now clear that some controlled flex makes a fundamental difference to the way the chassis works when the bike is leaned right over. Most factories were working this out to various degrees by early 2003, but it is fair to say that Kawasaki's 2003 chassis did not heed this lesson. The bike's wheel spinned easily, lacked traction coming out of corners and, if there was a bump anywhere in the middle of the corner, the entire chassis seemed to jump vertically up, clean off the

ABOVE: Andrew Pitt's ZX-RR with the fairing off. Note the second version of the 2003 chassis with the extended aluminium beams and the shorter cast sections at the headstock and swingarm pivot.

BELOW: Garry McCoy's early year bike (at the IRTA test at Jerez) with the short fabricated chassis beams but with the 2003 race bodywork. The exhausts lost their mufflers as the season started.

Alex Hofmann ran a third bike at Mugello. One of the frames he used was clearly of very different construction to the normal team issue, and it helped him beat both of the normal team riders.

Hofmann had a different swingarm too. This used a much shorter cast section and a smaller section arm in an effort to increase swingarm flex in corners.

Standard kit. One of the beefiest swingarms ever put on a motorcycle.

The short cast headstock version of the chassis. To increase flex, substantial amounts of the casting were also machined away from the inside of the frame.

ground. The bike wasn't quite unrideable, but it must have been close. It very quickly became apparent that the initial chassis, with its very stiff test headstock and swingarm sections, was going to be very difficult to continue with. During the year, many experiments were carried out on changing the flexibility of the chassis. Several different swingarms came and went and, later in the year, experiments were tried on the rigidity of the steering head, with substantial parts of the headstock castings being removed on the inside to try to allow some flexibility, and thereby give the forks a chance of maintaining grip even when leaned right over.

The bodywork changed as well. Kawasaki's initial 'Star Wars' look was replaced with something slightly more conservative, albeit still quite avant-garde by the standards of the MotoGP pit lane. The bike developed a reputation for being extremely hard to change direction, and at circuits with high-speed changes of direction, like Assen and Donington, the problem was particularly acute, with the riders looking quite exhausted by the end of each session.

This bike was also the first Kawasaki to use fuel-injection in a race situation. Using flat-slide (or guillotine) throttle bodies, and two injectors per port, they were designed to allow maximum possible horsepower without any flow restrictions at high revs. For the ECU, Kawasaki used one of their OEM manufacturers, but this proved to be quite unwieldy. To facilitate retuning the bike, race computer systems require flash load capabilities – the ability to write a new fuel or ignition map into the computer at will, and preferably while the bike is sitting in the pit lane. To change the fuel-injection computer, so that the entire unit could go inside the garage to be remapped, the crew had to lift the lid, remove the computer and replace it with another one.

For 2004 a radical new short wheelbase chassis was introduced. Designed by Swiss ex-racer, Eskil Suter, and his SRT race organisation in conjunction with Kawasaki, these bikes looked just like 250s the first time they were seen. Outwardly the engines appeared the same, even the machined-from-solid crankcases were still present, although they were progressively replaced with cast versions later in the year. In addition to changing the chassis, the team moved from Dunlop to Bridgestone tyres. The new motorcycle used a combined seat, fuel tank and airbox moulding, with the airbox lid sitting just under the rider's chin.

The engine retained its classic 180° crankshaft spacing, on the basis that it had worked perfectly well in superbikes. It was somewhat puzzling that the bike appeared to have little grip under acceleration in MotoGP. What was also puzzling was the bike's excellent stability, arguably still too much for racing. This wasn't a particular problem, except at circuits like Donington Park where there was a need to be quick turning in the Melbourne Loop chicane section and light enough for high-speed changes of direction down Craner Curves. Another circuit that was a problem was Assen with its high-speed cornering giving the Kawasaki riders a very heavy workout indeed.

These were problems that were supposed to have been solved by the shorter lighter chassis, so clearly there were other effects at play here. The most logical would appear to be the long in-line four crankshaft giving the bike substantial gyroscopic stability at high speed. In an effort to make the bike easier to turn, Kawasaki specified lighter crankshafts. This worked, but the quicker-revving engines lost traction more easily. During the course of the year the Mitsubishi fuel-injection system was replaced by a Magneti Marelli system. This made quite a difference, not least because the team could now use Marelli's 'missing cylinder' traction control system, in addition to the simple advance curve control in use before. By the time we came to the end of the season, with the combination of this system and the lightweight crankshaft, it seemed like cylinders cut out every time the engine went over 14,000rpm and the bike was not perfectly upright.

Even in early 2004 Kawasaki were using fuel injection computers from one of their OEM suppliers. These were fitted to the underside of the airbox top and needed to be removed and reflashed with new maps off the bike.

BELOW: The early 2004 bike. A completely new chassis made the bike seem a lot smaller. Note the 4-into-2-into-1 pipe of the screamer engine.

© KRT MEDIA

© KRT MEDIA

Nobody could accuse Kawasaki of not trying, however. Several times during the course of the year they attempted to modify their engines so that they would accept more revs and make more power, most notably at Le Mans and Motegi, where their efforts resulted in either piston-ring or valve failure and rather smoky DNFs. Bridgestone tyres did help Kawasaki to an excellent podium finish at Motegi, where the tyre company's knowledge of the circuit gave Nakano an excellent shot after the seriously quick bikes all got caught up in a multiple pile-up in the first corner.

For 2005, things were supposed to change dramatically. Another new chassis had been prepared by Suter, and the team were hoping for substantial engine modifications from the factory. In addition, it managed to hire Ichiro Yoda, who had left Yamaha late in 2004. Yoda had been project leader of the M1, and he brought with him intimate knowledge of Yamaha's progress. After one brief practice in Malaysia, however, the new chassis was dumped; testing continued but all that was happening on the chassis front appeared to be a revised stiffness swingarm on Hofmann's test bike.

ABOVE: Alex Hofmann used this Akrapovic '1-into-2' extension to his basic exhaust layout several times.

BELOW: Kawasaki's motor was little changed externally after nearly three years. It still looked very big, but inside things were changing; Nakano had the use of two types of 'big bang' engines during the year.

KAWASAKI TRY BIG BANG

In the engine department things were different; the Kawasaki had no balancer shaft so it was not easy to make major changes to the crankshaft design. However, Kawasaki needed to get the benefits of an irregular firing order engine. They couldn't do it with a revised crankshaft, like most of the other factories, so they did it simply by firing two pistons together and having a long gap in the combustion sequence before the next pair of pistons fired. Two different specifications of engine were prepared. The first called the 'BB2' had each of its pairs of pistons firing together. This seemed likely to give either the primary gears or the gearbox a particularly hard time. A second specification 'BB3' engine was built, in which only one pair of pistons fired together, the other two acting in a conventional fashion. With only one pair of pistons firing together the primary gears and gearboxes would have a slightly easier time, and the tyre received an all-important space between firing pulses. As soon as the engines were fitted, the riders confirmed that they had more traction going into, and coming out of, all the corners. Initially, however, the BB2 variant was more popular with the riders.

At Shanghai, only four races into the season, Kawasaki were ready for their next jump forward; an experimental ride-by-wire system had been built by their electronics engineer, Danielo Casonato, and was put onto Olivier Jacque's bike. OJ, riding in place of the injured Hofmann, found the system worked immediately. Incredibly, a second system was available, and Nakano's bike was also equipped for the race. Olivier Jacque was undoubtedly aided by the atrocious conditions, and snatched second place from a dumbfounded field, but poor Nakano's ride-by-wire system failed in the rain. In one single outing Kawasaki had irrevocably transferred over to ride-by-wire.

Kawasaki's Marelli system was slightly different from Yamaha's, although it is probably more accurate to say they were lagging by one year in development, as only one butterfly was controlled by the computer and the other three by the rider. In Yamaha's case, with another year's experience, they had two butterflies controlled by the rider and two by a computer. The intention is the same, to use the computer-controlled throttle to smooth power delivery and to provide seamless assistance for engine braking. The strategy is quite simple – as soon as the rider has shut his throttles, the computer opens its fourth one sufficient to reduce the reverse torque within the engine to a

At Sachsenring in 2005 Kawasaki fielded extra bikes for Olivier Jacque. It made for a crowded garage, and then Hofmann and Jacque took each other out on the first corner of the race. Note that all the bikes have the four separate exhausts that characterised the big bang engine types.

FAR LEFT: 2005, the new Marelli fuel injection may be called ride-by-wire, but only one butterfly was under the control of the computer; the other three still used good old-fashioned cables.

LEFT: For the Shanghai debut of the new fuel injection and throttle system, Marelli flew in their own systems engineer to help the transition. While stand-in rider Olly Jacque scored an unexpected second; Nakano had his new throttle system fail.

The new 2006 bike was actually completely different, but until it got the new fairing it just didn't look it. This is Nakano's bike at Catalunya, the second race with the new big intake fairings. The bike is fitted with a special 2-into-1 pipe used only in practice.

level that the slipper clutch can deal with easily. This is the only time the computer can actually open one of the throttles more than the rider's request. The rest of the time the computer-controlled cylinder is acting as a traction control device, shutting off power at times when the rider cannot react quickly enough or where the engine's power delivery is so rough as to make it almost unusable.

As 2005 drew to an end, we finally saw the reason why the chassis, spied at Sepang at the start of the year, had been withdrawn. Over the course of the year, Kawasaki had built an entirely new motorcycle in Japan, purely for the last year of the 990cc MotoGP formula. The new engine and the new chassis were not revolutionary

changes, but they were certainly an evolution. The engine is slightly narrower and the cylinders are pitched forward, probably an additional 15°. As a result, the area behind the top of the radiator is more fully utilised. To keep the centre of gravity in the same place, the gearbox is slightly stacked, the crankshaft having come backwards slightly. On top of the gearbox there appears to be an alternator, now reverse rotating, just like Kawasaki's own ZX10 street bike. The bike had the balance shaft to allow an irregular fire crankshaft, but this was not fitted until the Malaysian race in September. Once it was in, the Kawasaki found a new level of grip.

Kawasaki's new ZX-RR had problems delivering during 2006. The bike was a natural progression from the Eskil Suter-influenced 2004 and 2005 bikes and brought with it a more rationally packaged engine. There was some criticism of the previous chassis insofar as it was too stable; the handling of a racing motorcycle needs to be, shall we say, creatively unstable and the new chassis was supposed to correct this. Unfortunately, experience during the first half of 2006 showed no real change in the bike's reluctance to change direction.

As with the previous two years, Kawasaki remained loyal to Bridgestone, who reciprocated by producing some quite special tyres for them,

ONE OF THE MAJOR AREAS WHERE MotoGP HAS CHANGED MOTORCYCLING IS IN CHASSIS DESIGN. THE MANTRA UNTIL THE EARLY PART OF THIS CENTURY HAD BEEN THAT RIGIDITY WAS EVERYTHING, BUT IT IS NOW CLEAR THAT SOME CONTROLLED FLEX MAKES A FUNDAMENTAL DIFFERENCE TO THE WAY THE CHASSIS WORKS WHEN THE BIKE IS LEANED RIGHT OVER

including a special 16-inch rear for use mid-season. The Kawasaki's power is quite different in both nature and size to the V-engined Ducatis and Suzukis, which were quite often able to share tyre designs. Bridgestone make their 'high power tyres' with a larger overall diameter for a larger contact patch, and, while Suzuki migrated to the larger diameters, Kawasaki didn't seem to need this enhancement.

The Kawasaki motor, although differently packaged, appeared to be quite similar inside. It seemed to be a problem to get the motor to rev to the same level as the opposition and on several occasions engines have failed. The crankshaft on the new bike remains turning forwards – you will note from the chapter on the Yamaha that that bike has its crankshaft turning backwards, primarily to reduce the overall gyroscopic stability of the bike and to allow the bike to roll into corners more quickly. Why Kawasaki did not change the rotation of their crank is unknown. While, mathematically, the effect is quite small, it is quite possible that it substantially affects the handling of the bike.

At Mugello new bodywork was introduced with a larger air intake at the nose and slightly narrower fairings, these last required new radiators as well as the bodywork itself. During the course of the year, several excellent results

came from a combination of a racetrack that Nakano particularly liked, especially those with long, high speed flowing corners, and a good tyre, but these occasions were less frequent than expected. New parts were made available all the way through to the end of the year, with a revised firing sequence engine and yet another new exhaust pipe finally becoming available at Sepang in early September.

The 2006 chassis goes higher over the cylinder heads while the motor tips forward slightly. This allows better inlet port angles and weight distribution.

Kawasaki arrived at Motegi with a third bike for their test rider. This finally had a reverse-rotating, irregular-fire crankshaft.

TEAM ROBERTS

And the Proton, then the KTM, and then the Honda

© MARK WERNHAM

ENGINE: Honda four-stroke, 75.5° V5

CAPACITY: 990cc

POWER: Over 240bhp

TOP SPEED: Over 216mph (347km/h)

TRANSMISSION: Six-speed extractable

IGNITION: Electronic programmable CDI

CHASSIS: GP Motorsports/Alloy

SUSPENSION: Ohlins

WHEELS: Marchesini

TYRES: Michelin 16.5in front and rear

BRAKES: Nissin, two carbon front discs, single steel rear disc

WEIGHT: over 148kg

Specifications based on 2006 Honda-powered Team Roberts bike

Jeremy McWilliams steps out to try the untested KR-Proton V5 at Le Mans in 2003. For the race though the team's old two-strokes were back out.

© HENK KEULEMANS

Kenny Roberts has had a torrid time in MotoGP. In an attempt to emulate David and Goliath he set out to not only build his own chassis and bike, but to build the engine as well. Even in Formula 1, only major manufacturers do this but, at the time of committing to the project, Roberts was seeing a renaissance in his two-stroke project that used an in-house built and designed engine. Perhaps the comparative complexity of a four-stroke project was overlooked when the decisions were made, and operating without the benefit of 20-20 hindsight, there was a chance.

The original thinking behind the 990cc MotoGP formula was that it would be so easy to make enough power that everyone would be dealing with an excess of power. The competition, therefore, was intended to be about the handling, and learning to use the power, rather than a power race. As with all grand plans, however, there was a snag, and that turned out to be the tyre companies. If grip levels had remained where they were in the late '90s it would have been impossible to use the power that has now become commonplace. But the grip levels didn't stay the same; indeed, they increased dramatically – as a result much more power could be used, if you had it to use.

On the chassis side, it was a very different story. The initial chassis was a pure KR design and

fabricated in house. Over the next few years very high quality chassis were developed using high degrees of sophistication based on initial designs and techniques introduced by the celebrated Formula 1 designer John Barnard.

Roberts sat out the first year of four-stroke competition, choosing to stay with their by then very competitive two-stroke triples. Engine designer John Magee had designed new crankcases for the mercurial bike, which had dramatically improved the way it worked, and in its very last race at Phillip Island it qualified on pole. Roberts secured funding from Proton in Malaysia to 'go four-stroke' late in November of that year, and at that point the team had to decide what to build. There were many comments at the time about the choice of a five cylinder, and much debate within the team, but in the end the logic appeared to mirror that of Honda; if you had more cylinders you could rev it more and make more power relatively easily. Roberts effectively committed to build from scratch a complete four-stroke racing motorcycle in less than six months.

While having the capacity to make power was one thing, having a chassis that would allow them the best use of it was another, and Team Roberts chose to focus on building their engine as small as they could, just like they had with their V-3 two-strokes, rather than chasing immediate power. The size of the engine gave them the ability to move the engine around in the chassis so that they could find the best possible position for optimum handling. The logic was that there was no point in having more than 200bhp if you couldn't get through the corners quickly. Also, the use of a balancer shaft would allow different firing orders to be tried, giving Team Roberts far more choice in how the engine affected handling.

The very short timescale put pressure on the project from the beginning. Magee started off with the intention of making the most compact package he could. The initial layout decisions – from the number of pistons to the V-angle, from the crankshaft to what bore and stroke ratios would be appropriate, and whether the engine should use a balance shaft and, if it did, where it should be placed – were taken, and all those decisions are very expensive to change once the initial castings are made.

The bike's first time on any racetrack was at Le Mans practice for the 2003 MotoGP, a move that was as impressive as it was foolhardy. Lack of test time condemned the team to being in a permanent state of trying to fix initial problems rather than developing the bike on track. This was also the year where MotoGP really clicked into

gear. Yes, the Hondas were already superior, but all of a sudden the Yamahas were capable of making it to the front, and the Hondas were improved to stay ahead. The level of competition had moved up, and KR was just getting onto the track. Very quickly it became apparent that the decision to build an extremely compact engine meant that to boost power through additional revs was going to be difficult.

The first year was hard work, several times the two-strokes were brought out of storage while new parts for the four-strokes were being made.

ABOVE: By Mugello the two-strokes were history; both bikes pulled out due to fuel injection problems.

BELOW: In 2004 Team Roberts ran Dunlop tyres, their Bridgestones having defected to Kawasaki. The bike spec was improving, there was a new Barnard-designed chassis and a different cylinder head design.

KENNY ROBERTS' HOME GROWN V5

Magee's design was a counterbalanced 60° V5, three cylinders at the front and two at the rear. Using a 75mm bore and a stroke of 44.8mm, the engine was reasonably oversquare. The initial crank was arranged so that the front three cylinders acted as a 120° triple (for exhaust tuning purposes), and the rear two shared crankpins at each end of the crank. The balance shaft was on the front of the block, gear-driven from the crank, and the cam drive was by two gear trains up the left-hand side of the engine. The gearbox was 'semi-stacked' in much the same way the RC211V became in its final iteration. The entire engine was tiny, really compact. The initial design had additional metal around the ports and valve seats to allow for tuning once the basic package had been run, and the balance shaft meant that the firing order was completely adjustable.

The problems suffered at the start were exactly those you would expect in a new and untried design – irritatingly small issues with big impacts, including problems with oil leaks, especially from around the carbon cam covers, and seals. The plan was for ex-Kawasaki guru Rob Muzzy to tune the engine, once the initial design points had been passed, but before long the team took on the services of some very experienced Formula 1 veterans: designer John Barnard and ex-Cosworth engineer Stuart Banks. In the middle of such quick personnel changes, Magee's original plans for the development of the engine were derailed.

1 Double overhead cams and four valves per cylinder were the MotoGP norm.

2 Normal cable throttles use a small kicker motor to increase effective tickover level to reduce engine braking going into corners.

3 The engine used a balance shaft to enable the team to change the crank firing timing by fitting different cranks and balance shafts.

4 In race trim the slipper clutch was a diaphragm clutch provided by Japanese OEM manufacturer FCC.

This is an early PR shot and by the time the engine reached the track such details as clutch and throttle bodies had been changed.

© HENK KEULEMANS

The team was operating on an unbelievably short timescale to build engines, get them to the circuit and then try to compete against the best factories in the world – all the time learning the foibles of racing four-strokes on a racing circuit for the first time.

One of Kenny Roberts' most famous quotes is 'time and money'. This project got to the track remarkably quickly and, compared to what the rival factories will have paid, for not a lot of money. It was probably the last time anything went to plan.

The bike initially had a KR-designed and KR-built twin-beam fabricated aluminium chassis. The engine's 60° V-angle meant that, while the engine was shorter than the Honda, the main chassis beams had to be very wide to go around the front cylinder head. Instead of Honda's side-entry airbox, the air intakes were carbon tubes that swooped up over the spars into the airbox.

Kenny Roberts had hired John Barnard for new ideas and execution in the chassis and packaging of the race bike, and in 2004 he certainly got what he wanted. With inventive use of materials and a careful rethink of basic concepts, the bike was very neat and nicely manufactured. The chassis was constructed of machined aluminium spars, with the centres spark-eroded away. Unlike the growing consensus amongst the rest of the

paddock, the front engine mounts were high up and the chassis was tied to the cylinder head quite close to the steering head. The bike's careful design showed itself in the way everything did at least two jobs, oil and water being sent through the frame at various points, and the rear head providing structural support for the chassis.

In an effort to boost the power, a new cylinder head was approved for 2004. Designed by Stuart Banks, this was intended to maximise output by allowing the engine to rev significantly higher. As well as being a new design from a power-producing point of view, Barnard included the rear head in his design of the chassis, using it as a stressed member.

Unfortunately, by building the engine into the structure of the chassis in this way, the Proton was committed to using the new-design cylinder head, and that's where it all went horribly wrong. Initial calculations on the benefit of a new head showed that there was the possibility of at least another 20 to 30bhp. The trouble was that the previous design direction had sacrificed everything for small size, and a side-effect of that was a high level of internal friction from the close proximity of some of the parts. As the engine was revved harder, more power was needed to overcome the drag than was being generated by the new cylinder head.

TOP LEFT: The 2004 version of the motor used the rear cylinders as a structural member. You can see the machined-from-solid construction of the main spars quite clearly here. The swingarm too is fabricated from several large lumps of alloy, CNC machined for accurate wall thicknesses.

TOP RIGHT: The injection system used a single overhead injector for each cylinder. The fueling was controlled by electronics from EFI who specialise in the Formula 1 market.

BOTTOM RIGHT: The lower triple clamp was made out of six pieces of titanium and welded together. Each clamping part, the bit that goes around the fork leg, took eight hours to machine.

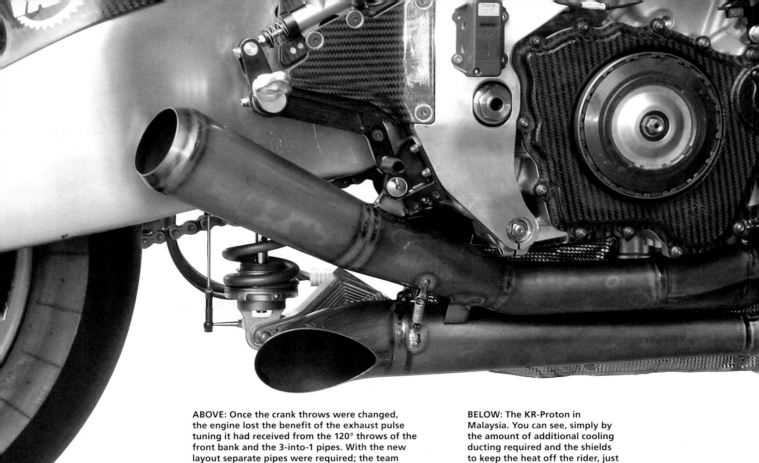

ABOVE: Once the crank throws were changed, the engine lost the benefit of the exhaust pulse tuning it had received from the 120° throws of the front bank and the 3-into-1 pipes. With the new layout separate pipes were required; the team used megaphones to try and replicate some of the scavenging effect.

BELOW: The KR-Proton in Malaysia. You can see, simply by the amount of additional cooling ducting required and the shields to keep the heat off the rider, just how much heat, instead of power, the engine was generating.

BY EFFECTIVELY HAVING TWO DESIGN TEAMS INVOLVED IN ONE ENGINE, EACH WAS HINDERED BY THE DECISIONS OF THE OTHER...

As experience of MotoGP increased, the original choice of firing order was seen to be less and less appropriate. What was right for exhaust gas tuning was causing major torque fluctuations on entering corners and unsettling the bike on its suspension, regardless of the best efforts of the engine management system and its slipper clutch.

Early in 2004 (as soon as the limitations of the engine became apparent) the bore and stroke were modified to 72mm x 46mm. The reasoning behind this was that the slightly longer stroke engine felt better to the rider, and a revised firing order gave the clutch an easier time, allowing the bike to roll into corners more smoothly. Depending on the stroke and firing order of the engine, different exhaust pipes were tried. The team settled on a system for the 72mm bore version with a 2-into-1 and a 1-into-1 from the front three cylinders. The rear pair were either linked 2-into-1 or had an exhaust pipe each.

By effectively having two design teams involved in one engine, each was hindered by the decisions of the other, and that's before the time pressures are taken into account. It is quite possible that it would have been more successful had Magee been allowed to develop the engine as he had wanted, or equally if Banks had been given the budget to build his preferred bottom-end design. In either case, more time and money would have helped. As it was, the engine's potential was never seen.

During the first year, the team carried on with the Bridgestone tyres they had helped develop on their two-strokes. After that, however, Bridgestone moved over to the works Kawasaki team, and KR-Proton signed to use Dunlops. Dunlop, at the time, were not the best tyre available in the MotoGP paddock, and on several occasions Kenny Roberts commented that it would not be worth his while coming back to racing if he had to do so on Dunlops. Given the sheer amount of work and determination put into the project, the outcome was pretty disappointing.

KTM

KTM made an ill-fated effort to get into the world of MotoGP. When the class was introduced, KTM announced that they would take part – bikes, riders, a full works team – and they started hiring people on that basis. Development of the engine was started under the guidance of Kurt Trieb, an ex-BMW Formula One engineer.

Development started in early 2003 with staff recruited all through the year. However, the desire to run their own team reduced dramatically when they saw the massive expenditure being incurred in the first year of MotoGP. At the same time, sales in the USA of KTM bikes were slumping because of the devaluation of the dollar and the Bush administration's desire to export its recession. So, the idea of running their own team was over, but with most of the work done on the engine the company announced it would complete it and put the engine up for sale – perhaps someone else would like to mount it in a chassis and run it.

The engine was a 70° V4 with a dry sump, water cooling, fuel injection and pneumatic valves. The throttles were by a normal cable, but with a kicker motor attached to the pair of butterflies serving the rear cylinders. Pistons were

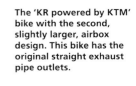

The 'KR powered by KTM' bike with the second, slightly larger, airbox design. This bike has the original straight exhaust pipe outlets.

The original engine: a 70° V4 with an 84mm bore and a 44.6mm stroke. The engine castings were by Zeus, pistons by Mahle. Pneumatic valve springs were used. The motor is dry sump with a single pressure pump and two doubled-up suction pumps. For the best packaging, the oil tank was placed under the engine. This version is fitted with KTM's own clutch.

ABOVE: The KR powered by KTM was warmed up using a car style coolant heater – a small electrical pump and a glorified kettle – before being started, which was significantly more peaceful than the usual MotoGP throttle blipping session at 8.00am in the morning!

BELOW: The original schematic for KTM's own bike, not a million miles from an RCV.

© KTM

by Mahle, and rods by Pankl. A six-speed gearbox in a semi-stacked arrangement, similar to that ultimately selected by Honda for their Evo RC211V, was fitted. The dry sump used a four-section oil-scavenge pump (two pumps paired up, actually) and a single pressure pump. The oil tank was situated under the engine, looking just like a normal sump, but the dry sump design ensured that there could be no windage losses on the crank. All the gearbox gears were individually served with oil jets, as were the base of the pistons. The pneumatic valve-spring

system was built in-house to Trieb's specifications after the decision was taken not to pursue the Del West 'off the shelf' option. This used pressures in the 11 to 14bar range.

By November 2003 the engine was being turned over on the Dyno prior to being run for the first time. Once the idea of building a bike had been discounted, the engine team quietly continued building the first four engines. At the same time it was becoming apparent that Team Roberts' V5 wasn't going to make its hoped-for power outputs, and they started looking around for more power. Would the KTM fit in their chassis?

Initial tests took place during a practice day at Brno in the Czech Republic, and there were more public tests a month or so later at Estoril in Portugal. For 2005, following some very complex negotiations, Shane 'Shakey' Byrne was taken on as the rider, Michelin provided tyres, KTM gave the engines and Roberts provided the chassis and infrastructure. Full KTM support went with the project, with a team led by Heinz Payreder travelling to each GP.

The first chassis for this project was a redesigned Barnard-style one. Byrne had difficulties with the first version, and a radical redesign saw the engine effectively moved forward 20mm. This chassis debuted at Le Mans but didn't bring the required improvements.

Although it was very powerful, the power delivery proved to be difficult to control. To try to slow the engine's desire to rev, a higher-inertia crank was specified. With careful design, this would have been only 0.5kg heavier than the 7kg weight of the original. Unfortunately, though, there was insufficient cash available to the project to get the cranks made. KTM had not gone ahead with their own bike project because of worries on costs, and the cost of a new crank design was deemed prohibitive. This led to Roberts building a new front-biased chassis.

At the same time, however, KTM produced an additional run of ten engines to ensure the team could compete for the entire season. The engines used in the first few races were the original prototypes, and these were close to their time limits. Unfortunately, those new engines had the crankpins made with too low a main bearing clearance, and a series of engine failures finished the teams hopes at Le Mans; the problem was sorted by the next race.

Development of the peripherals continued – new exhausts from Akrapovic, a bigger airbox and KTM's own coil-spring slipper clutches all making appearances, but without the high-inertia crank the bike remained stubbornly uncompetitive. At the same time, relationships

KTM MADE AN ILL-FATED EFFORT TO GET INTO THE WORLD OF MotoGP. WHEN THE CLASS WAS INTRODUCED, KTM ANNOUNCED THAT THEY WOULD TAKE PART – BIKES, RIDERS, A FULL WORKS TEAM – AND THEY STARTED HIRING PEOPLE ON THAT BASIS. DEVELOPMENT OF THE ENGINE WAS STARTED UNDER THE GUIDANCE OF KURT TRIEB, AN EX- BMW FORMULA ONE ENGINEER.

between KTM and Team Roberts became fraught. By Brno they broke down, and KTM withdrew their engines. Foreseeing such a possibility, KR had one of the old five-cylinder bikes available for Jeremy McWilliams, and that is what rolled out of the front of the garage. By Saturday afternoon all of KTM's engines were in their truck and KTM's MotoGP adventure came to an end.

There was some talk of the engines being lent to WCM for the last year of the 990cc competition, but this came to naught when it was realised there wasn't the money to run them.

BELOW LEFT: The titanium rear exhaust had a few unusual bends in it to get the right primary pipe length under the seat.

BOTTOM LEFT: The through-the-steering-head air inlet of the Barnard chassis design was very direct. You can see the fuel injectors in this photo.

BELOW: The end came at Brno. By Friday's practice session Byrne's bikes were parked and the old Proton V5 was back on track. Byrne was contracted directly to KTM so McWilliams turned up to ride for Roberts.

KR HONDA

ABOVE: The KR211V. This is an early chassis with an old style swingarm in a year where Roberts' chassis development expertise was given its first real test. A reliable and powerful engine meant the Roberts clan could concentrate on the handling.

RIGHT: Honda 'suggested' long front engine mounts. This allowed the whole headstock to be quite flexible and Roberts slowly added bracing around their Barnard-style headstock until the chassis felt right to Kenny Jr.

MIDDLE RIGHT: The chassis that Roberts seemed to like best was a fully braced headstock chassis with a new Barnard-style, CNC'ed-from-solid, swingam.

FAR RIGHT: The final version of the frame had extended sidebeams rather than a reinforced head area. This meant a return to Roberts' old methods of fabrication as the spark erosion technique could not be used on beams this long.

In 2006 Roberts had the use of Honda RC211V engines, possibly the ultimate MotoGP engine. The version Team Roberts uses is the same as those in the Honda 'customer' bikes. Honda even allows the team to service the motors in-house, something that would have been unthinkable just a couple of years ago, and something that must be quite fascinating for mechanics who worked on Roberts' own V5.

The team has finally found a power plant to challenge their chassis designing and setup capabilities. The early versions of the bike (six in all!) all used the same basic design put together by noted F1 engineer John Barnard in 2004. This used some unconventional techniques to minimise weight and maximize the accuracy of the construction. The major change was the adoption, at Honda's suggestion, of long front engine mount spars to allow the chassis flex needed for grip in corners to occur over a bigger part of the chassis. As a result, each version has used a stiffer and stiffer headstock area as, with the long engine spar modification, this area does not have to flex as much. By Le Mans the team had a chassis setup that was broadly right and so they built a new version that mounted the top of the shock directly to the frame rather than to the underside of the top of the swingarm. The main reason for this was the

In the absence of real sponsors, dummy ones would do. Venture Petroleum was on the bike as part of its role as an extra in the movie *Velocity*.

time it took the mechanics to change rear shocks, and with the new design it was a lot quicker.

However, the fastest bike saw Roberts reverting to their old fabrication techniques, mainly because the long main beams have to be longer than can be manufactured using Barnard's preferred spark erosion technique. While this chassis seems capable of being faster, it doesn't make the rider feel as comfortable, nor is it as quick or as easy to set up. The team did not stop modifying chassis to the end of the year, finally combining a modified 'long beam' chassis with one of their earlier swingarms, giving Kenny Junior the best feel and the best performance.

HONDA EVEN ALLOWS THE TEAM TO SERVICE THE MOTORS IN-HOUSE, SOMETHING THAT WOULD HAVE BEEN UNTHINKABLE JUST A COUPLE OF YEARS AGO, AND SOMETHING THAT MUST BE QUITE FASCINATING FOR MECHANICS WHO WORKED ON ROBERTS' OWN V5.

FAR LEFT: The preferred style of swingarm. The mounting system made changing the shock a very slow job but KR Jr simply preferred the overall feel.

LEFT: The team built two chassis that mounted the shock top mount to a frame cross member, speeding the shock absorber change time. This design was introduced at Le Mans, but it took to the end of the season for it to feel as good to the rider.

SUZUKI

Catching up fast

ENGINE: Liquid-cooled, 4-stroke V4, DOHC 4-valve

CAPACITY: 990cc

POWER: Over 240bhp, 16,000rpm

TOP SPEED: Over 206mph (330km/h)

TRANSMISSION: Six-speed constant mesh

IGNITION: Mitsubishi ECU

CHASSIS: Twin spar aluminium alloy frame

SUSPENSION: Ohlins, inverted type telescopic front, link type rear

WHEELS: JB-Power Magtan

TYRES: Bridgestone 16.5" front and rear

BRAKES: Brembo, two carbon front discs, single steel rear disc

WEIGHT: 148kg

Over at Suzuki the philosophy was slightly different, but the outcome was similar. Suzuki didn't want their MotoGP engine to be a road-bike-like design, and they wanted to use their tried and tested two-stroke chassis experience. So their new engine had to be small enough to fit as near as possible into the same space as their old two-stroke 500.

Having seen Honda's and Yamaha's exhaustive race programme over the previous year, Suzuki's initial decision was to continue with their two-strokes for another year and get their four-stroke working well away from the rigours of the GPs. As soon as they had it running, though, they found it went a lot better than they expected – and at the November tests in Malaysia the team were amazed to discover they were going four-stroke a year earlier than they had expected.

The bikes were XRE-02 60° V4s. As a design it lasted just one year, but, given the timescale of its construction, it was very effective. Although using a different configuration, bore and stroke to the

GSXR1000, it did have a bucket and shim valve operation design borrowed from the road bike. 'We had a lot of experience with that design, and we didn't have time to think of anything else,' said Masahito Imada, head of Suzuki's MotoGP programme at the time.

The choice of a 60° V meant that the engine fitted into a chassis built to the old two-stroke 500cc specifications, but with that came a whole bunch of other issues that stopped the engine from being developed further. At 60°, it needed some form of balance shaft to minimize vibration, but this would use up power. Also, at 60°, the cylinder heads were so close together that Suzuki couldn't get a decent design of throttle body or inlet port between the angles of the V.

To resolve these issues, Suzuki opened the V-angle of their engines up to 65° for 2003 – not a small operation! That motorcycle, the XRE-03 also came with a full electronic package, including a ride-by-wire throttle. The engine never did make much power, but any chance it had of being competitive in its first year went straight out of the window with the difficulties the team and the riders had in coming to terms with the electronic control package. Suzuki had entrusted their ride-by-wire technology to Mitsubishi, one of their major OEM suppliers. That meant that the package that was put onto the bike was a first

Apart from a fourth in Brno, Sete Gibernau had a disappointing year, but the team was always going to struggle to meet the factory's expectations after Akiro Ryo's surprise second in the first race at Suzuka. The 2002 bike was a rush job, but it worked surprisingly well in the wet.

> ## 'WE HAD A LOT OF EXPERIENCE WITH THAT DESIGN, AND WE DIDN'T HAVE TIME TO THINK OF ANYTHING ELSE.'
> **MASAHITO IMADA**

© HENK KEULEMANS

attempt by a supplier who had no experience of similar technologies within Formula 1 or other forms of motorsport. As a management decision it probably had some advantages – you maintain good relations with your suppliers; they probably charge you less; and one of your suppliers gets massive education in some potentially very profitable technologies. But, from a racer's point of view, it means you are part of a, quite possibly painful, experiment.

Chassis behaviour wasn't everything the team wanted either. Tests would be carried out using

swingarms of slightly different flexibility – the precise degree of flexibility being critical to the way the bike worked when leaned right over. Unfortunately, the manufacturing processes used in building the swingarm up from a series of sections of extruded aluminium did not allow the factory to accurately repeat the precise flexibility of the structure.

ABOVE: The 2003 bike was brand new. An engine with a bigger 65° angle between the cylinders, and a new beam chassis with a longer swingarm.

The new bike used a prototype ride-by-wire throttle system and was clothed in new bodywork. Suzuki also joined the noisy squad with a tiny open pipe exhaust system. This was different to the system used on the test bikes in Japan; by the end of the year the mufflers were back, if only for consistency.

© DORNA

Later in the year Suzuki changed the firing sequence of their engine in the search for more traction, and with that change came the coolest exhaust in the pit lane.

The biggest chassis change for 2004 was a new swingarm made using large sections of CNC machined aluminium. The new consistency of manufacture allowed Suzuki to fine-tune their handling. On this early 2004 bike you can see the screamer 4-into-1 pipes.

The 2004 Suzuki airbox couldn't get down between the cylinders, so it was both too small and perched up on top of the engine, and that meant the fuel had to go elsewhere.

For 2004 Suzuki changed over to a swingarm design where the main parts were machined from solid. This enabled them to make revised swingarms that flexed precisely to order and on a repeatable basis. Masahito Imada commented, 'It wasn't easy, there was a lot of effort put into getting that technology to work for us.'

Suzuki was the only manufacturer with a V-configuration bike still mounting the top of the shock absorber to the frame, all the others having chosen to save space by mounting the top of the shock to the swingarm. This meant that Suzuki used a long fuel tank going back under the rider's seat, rather than down close to the top of the swing-arm. Because of their narrower-angle V-configuration, their airbox and inlet system sat higher than the others too, again squeezing the available space for fuel. The weight distribution issues the V-angle forced on the designers were offset to some extent by the very centralised nature of the engine's weight. Like Yamaha, Suzuki also changed to a conventional six-spring slipper clutch using ramps and springs. Although it looks externally similar to Yamaha's, the earlier 'part slipper' version of the new clutch allowed the plates to slip without half of them being clamped tight.

In 2004, Suzuki reduced the complexity of the control system, and the bike worked a lot better. That still wasn't enough, however. Good pre-season test results didn't reflect the real picture and, as soon as the season started, the Suzukis struggled. From day one, the engine, with its new rocker cam followers, had a very fragile top end. The team had to change valve springs every day, and the engine consistently lacked sufficient power to be truly competitive. Both bikes were using the original 180° crankshaft. This gave the slipper clutch and tyres a very hard time on corner entry. So while Yamaha and Ducati were looking for irregular firing for better traction, Suzuki were going the other way to ease engine braking. Revised parts were made, and an engine and the appropriate exhausts were flown to Estoril for a test. Following those tests, the new 360° crank was introduced – this spread out the firing pulses and meant that the firing intervals became 0°, 65°, 360° and 425°. Both riders found this engine much easier to use, especially in a corner entry.

One detail that seemed likely to change, though, was the airbox. It looked quite small for the power they needed. Suzuki did use quite a few different exhaust systems, the 360° crank version of the engine using a pair of 2-into-1 pipes. The one from the front cylinders was longer and used a spectacular sectioned megaphone, but the other pipe, which was from the rear cylinders, used a much shorter small-

diameter pipe. Suzuki personnel said at the time that the combination of the two pipes got the best result on the dyno. While the idea of using different diameter pipes to equalise the way different length exhaust pipes work is not new, it seems just as likely that the decision was driven more by manufacturing expediency.

Each rider and his crew chief had different preferences on chassis set-up. For 2005, the basic bikes looked very similar to the 2004 versions, but Hopkins' bikes, under the control of Stuart Shenton, had both the headstock and swingarm positions welded in place for most of the year. At particular circuits, where Shenton thought a change might be advantageous, an adjustable chassis was used, but wherever possible he preferred the major locations to be welded in place. The reasoning was that, with less opportunity for movement, chatter was less likely to be a problem. Noticeably, Kenny Roberts' bikes, under the control of returning crew chief Erv Kanemoto, remained fully adjustable. There were a few other differences in the braking department, though, with Hopper's machine using a very small Brembo Motocross master cylinder for the rear

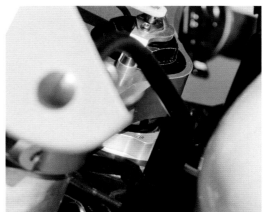

Roberts always had an adjustable steering head on his frames but Stuart Shenton, Hopkins' crew chief prefers to keep things welded up if he can as a precaution against chatter. Some times, however, new settings need to be tried and an adjustable chassis is necessary. This is Hopkins' bike at Brno in 2005.

Roberts also likes an adjustable swingarm pivot, different spacers are used to raise or lower the pivot point in relation to the front sprocket. Here it is being tightened up again at Brno in 2005.

MOVING FUEL FOR THE AIRBOX

As recounted earlier, one of the packaging difficulties a 65° V engine brings with it is the height of the engine once the airbox and throttle bodies are taken into account. It makes the constructor have to choose between fuel tank and airbox as to what goes at the top of the bike – it's easier to move the fuel, but this has a greater effect on the weight distribution. Suzuki spent the early part of 2005 experimenting with different airbox volumes, airbox intake ducts, fuel tanks and intake and exhaust lengths. Airboxes resonate at certain frequencies, and their resonant frequency can work either with or against the engine. In a perfect design, the airbox provides a positive pulse just as the engine hits a flat spot, without damaging power anywhere else in the range. The frequency is a product of several features, which include the volume of the airbox itself and the length and cross section of the airbox intake tubes. Suzuki's solution was to include a temporary increase in airbox volume by removing the airbox top and relying on a seal between the airbox base and the fuel tank, using the fuel tank as the airbox top.

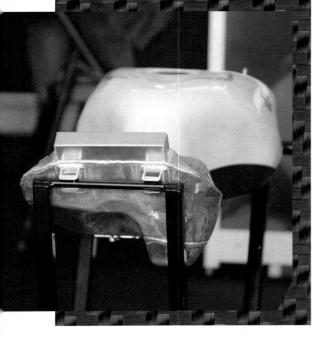

TOP LEFT: Suzuki use a Mitsubishi throttle system, this uses a small flashload unit to transfer revised throttle settings from the data technician's PC to the onboard ECU.

TOP RIGHT: Paul Denning took over from the long serving Garry Taylor in 2005 initially bringing his own Crescent Suzuki brand as a sponsor and then following that by bringing on board Rizla, one of the sponsors of his UK-based BSB team.

ABOVE: Roberts' bike is warmed up at Sachsenring in 2005, the 2D dash gives a full display of engine data and is redlined at 16,000 rpm.

brake. This is because Hopkins very rarely if ever touches the rear brake, and the decision was therefore made to provide the lightest and smallest rear braking system possible.

2005 brought more revs and more power but, again, Suzuki had fixed their problems for the previous year and hadn't been able to take the extra step to compete head-on with the majors. Cylinder head modifications boosted top-end power, maximum revs were up over 1000rpm, but the mid-range hadn't improved.

With a bike looking very similar to last year's, albeit with a new Paul Denning-inspired paint scheme, Suzuki were the sensation of the tests. The chassis looked very similar to the 2004 version, with, we are told, a little more rigidity. The fairing, seat and fuel tank also looked very similar. Suzuki tested a completely new chassis early in the year at Malaysia which was not successful, but the current chassis had a very good reputation. The new one was sent back to the crusher and the older version was given another year.

The major changes were in the engine, with another 1000rpm and 20hp to play with. Kunio Arese, the engineer in charge of engine development at Suzuki's racing division, confirmed that most of the changes were in the inlet and exhaust porting, but new and lighter parts had been used in the valve train to keep the engine reliable at higher revs. 'The latest evolution of the GSV-R has improvements in power and rider controllability. We improved the inlet port a lot, to increase the airflow, and we have a little more compression to work with it. The engine has new fuel-injection technology that uses overhead injectors, and which has given us an 8% improvement in fuel efficiency. We have also improved throttle response, with changes to the fuel-injection and exhaust system. We still have the same ride-by-wire system on the bike as was on the XRE-1. We modified the electronic clutch, but the system we now have is well developed. We still use the slipper clutch, but we have new software to help control the engine braking. We would like to improve the engine a little more, possibly with a bigger V-angle. The engine we now have is 65° V; 90° makes it difficult to get the right chassis balance, so maybe somewhere between the two. This may be available later this year.'

Although Suzuki did not claim any increase in mid-range power, the simple fact that the engine revved 1000rpm more meant the gearing could be lower in nearly every situation, meaning that more power would be available at any given speed. Hopkins clearly enjoyed the bike, and got up to fourth in the televised shoot-out at

'WE ARE UP AGAINST BIG MOTOCROSSERS OUT THERE, WE JUST DON'T HAVE THE MID-RANGE GRUNT THEY DO.'
PAUL DENNING

Catalunya at the start of the year.

With Erv Kanemoto off to Honda, Suzuki hired a new crew chief for Kenny Roberts Jnr, Tom O'Kane, one of the stalwarts of the original Roberts team. Bridgestone's rear tyres made a tremendous step forward, with the Suzuki's having so much additional rear grip that the team had to do additional tests on the front to get it to work better and to balance out the bike again. The year ended in frustration, however, as the bike was still not able to compete with the top runners except when the conditions were so bad that no one else could use their higher mid-range power capabilities. New Suzuki MotoGP Manager, Paul Denning, said it best: 'We are up against big motocrossers out there, we just don't have the mid-range grunt they do.'

For the final year of the 990cc fours, however, Suzuki went back to the drawing board and built a 75° V4 with pneumatic valve actuation. It was always going to be difficult to develop the engine sufficiently to be competitive in just one year, but

Hopkins' bike at Sachsenring. Note the loose airbox cover, used just to shield the injection system from prying eyes; the foam on the lower airbox forms a seal with the bottom of the fuel tank, increasing airbox volume. This bike has a set of short megaphones.

Suzuki tried. The new engine allowed the intake system and the airbox to be moved down inside the V, and a new chassis and swingarm were required. Initial testing with the chassis took place in Sepang in late 2005, but this was without the new engine. Instead, the old engine was used with custom-built engine side-covers. This test allowed the team to find a combination of chassis and swingarm that would take the new engine and also duplicate the feel of the old chassis.

The new engine's debut was at Sepang in early February 2006. It wasn't an immediate success, with software problems making the bike difficult to ride. By Qatar a week later, however, that had been resolved and, on his first day at the desert track, Hopkins was over a second quicker than his previous qualifying time.

In the second race at Qatar both bikes failed to finish because of a previously unheard of failure of the water pump impeller. This small propeller-like device is the core of the water pump, and during the race the drives to both bikes' impellers failed. As a result, no water was circulated and the bikes quickly overheated.

During practice, though, the Suzuki had suffered a problem with its new-for-2006 pneumatic airvalves. These systems use a pressure of around 20bar inside the bucket over each valve. Replacing the metal spring, this air pressure provides a progressive spring for each valve. Obviously, should this pressure drop it's possible for the valves to become tangled with the pistons. To prevent this, a small canister is fitted to the bike that tops up the system should any leaks occur. With a system like this it's normal to see some leakage, but it shouldn't be a problem over the short duration of a practice

Suzuki's new bike was in Europe for the first time at the Catalunya pre-season test. Radically different construction and a 75° V engine with pneumatic valve springs showed Suzuki were getting serious.

or a race. To prevent disastrous failures, the ECU monitors the amount of topping-up required, and should this rate exceed a certain level, the system comes to the conclusion that the airvalves will ultimately fail. To prevent any problems it triggers an automatic shutdown of the engine.

Suzuki pulled out all the stops to fix it in the three weeks up to the Turkish round. The factory produced and delivered new seals for the valves, along with revised plating for the buckets. These two measures helped reduce leakage, and as a final measure they also provided camshafts that closed the valves less violently. In all, these changes made sure that the bike's pressure monitor was not triggered, and reliability returned.

The slightly softer cam timing probably helped give Suzuki a very tractable engine, perfectly suited for the wet qualifying conditions of Turkey. One modification that may have helped was a small keel attached to the bottom half of the fairing, designed to deflect some water away from the rear tyre. Whatever it was, the rest of the pack had no match for Vermeulen in the rain. As soon as anyone came close he was able to improve his time by half a second.

Turkey was also bitter-sweet for Masahito Imada, head of Suzuki's race effort for all of the MotoGP years. He moved on to head the development programme for the GSX-R road bike range. His replacement in the race programme is the previous head of that same GSX-R programme Fumihiro Ohnishi – they essentially swapped jobs. It's difficult to think of a more effective way of injecting MotoGP know-how into road bikes.

Once Suzuki had regained their reliability, they had to use their new-found top-end power as well as they could, the continuing lack of mid-range grunt on a par with Yamaha and Honda meant the their setups worked better on circuits where they could use their high corner speeds. On Bridgestone qualifiers with their outstanding edge grip they were consistently competitive, but that success was only available if that edge grip was maintained.

Typically a good final qualifying was followed by a good start and a slow fall back through the pack. Suzuki worked hard on their engine; a new motor setup was tested after the Brno race. That got the attention of the riders and this version of the motor was used at the end of the season.

At that same Brno test several experiments were carried out on fork and swingarm flexibility, three different swingarms were tested together with fork legs that had been machined down for additional flexibility.

After the warm-up lap the data-logging is double checked.

The sailing contingent in the team added this small keel to the fairing for the wet sessions in Turkey. It's clearly effective at keeping the water thrown up by the front tyre away from the rear tyre.

© SUZUKI PRESS

The new 75° engine was an opportunity to repackage a lot of things. Compare this with the 65° motor in the 2005 bike on the previous page.

With no enrichener circuit the Suzukis get special richer maps for the warm-up session in the morning; producing some gratifyingly large backfires.

YAMAHA

**The Mission One
journey**

ENGINE: Liquid-cooled in-line four-cylinder, four-stroke

CAPACITY: 990cc

POWER: Over 250bhp at 16,000rpm

TOP SPEED: Over 206mph (330km/h)

TRANSMISSION: Six-speed cassette with alternative gear ratios

IGNITION: Magnetti Marelli ECU with adjustable mapping

CHASSIS: Aluminium delta box, adjustable geometry

SUSPENSION: Ohlins upside down front forks and Ohlins rear shock, alternative rear linkages available

WHEELS: Marchesini

TYRES: Michelin 16.5in front and rear

BRAKES: Brembo, 320mm carbon front discs, two four-piston calipers. Single 220mm steel rear disc, two-piston caliper

WEIGHT: 148kg

Yamaha launched Mission 1 (M1) in the autumn of 2000. The bike was designed from the start to be a well-balanced rider-friendly motorcycle. By March 2001 testing was underway with ex-World Superbike and GP250 champion John Kocinski. By the middle of that year Yamaha's regular GP riders, Biaggi and Checa, were riding it in tests at Catalunya.

Using their well-developed 500cc two-stroke chassis layout as the basis, Yamaha stuck with proven ideas: 'If you consider that all the top 500s are similar in layout and dimensions, this suggests that it is an ideal configuration. That's why we wanted to continue using our YZR-style chassis with the YZR-M1 – the engine was designed to fit within the package, not the other way around.'

Yamaha decided that the very compact configuration of the in-line four would fit best. There was no second bank of cylinders to squeeze in at the back and, although the engine was wide, it was wide where there was room for it to be wide – in front of the rider's legs. And, with one cam drive, one set of cams and one block, it was relatively light. Marketing considerations were also taken into account – most of Yamaha's sport bikes were across-the-frame fours. The

M1 initially came in at less than the full 990cc allowed; engine designer Masakazo Shiohara having designed a 942cc engine to be compatible with the 500 two-strokes of the time, and with the grip available from the Michelin tyres. Yamaha's reputation has always been to produce real-world racing motorcycles that are designed from the start to maximise their cornering ability and their initial acceleration out of those corners, and everything about the first M1 said that they were following that philosophy. Yamaha's engines were carburetted, even though the factory had spent several years in World Superbike with their fuel-injected R7 750-4. They decided that it would be easier to produce a more human response from the throttles by using carburettors on the MotoGP engine.

Ichiro Yoda went further: 'Considerable

Yamaha's first four-stroke M1s displaced 942cc, more than enough to make the right sort of power to be competitive thought Yamaha. Initial designs used a chassis with very similar dimensions to the previous generation of 500cc fours.

experience has taught us that the best measure of the overall performance of a race machine is expressed in the concept of "drivability". Naturally, this was also the concept we stressed in the development of the YZR-M1. In other words, we placed top priority on developing more usable power development character in the engine. If we were only focusing on max power output, we could have raised the output. But that would not necessarily mean better lap times or competitiveness on the racetrack. We sought to develop engine and chassis characteristics that would communicate the drive force of the rear tyre to the rider more directly, create better contact between the rear tyre and the track surface and produce more efficient tyre performance.'

Yamaha's initial ideas of matching torque curve to tyre grip, and agility to power, took a heavy battering in the first few races of the first season, and the rest of the first year turned into an unseemly scrabble for more power, better clutch control and changes in weight distribution. By the end of the year, however, Yamaha had gone from being embarrassingly outclassed by the old two-strokes to qualifying on pole at Valencia. Even now, it's difficult to get from Yamaha the process by which they improved their bike, but improve it they did, and the story is a classic case of showing

how a revised engine formula totally changed the shape of motorcycle racing.

By deciding to build an engine to fit the 500 two-stroke space, Yamaha had fallen into the trap of assuming that the new formula would be the same, only four-stroke and noisier. Yamaha had also duplicated the power outputs of the 500 two-strokes, but being a four-stroke this meant it would carry with it some disadvantages, especially on the engine-braking front. Two-strokes simply don't have enough cylinder compression to jerk the rear suspension around as the throttle is shut going into a corner. Powerful four-strokes, however, most certainly do. By building an engine that performed similarly to the two-strokes on track, and not doing enough to eliminate the difficulties going into the corners, meant that the Yamaha was outclassed by the old two-strokes during the first three Grands Prix. Rapid development of an active computer-controlled pump to emulate a slipper clutch action – together with a throttle-kicker motor opening one of the carburettor slides as the throttles shut, just enough to eliminate some of the engine braking but not enough to drive the bike forward – helped, but didn't solve the problem.

Several different versions of the chassis were seen during the first year, all moving the engine around so that different centre-of-gravity heights

By the second year the Yamaha was expanding. Now a full 990cc, the search for power was really on. Note the experimental 'muffler' on this bike and the mounts holding the cylinder head to the chassis.

© HENK KEULEMANS

YAMAHA'S BACKWARDS CRANK M1 ENGINE

Yamaha's initial M1 engine, while appearing to be a simple across-the-frame four-cylinder four-stroke just like their street bikes, was in fact a very complex rearrangement of that formula, specifically designed for the Grand Prix track. All the engines had crankcases machined from billet, and some experimental barrels had also been cut from billet, but most were cast, as were the cylinder heads. To start with, the engines came with five valves per cylinder, just like Yamaha's big street engines, but the bottom ends were very different, in so far as the crankshaft turned backwards. This decision necessitated an additional shaft across the back of the engine taking the power from the centre of the crank to the primary gear next to the clutch basket, just to get the engine final output rotation in the right direction to drive the bike. Taking the power from the centre of the crank had other advantages – less flex, less load and less chance of the crank twisting under power – but the main advantage seemed to be the torque reaction and gyroscopic effects.

An additional gear set like this probably cost Yamaha 2–3% (say 5bhp) of their power output, so there has to be a very good reason to decide to rotate the crank backwards. (See the section on the effects of crankshaft rotation on motorcycle handling.)

and front-to-rear weight distributions could be tried. All shared the same basic deltabox layout, with the steering head attached rigidly to the cylinder head.

At the start of the second year, Yamaha moved from carburettors to fuel-injection but, just like their experience with the R7 750, the throttle response was not as good as they wanted. They also ditched their computer-controlled clutch and went back to a simple slipper clutch, but with a more active throttle-kicker system. At the final IRTA test at Jerez, before the start of the season, it was quite amazing to hear Barros arriving at the final corner with the wailing four-cylinder engine suddenly changing into a blubbering 500 twin. This was that new kicker mechanism keeping one cylinder sufficiently on an open throttle to destroy most of the damaging effects of engine braking.

New bodywork was fitted for 2003 – much more aggressive than the older more aerodynamic fairing and seat. In the search for more power there was constant experimentation with airbox sizes. (It can be quite difficult to increase the size of an airbox when there is little room to put the fuel elsewhere.) Airbox size is a fundamental part of the way an engine works – too small and it can affect not only peak power but also, because of the pressure fluctuations that occur within it at different rev ranges, the shape and smoothness of the torque curve. At Yamaha they increased the size of the airbox but initially had to raise the top of the tank to retain the fuel capacity they needed to finish the races.

Again, though, it was obvious that Yamaha had underestimated the amount of power they needed, and throughout the season they were revising engine parts in an effort to get on the pace.

During 2003 there was a massive shake up in Yamaha's race engineering department, putting Masao Furusawa in charge. He was determined that, to properly celebrate Yamaha's 50th anniversary two years hence, they would capture the MotoGP title in 2005. By the end of the 2003 season it was obvious something was up, but it wasn't until Valentino Rossi announced his defection from Honda to Yamaha that things started to come together.

For Rossi's initial test session four engines were used – a five-valve four-cylinder with a conventional crankshaft, a five-valve four-cylinder with a modified crankshaft giving an irregular-firing delivery, a conventional crankshaft four-valve engine and finally, the one that Rossi took forward, a four-valve engine with an irregular-firing crankshaft. The chassis set-up was radically changed – the bike being made longer and higher, the forks extended by nearly 25mm and the swingarm stretched by the same amount. These

'ALL BIKES OPERATE WITHIN A CIRCLE, AND THE CIRCLE WASN'T ANYWHERE NEAR WHERE I FELT IT SHOULD BE… TO RIDE ONE OF THESE THINGS, YOU NEED TO HAVE ENOUGH FEEL TO GET THE BIKE TO SLIDE; YOU MUST BE ABLE TO FEEL YOUR WAY INTO A SLIDE AND THEN BACK OUT AGAIN SAFELY.'
JERRY BURGESS

modifications were made to a chassis that had even more radical front engine mounts than the prototypes seen at the end of 2003 at Valencia. Front forks don't work so well when leaned over, and to try to maintain grip the new chassis allowed the whole headstock to flex a little when the bike was deep into a corner and leaned right over.

Yamaha had provided a new kit of parts, but it was Rossi and Burgess who made things work. Jerry Burgess said: 'We identified fairly early what the problems were. The bike was developed by two very good 250 riders. No slur on them, but what you want for a big bike, a 500 or a four-stroke, is something different. All bikes operate

TOP LEFT: In addition to experimenting with chassis, engines and exhausts Yamaha tried different airbox sizes looking for more of the right sort of power.

BOTTOM LEFT: Abe used a 2002 bike complete with carburettors at the IRTA tests at the start of 2003.

BELOW: Melandri's 2004 bike has the old 5 valve cylinder head and short swingarm but has received the new long front engine mount main chassis. Yamaha uprated all their bikes to the top spec by the second GP.

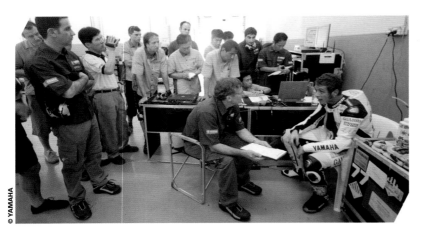

© YAMAHA

ABOVE: Rossi brought most of his crew with him from Honda, Jerry Burgess in particular bringing many years of championship winning experience.

BELOW: Rossi was quickly on the pace in testing. New features included four-valve heads, TT25 Ohlins forks; a swingarm with its bracing underneath, and, most importantly, a revised firing order engine for traction.

within a circle, and the circle wasn't anywhere near where I felt it should be... To ride one of these things, you need to have enough feel to get the bike to slide; you must be able to feel your way into a slide and then back out again safely.'

A longer bike required more rider input to get perfect traction, but the point of having the bike longer was that the rider could choose to increase or reduce traction by moving his weight forwards and backwards. By having the bike taller they could run it as a more stable chassis, but one whose higher centre of gravity would still allow it to turn into corners quickly. Masao Furusawa: 'For sure, we have built a bike that Valentino has to move

around on to get the best out of, but our final goal is to build a bike where the rider doesn't need to move as much.' Burgess, too, revealed something of the way the bike had been developed, 'Valentino could never understand why he could outbrake the Yamaha when he was on the Honda, both bikes have the same basic braking system, and the same tyres. But then we realised the Yamaha was too low, it couldn't pitch its weight forward on braking like the Honda could.' Honda were using the tendency of a bike to pitch forward under braking to load up the front tyre more, squashing it onto the track and increasing the size of the contact patch. This allowed the rider to further increase the braking forces, further increasing the contact patch.

Once a basic set-up had been found, and used for the South African win, the team revisited the settings – the longer wheelbase variant was clearly easy to control, but possibly didn't offer the best traction. During the next few races they struggled to find the right combination of chassis and suspension settings, and the bike was a real handful in the wet. By Le Mans, the Weber Marelli ride-by-wire

© YAMAHA

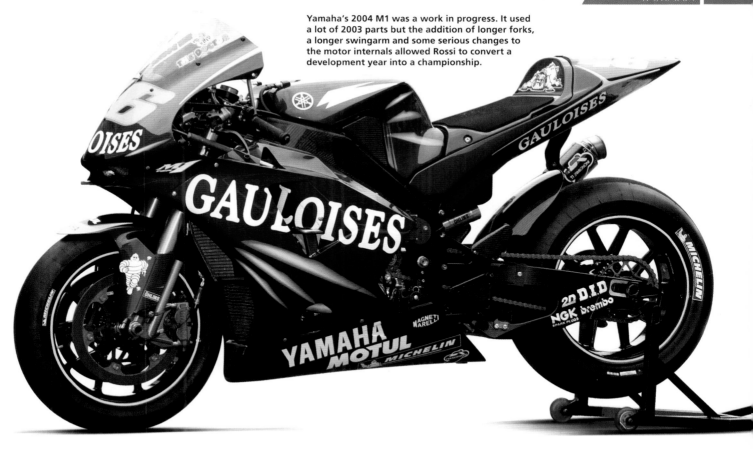

Yamaha's 2004 M1 was a work in progress. It used a lot of 2003 parts but the addition of longer forks, a longer swingarm and some serious changes to the motor internals allowed Rossi to convert a development year into a championship.

throttle system, having being tested on Melandri's and Abe's bikes, was transferred to Rossi and Checa, with a great improvement in driveability.

By Mugello there was a new swingarm, and another was tested after the Catalunya race – with chassis composure increasing each time. At Assen a new chassis was delivered. From the outside Rossi's set-up didn't appear to change much more until the last few rounds, but it was certainly being changed inside.

Towards the end of the year we saw more evidence that the 2004 bike was still a 'work in progress' project. Yamaha wanted Rossi and his crew to show what was needed before designing

the bike destined to celebrate 50 years of Yamahas in proper style. Qatar held its first GP in previously unheard of temperatures – over 55°C on the track. To help cope with these temperatures, the works Yamahas suddenly sprouted additional air dams, side-fairings designed to deflect more air into the radiator, and spoilers to help drag hot air out. While the engine would be cooled better, all these things add drag and slow the bike down.

These modifications were evidence that the new Rossi-style long front engine mounts were using valuable space previously available for the radiator exhaust ducts. All motorcycle design is

BELOW LEFT: Yamaha tried new bodywork at a test at Brno after the GP. Somewhat slimmer, it was rejected by the riders because it didn't provide enough wind protection.

BELOW: Rossi tried two different new swingarms at a test on the Monday morning after the Catalunya GP.

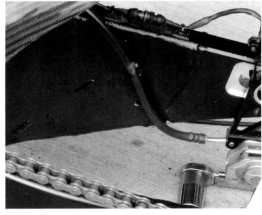

ABOVE: Yamaha used special fairings designed to duct more air into the radiator and back out again at Qatar and in practice at Malaysia. Look at the shape of the leading edge of the fairing and the air dams by the radiator exhaust ducts.

ABOVE RIGHT: Rossi's swingarms had different welds on their inside walls for different rigidities compared to his team-mate's.

BELOW: Rossi's Yamaha is prepared for battle at Estoril in 2004. Note the 2004 exhaust routing and long front engine mount frame.

BELOW RIGHT: The 2005 engine used the same clutch, but that was about it. You can see the different pipe routing, sump design and the absence of the cam chain housing on the extreme right of the cylinder block.

compromise, but the temperatures of Qatar showed where the 2004 M1's limits were.

The cam drive, situated at the far right of the crankshaft, was still by chain, and this was becoming a problem. The revs now required to make competitive power were above the chain's safe limit and, as a precaution, the cam chains were changed every night of each GP weekend. At the end of 2003 Yamaha still had a guillotine slide fuel injection system. We don't know whether Yamaha went across to the butterfly valves at the start of 2004, but they most certainly changed to a full Weber Marelli system at Le Mans in 2004. This system has gone on to become the definitive ride-by-wire system. It was now clear to Yamaha what they needed to do to win the championship in 2005 and after the last race at Valencia a new bike was debuted.

Yamaha's 2005 M1 had a completely new engine and chassis, using some really neat ideas. The six-spring slipper clutch was probably the only part unchanged. The new design necessitated a very complex split in the crankcases, with the front half of the engine split at nearly 45° to allow the revised shaft assemblies to be bolted into place. The cam drive was different, too. Obviously, you have to drive the cams somehow, but all conventional designs put the 20mm-wide gear or cam chain assembly in line with the cylinders,

either at one end or in the middle, and that makes an in-line four quite wide.

The 2005 engine was optimised for higher rev capability and, to raise the centre of gravity while still allowing the preferred swingarm pivot countershaft relationship, a stacked gearbox was used. To make the engine as narrow as possible so that the radiator exhausts worked with the chosen 'long front spar' chassis, Yamaha redesigned the cam drive to the back of the engine, just behind the two central cylinders. Driven off an abbreviated jackshaft, the new cam drive was a train of gears, replacing the combined chain and gear drive used since 2001.

This latest M1 engine was probably one of the smallest 990cc four-cylinder engines ever built. While the crankshaft was no narrower than in the engines of 2004 and before, the revised cam drive allowed the engine to be made narrower immediately above the crankshaft. This permitted the chassis spars that attach just above the crankcase to be moved inwards, and allowed bigger, more efficient radiator exhaust ducts to vent more hot air out of the radiator. With the potential for less drag in the radiator area, and a reduced frontal area, this was one modification that promised to translate immediately into increased top speed.

The basic specification of the latest engines

started out at the same level as the successful 2004 engine. During 2005, however, the engine benefited from new cams and valves, allowing it to make power reliably higher up the rev range – something that could not be done with the older chain cam drive system.

The factory has never released bore and stroke figures. Initially, the engine was only slightly more oversquare than the R1 road bike. Certainly the long path towards more revs had not given the impression that the engine was particularly oversquare. When it was first released the rev limit was around 14,500rpm, but by mid-2005 the factory conceded that 16,000rpm was normal

THIS LATEST M1 ENGINE WAS PROBABLY ONE OF THE SMALLEST 990CC FOUR-CYLINDER ENGINES EVER BUILT. WHILE THE CRANKSHAFT WAS NO NARROWER THAN IN THE ENGINES OF 2004 AND BEFORE, THE REVISED CAM DRIVE ALLOWED THE ENGINE TO BE MADE NARROWER IMMEDIATELY ABOVE THE CRANKSHAFT.

The 2005 bike used this spectacular retro-Yamaha USA paint scheme for Yamaha's 50th Birthday celebrations at Laguna Seca. The bike itself doesn't look that different to the 2004 one, but in reality every part is new.

© YAMAHA

and that figures in excess of this were used occasionally. Power figures also released at Motegi in 2005 clearly showed the additional power being quite peaky in nature. The throttle system – by now equipped with dual rider-controlled butterflies, and dual computer-controlled ones to help deal with a less stable power delivery – was now earning its keep. The riders acknowledged that the bike would be unrideable without the throttle system calming the engine's power at appropriate moments.

The changes didn't stop there. All the works Yamahas were using newly-designed Ohlins forks – the gas reservoirs that previously lived behind

the fork tubes were gone. For some years Sachs and Ohlins had been perfecting new twin-tube 'constant volume' shock-absorber technology for cars. The technology is not dissimilar to that on a typical steering damper. As only very low gas pressures are required, there is no need for a gas reservoir, thus saving weight and space and giving very precise, easily adjustable damping. Yamaha didn't stop looking for every advantage they could find, and at Mugello they debuted a new Ohlins rear shock using the same constant-volume TTX 44 technology as the 2005 forks.

The decision to make a new bike for what was

ABOVE: Sachsenring 2005. Rossi's bike is rebuilt following his practice crash. Note the 2005 chassis and in particular the shape of the join between the main frame beam and the front engine mount.

possibly the most important year of competition for Yamaha since they won their first World Championship shows staggering self-confidence. Usually you don't expect a new design to work perfectly until at least the second year, and the 2005 M1 was effectively a new design.

For 2006, Yamaha further refined the M1. First seen at Sepang at the end of November 2005, the new bike looked very similar to the old, but it was in fact almost completely new. A revised frame had different sections in the headstock area, undoubtedly to make the bike more stable under braking. The swingarm was

also new, being both lighter and stronger, and having a gussetted hole cut into it, which was filled with a carbon-fibre plug. The airbox and ECU area were also different, with the fuel load dropped down into the area that used to be allocated to the old design of rear shock. As a result, the airbox could be slightly bigger, potentially improving the bike's power. While the engine looked similar, a careful examination of the crankcases showed additional blanked-off passageways, probably to improve oil feed to the crankshaft. Masao Furusawa confirmed that the new engine had a shorter stroke and bigger bore than before, in the search for more

RIGHT: Rossi's Marelli dash readout includes a best lap function in addition to a myriad of other detail. Here we can see that Rossi has just set a 1:48.39 time, the fourth fastest warm-up lap at Motegi in 2005.

FAR RIGHT: From Mugello 2005 on, the works Yamahas used this Ohlins through shock. With minimal oil displacement, only a very small reservoir is needed.

power, but he declined to say what the actual figures were.

Yamaha had a very successful winter testing, with only a few problems with chatter surfacing on one or two corners in Malaysia and Qatar. At the GP zero at Catalunya in March, the Yamahas showed themselves right at the top of their game, and Rossi only had to do a few laps to prove he was the fastest. One week later, however, at Jerez everything went wrong. The bike suffered badly from chatter, undoubtedly a combination of Michelin's new super grippy tyres and the changes Yamaha had wrought to their chassis over the winter. The team had three days testing at Jerez to try to isolate the problem, but when they returned for the Grand Prix two weeks later they still had chatter as violent as had been seen for many years.

Three days of the Grand Prix didn't cure the problem, and neither did an additional day's testing. Jerez is an unusual track – the corners are all in the speed area that seems to encourage the onset of chatter, possibly 140kph – and Yamaha must isolate the problem and cure it because next year they will be back at

Jerez, and there will be many other circuits that have quite a few corners in the same speed range. Two weeks later, in Qatar, they were still suffering some chatter, but not quite as badly. Rossi managed to win the race, but it was clear that Yamaha did not have that great advantage over either the Honda or the latest Ducati.

The design of the Yamaha chassis is such that the team can easily change its rigidity and, they hope, its harmonic frequency when attempting to eliminate the frequencies that are colliding with those emanating from the tyres. One of the main weapons is an adjustable engine mount just behind the cylinder head. This normally exists to provide a solid location on the chassis at a point in a straight line from the rear tyre contact patch. Loosening the bolts attaching the chassis to the engine or, even more dramatically, changing the material and fit of the brackets, would all change the frequency of the chassis. We know Yamaha was experimenting with these changes at Jerez and Qatar, but to no avail. Once the scientific solutions had been exhausted, the older systems were tried. Rossi went to the line at Jerez with the rear axle filled with lead (not because he wanted to increase unsprung

The 2006 M1 looked very similar on the surface, but some critical differences in rigidity made it very susceptible to chatter.

© YAMAHA

JEREZ IS AN UNUSUAL TRACK – THE CORNERS ARE ALL IN THE SPEED AREA THAT SEEMS TO ENCOURAGE THE ONSET OF CHATTER, POSSIBLY 140KPH – AND YAMAHA MUST ISOLATE THE PROBLEM AND CURE IT BECAUSE NEXT YEAR THEY WILL BE BACK AT JEREZ…

ABOVE: Rossi's Yamaha at Assen. Now using a 2005 chassis, you can see the straight join between main frame and the engine mounting spar, and airbox. Compare this with the original 2006 chassis shown in our main ghosted image on page 80/81.

BELOW: At the IRTA tests in 2003, Abe used this 'twin shock' M1. The main point was not the redirected exhaust or the pair of shocks, however. The main reason for the bike's existence was the two long dampers set above the main frame beams. These are used to damp out chatter. The project was cancelled later that year, but after the Jerez 2006 experience it will be back.

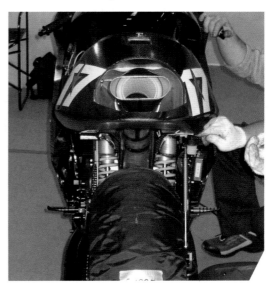

weight, but purely to try to change the harmonic frequency of the chassis) and Edwards started with a solid front axle. During testing over the next few days different tyres, weights and rigidities were tried, all to no avail.

There had clearly been a problem like this at Jerez before. One of the bikes seen in March 2003 was known as the twin-shock bike. This was an M1 using two very small Ohlins dampers, and a chassis that appeared to have long struts from the top shock-absorber mount up to the headstock, alongside the main frame spars. This bike was never seen again but, in retrospect, it is just possible that Yamaha was trying as long ago as that to build a chatter-proof chassis for Jerez.

It is pretty rare to have a pre-season favourite fail so spectacularly once the season starts, but Yamaha simply could not get their bike to stop suffering from chatter. The works team of Rossi and Edwards ran Jerez, Turkey and Shanghai with the 2006 chassis using various forms of rear cylinder head mounts and weight in the axles. By Le Mans and with two really bad results under their belts, Yamaha had decided to raid their museum. In complete secrecy a 2005 bike was modified at the factory to take the shorter stroke 2006 motor. The project was not without its problems; the 2005 frame wouldn't take the 2006 airbox, but although this limited ultimate power Yamaha decided this was the least of their problems. The new/old chassis was tested and used at Le Mans by Rossi, the bike suffering a valve gear failure while leading the race.

Yamaha had adopted two strategies however: the first to get Rossi onto a usable bike, and a second to resolve the problems they were having with the new chassis and the latest Michelins. The first strategy, using the older 2005 design, was reasonably successful, but the 2005 chassis still didn't like the high grip tyres, especially the qualifying versions, but it was significantly better than the stiff 2006 version. The second part of the strategy was to work on a completely new chassis to compliment Michelins with revised constructions. A special Yamaha/Michelin test team was formed with Jurgen van der Goorbergh as test rider to ensure the revised chassis and tyres did not suffer from chatter. This test programme concluded with a three-day tyre test at Brno in mid-July.

Until Michelin made the new tyre constructions available at the Brno GP, we got used to seeing Rossi in the middle or towards the back of the grid. There was nothing wrong with his abilities under braking, however, and he scored several notable podiums despite his bike not because of it. However, at Brno the new Michelins did seem to work with the older chassis and Rossi was on the front row again.

Rossi tested two new chassis after the Brno race, one using the early season 2006 seat and tank and one using the 2005 version with its different seat unit mountings; his times on the 2005 seat version were quickest. Both chassis used different rigidities in the frame and swingarm, the front engine mounting spars resembling the 2005 chassis and the swingarms following the 2005 design. A third chassis using a revised 2006 swingarm was given to Carlos Checa.

The cost to Yamaha of re-engineering the 2006 chassis was high though. Their 'new' 800 shown for the first time in the same test appeared to be merely an 800 motor in a version of the 2006 chassis used for most of the year by Checa. The race department is only so big, and the 2006 project was supposed to have gone away in March, instead new chassis were being tested in mid august. The good results at the end of 2006 were bought at the cost of 800cc development, but we will not see the true consequences until the 2007 season is underway.

Yamaha effectively turned up with new bikes for every single year of the MotoGP championship, and each year has seen a significant improvement. Each modification has addressed specific issues that had become critical in the year before, and Yamaha has not hesitated to make fundamental design changes to resolve these issues. But, to put things in perspective, it was the combination of Rossi and the Yamaha that was effective; the whole Yamaha effort was geared to providing him with a bike he could use against the Hondas.

Carlos Checa on the special combination chassis bike he used for most of the middle of 2006. This used a 2005 fuel tank and swingarm fitted to a 2006 chassis. By having Dunlops on one of their two teams, Yamaha had lost the ability to have four riders testing for solutions to problems.

WCM

Basic racing at the highest level

ENGINE: In-line four-cylinder, four-stroke, DOHC four-valve

CAPACITY: 990cc

POWER: Over 210bhp

TOP SPEED: Over 190mph

TRANSMISSION: Six-speed cassette

IGNITION: Programmable CDI

CHASSIS: Twin spar aluminium alloy frame

SUSPENSION: Ohlins, inverted type telescopic front, link type rear

WHEELS: PVM

TYRES: Dunlop 16.5" front and rear

BRAKES: Brembo, two carbon front discs, single steel rear disc

WEIGHT: 148kg

WCM made it into the four-stroke racing world in a rather painful fashion. A team that had grown sufficiently successful to be provided with works Yamaha two-strokes towards the end of the 500 GP era, WCM had managed five Grand Prix victories over the previous few years. As the four-strokes arrived, though, fewer bikes were to be built by Yamaha, and there was no room in their plans for WCM.

WCM had good sponsorship in the shape of Red Bull (the energy drinks company) and, using that, sought to partner Moriwaki with their tubular-framed Honda RC211V-engined 'Dream fighter' bikes. Red Bull, however, then decided to go their own way. WCM, effectively a partnership between American millionaire, Bob MacLean, and ex-journalist, Peter Clifford, decided that, in the absence of bikes that they could afford to buy and use, they would have to build their own. That's not a small project, and certainly not one that can easily be put into place when the decision is only made after the end of the previous season. WCM, though, had quite a valuable asset to protect – their allocation of grid slots, which should have been saleable if another factory decided to enter. And, they had to be on the grid to ensure the continuation of support payments from Dorna.

The creators of the rulebook thought they'd been quite specific when they included a phrase that only bikes 'not from industrial production' could be used on the MotoGP grid. Quite why there was the need for such a distinction is open to some debate, but it does seem likely that it had something to do with the various contracts signed by the FIM regarding World Superbike and MotoGP, and the definitions used within those contracts for the sort of bikes that could appear on the relevant grids.

The requirement to have a race bike that was not obviously based on a production road bike meant that WCM would have to start from the ground up. Expediency meant that WCM would, then, have to build something simple, inexpensive and effective. As far as the engine was concerned, it almost designed itself – it had to be an across-the-frame four, just like several current Japanese 1,000cc street bikes, with as many parts as possible sourced from the race kits originally built for mass-produced engines. The original series rules (they were changed for the second year) were particularly specific in banning the use of castings 'obtained from 'industrial production', and they also required that the new parts be of original design. In particular, the crankcases, the cylinders and the cylinder heads had to conform to these rules. To speed development, the team brought in Harris Performance Products, the noted UK-based chassis builders.

Early days: Chris Burns and David de Gea had spare bikes.

© Dorna

The WCM engine was a classic inline four using parts from several different original equipment manufacturers as well as their own in their own castings.

Peter Clifford himself drew up the basic engine layout and used an early-type Yamaha R1 crank and piston design, with slightly shorter stroke and a larger bore to bring the bike in just under the 990cc limit. The cylinder head layout eschewed Yamaha's five-valve design (way before they did so themselves) with a four-valve design, taking elements from several Japanese superbikes. Gearbox internals were manufactured by Hewland to fit the same dimensions as the Yamaha box, allowing the engine to use Yamaha's very compact vertically-stacked design, but with the inclusion of a cassette gearbox and a dry clutch.

The contract for the production of engines to this design was initially given to Dave Hagen. However, something went wrong with that relationship, and the contract had to be reissued several months later, with Jan Roelofs and Coen Baijens in Holland taking over the further design, production and development of the engine. The chassis was built by Harris performance, using Ohlins forks and suspension; it was a simple aluminium beam structure with a carbon-fibre subframe acting as the seat.

'The fact that the engine worked at all, and indeed worked so well, is a testament to the people involved. Coen Baijens took my initial crankcase SolidWorks CAD and made it into something that worked in metal,' said Peter Clifford.

> 'THE FACT THAT THE ENGINE WORKED AT ALL, AND INDEED WORKED SO WELL, IS A TESTAMENT TO THE PEOPLE INVOLVED. COEN BAIJENS TOOK MY INITIAL CRANKCASE SOLIDWORKS CAD AND MADE IT INTO SOMETHING THAT WORKED IN METAL'
>
> **PETER CLIFFORD**

The WCM had a stacked gearbox and four valves per cylinder, concepts originating in the R1 Yamaha but predating the M1's use of those design aspects by two years.

'He also designed the four-valve head, building on a concept he created with Jan Roelofs. Roelofs then built the engines, assisted by WCM staff. Jan is a practical genius, drawing on his experience to build something that runs well and stays together.'

Because of the impossibly short time available to produce new crankcases and heads, etc. for the WCM engines, some early race engines were assembled using street R1 crankcases and cylinder heads. These were entered into the first round, the Japanese Grand Prix at Suzuka, but were withdrawn after an enquiry from the FIM as to their legitimacy. At the second Grand Prix in South Africa, the FIM technical commission attended, probably the first formal FIM attendance at a GP for ten years. Their team inspected the WCM bikes and announced that they were incompatible with regulations.

The rulebook used some slightly tricky definitions as to which parts were legal and which were not. 'Industrial production' and 'original design' sound like meaningful terms, but they seem woefully inadequate in pinning down what could and could not be used when considered in a strictly legal context. They existed most probably because they were similar to expressions or phrases in the FIM contracts of Dorna for MotoGP and Flammini for Superbike, and it was important to the FIM that there could be no 'accidents' as to

what was allowed on to the relevant grids.

WCM didn't have the required parts to simply become legal overnight so, not unreasonably, they challenged the choice of words in the rulebook. WCM proceeded to arrive at the GPs with their four-strokes all the way through to the middle of the season when their appeal was finally thrown out by the Court of Arbitration for Sport in late June. The required parts were still not available, so to remain operational the team resorted to picking old 500cc bikes out of team-owner Bob MacLean's personal museum in the US, and Peter Clifford's repository in New Zealand. By the Czech Grand Prix at Brno in August, the new parts were ready and the bikes were being assembled in the pit lane garage, and briefly tested on the Monday after the race. It was not until the Portuguese GP at Estoril that the bikes would be raced for the first time.

The WCM is a classic example of what you need to actually go racing. At the time of writing, at the end of the 990cc generation, it is clear that relatively small changes to the original design, meeting needs that only became fully apparent way after the WCM was designed, would have made a substantial difference to the performance of the WCM. All it would require would be the right money. It took Yamaha to understand the long-bang advantage, enjoyed

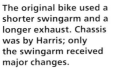

The original bike used a shorter swingarm and a longer exhaust. Chassis was by Harris; only the swingarm received major changes.

Michel Fabrizio's upper fairing was drilled full of holes to try and reduce sensitivity to crosswinds.

by Honda's V5 in mid-2003, for the importance of an irregular firing order engine to become apparent. Modifying the WCM fully would have meant a balance shaft, but Kawasaki, with a not dissimilar engine, managed to get a proportion of the benefits of the effect with revised ignition and cam timing, albeit in a way that stressed the rest of the engine quite highly.

The bike's design was a classic. An in-line four-cylinder set across the frame with a conventional 180° firing order. The engine control electronics were made by Life Racing and the data-logging came from 2D. The throttle bodies were quite conventional Suzuki GSXR1000 parts. With Wiseco pistons and Carrillo rods, the bore was set at 76mm and the stroke at 54.5mm, giving a bore stroke ratio of 1.395. The length of the stroke meant that engine revs in excess of 15,000rpm were unlikely to be seen. This was at the top-end of street specs when built, but by the time the WCM retired from the grid many street bikes had similar or more extreme set-ups. Electronic engine control was limited to programmable ignition and fuel maps, with no traction control. Idle could be set by the fuel map, but the most effective control of engine braking going into the corners was found to be simple manual adjustment of the throttle bodies.

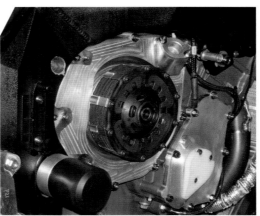

The clutch used in the first two years was a carbon based AP Lockheed item. This appeared to suffer from sensitivity to operating temperature, leading to differing setups being required from the beginning to the end of a race.

Standard Ohlins suspension was used, and although usually not the latest generation it was nevertheless perfectly adequate.

Roelofs kept things simple in the cylinder head as well. The original idea was to use titanium valves, but these created some problems. English company G&S quickly produced some stainless-steel valves (for a tenth of the price of the titanium ones) and they solved the problem. The cam followers came straight out of a ZX750RR Kawasaki, the valve guides were also Kawasaki, and the valve springs were a combination of ZXR400 Kawasaki outer and FJ1200 Yamaha inner.

'The fact that the engine never embarrassed us by cascading oil and broken parts all over the racetrack is also due, in a large part, to the great bunch of guys we had in the garage during those three years,' asserts Clifford. "Not fitters, but mechanics who could maintain the engines properly, with regular checks to make sure there were no problems. Through 2004 we had zero race stoppages due to mechanical failure.'

One interesting choice at the start was a carbon slipper clutch from sponsors AP. WCM ran an all-carbon slipper clutch which was to prove to be quite inconsistent in operation because of the large variances in grip from the carbon plates at different temperatures. The clutch would feel completely different off the start line from its performance going into corners in the latter stages of the race. The

team adopted an STM clutch in 2004, and its more normal metal plates made life a lot easier for the riders. The second big change was the arrival of James Ellison in 2005. His history was in endurance and superstock racing. Rather than a rider who demanded the perfect set-up, he was more comfortable with trying to ride around problems. With Dunlop starting their renaissance in the same year, the two were on several occasions able to get close to causing a big upset.

The team also benefited greatly from the support they received from the whole of MotoGP, as Clifford confirms. 'Racing is seen as a money business, but for most of the people we deal with, that is not their motivation. The list of people who helped us, with nothing to gain, is huge – the engineers from Ohlins and Brembo did so on an almost daily basis. They have a lot of equipment to look after, yet they still bent over backwards to give us real practical support.'

Ellison liked some quite extreme set-ups, with a preference for a very long swingarm. This moved the weight forwards, and he responded by lapping quicker. 'The longer we made the swingarm the faster he went,' confirmed Clifford. 'I must say that I was concerned that we might have just been making the bike feel

The throttle bodies were standard GSX-R1000K, no all-electronic throttles here.

In the last year James Ellison made the bike go a lot quicker with a few small but important modifications. The swingarm grew nearly 100mm and the seat height was raised.

more comfortable, and it was not necessarily a faster motorcycle, but his crew, Paul Trevathan and François Charlot were aware of that and made sure they were making a genuine improvement. In a year, the bike got more than 100mm longer.

'The relationship between bike and rider is obviously incredibly important, and the fact that James felt confident enough to ride the wheels off the Harris WCM was doubly essential, as we certainly weren't giving him horsepower!'

TOP: Shorter pipes soon made their appearance. By Sachsenring 2004 they were joined by an aftermarket STM clutch, which at least worked more consistently than the AP carbon one.

RIGHT: Ellison and the WCM clicked in 2005. On several occasions he got into the points, finishing the year with seven and impressing Dunlop with his feedback.

© WCM

APRILIA

**Outside the box with
Aprilia's Cube**

ENGINE: In-line three-cylinder, four-stroke, DOHC four-valve

CAPACITY: 990cc

POWER: Over 240bhp

TOP SPEED: Over 200mph

TRANSMISSION: Six-speed cassette

IGNITION: Programmable CDI

CHASSIS: Twin spar aluminium alloy frame

SUSPENSION: Ohlins, inverted type telescopic front, link type rear

WHEELS: Marchesini

TYRES: Michelin 16.5" front and rear

BRAKES: Brembo, two carbon front discs, single steel rear disc

WEIGHT: 148kg

Aprilia's decision to go MotoGP racing was taken very late, and the consequences of that late decision would haunt the bike until the project was finally stopped at the end of 2004. Just as the programme was launched, Aprilia found itself in a financial crisis that would ultimately resolve itself with the company's enforced sale to Piaggio. Given the financial constraints, the fact that there was any MotoGP programme at all is amazing; that the team developed the machines as they did, even more so.

Early on, it was decided that Aprilia would not design its own engine – instead the job was to be farmed out to Cosworth Engineering, the people responsible for the race version of Aprilia's V-twin superbike engine. The original layout of the engine was a collaboration between Aprilia and Cosworth. Cosworth's brief was quite simple – build a three-cylinder engine using as much technology as possible from the Formula 1 programme, where Cosworth made its name, re-engineered to work in a motorcycle chassis.

The original MotoGP regulations allowed a lighter weight for three-cylinder engines. Both two- and three-cylinder engines were allowed to be 10kg lighter than the fours, so a three seemed a logical place to be if you worshipped light weight above everything. Unfortunately, a three-cylinder engine, by its very nature, is quite bulky. The stroke is relatively long compared to an equivalent four-cylinder, and the combustion chambers and pistons are quite large in diameter – experience to date has shown that you end up saving very little in terms of width compared to a four-cylinder, and what you do save is lost in packaging, because the cylinders are generally taller. This becomes even more complicated when you take into account the rocking present in a typical in-line three-cylinder engine's crankshaft. When running, a triple has a particular tendency to rock side-to-side, and to counteract this force, an engine speed balancer is needed that rocks in exactly the opposite direction. Correctly designed, this balancer doesn't have to be anywhere near the same weight as the crankshaft; nevertheless, if you don't want to shake the chassis to pieces you have to have a balancer shaft. Balancer shafts soak power, correctly designed they might reduce overall output by 2%–3%, so there is a price to pay.

When the Aprilia triple was laid out, it quickly became apparent that they would need an inordinately large primary gear for the normal gear take-off from the crank. One option was to have an additional shaft between the crankshaft and the primary gear to reduce the diameter of the individual gears. It was decided that this

Regis Laconi had an exciting and quite probably uncomfortable year while Aprilia worked on the basic chassis setup.

© GOLD AND GOOSE

© DORNA

ABOVE: Colin Edwards joined for 2003. This bike has the longer swingarm but the earlier chassis and seat unit. The pipe was still relatively quiet.

LEFT: Haga was also on board in 2003, his bike was always one generation behind Edwards, but that didn't stop him trying.

© Dorna

additional shaft could also do double duty as the balancer shaft, and as a result of it being put between the crank and the clutch, Aprilia was also able to turn the crankshaft backwards. This last feature was not a necessary part of the initial calculations but, as we shall see, it was something that helped out in the handling department. The gearbox was essentially attached to three cylinders off a Formula 1 engine, with a specially cast aluminium dry sump at the bottom, and the machined plate holding the gearbox casing at the top. Bore and stroke stood at 93mm x 48.49mm, giving an exact capacity of 988cc. This is a slightly less oversquare engine than was current in Formula 1 during the same period, and is probably based on a mid-'90s design.

The clutch was an AP Lockheed ramp-type slipper clutch made of carbon-carbon, and the gearbox had a cartridge design to ensure the fairly easy changing of ratios. As one would expect from current Formula 1 practice, pneumatic springs were used on the valves, along with a double-overhead cam set-up to control the breathing. Aprilia decided not to proceed with Cosworth's own ride-by-wire systems, and instead used an advanced version of the control systems built for and used on the firm's two-strokes over the previous ten years. Aprilia are very proud of this system, developed with help from three northern Italian universities, because of its compact design and the manner in which it was quickly adapted to become the first true ride-by-wire system fitted to a MotoGP racing motorcycle.

Aprilia's use of pneumatic valves was also a first for motorcycling; since they debuted, the pit lane has not been without at least one entrant using pneumatic valves, but to date they have not conferred any race-winning advantage. The pneumatic valves use a pressure of around 15bar to act as a spring, but the seals that hold the pressure in place are prone to leak. The usual solution is to carry a spare supply of nitrogen on the bike – normally in a small canister containing a reserve at 200bar. The ECU monitors the pressures being used and, should the rate of pressure loss exceed a specified level, then the system shuts down. In the Aprilia's case, the small reservoir was situated behind the airbox and above the gearbox.

The chassis was no less inventive and unusual. By the end of the 990cc MotoGP formula it was quite common to see CNC-machined sections of chassis, but Aprilia was the first to use them. The technology came out of the 250 racing programme, where the CNC-machining of individual beams allowed the Aprilia to change flexibility and design

TOP LEFT: The Aprilia engine was a dry sump, the front of the engine was all oil pump and the oil tank ended up in the same place as a wet sump. This is an earlier version of the chassis and seat unit.

MIDDLE LEFT: The Aprilia was started by a plug in electric motor. For the first year or so this wasn't clipped to the engine so the mechanics had to brace their shoulders against the reaction. You could see the resulting 'Aprilia shuffle' from the other end of the pit lane!

BOTTOM LEFT: Again this is an early version of the chassis; later ones rolled the engine back, lowering the countershaft sprocket and raising the front of the engine. The triangular box in the centre of the picture is the water overflow tank. Note the Schraeder valve in the water line.

APRILIA DECIDED NOT TO PROCEED WITH COSWORTH'S OWN RIDE-BY-WIRE SYSTEMS, AND INSTEAD USED AN ADVANCED VERSION OF THE CONTROL SYSTEMS BUILT FOR AND USED ON THE FIRM'S TWO-STROKES OVER THE PREVIOUS TEN YEARS. APRILIA ARE VERY PROUD OF THIS SYSTEM, DEVELOPED WITH HELP FROM THREE NORTHERN ITALIAN UNIVERSITIES, BECAUSE OF ITS COMPACT DESIGN AND THE MANNER IN WHICH IT WAS QUICKLY ADAPTED TO BECOME THE FIRST TRUE RIDE-BY-WIRE SYSTEM FITTED TO A MotoGP RACING MOTORCYCLE.

Noriyuki Haga demonstrating that they still hadn't quite got the setup right. The front forks are right on the point of bottoming.

© HENK KEULEMANS

Another version of the swingarm, and you can clearly see where the end has been lengthened.

very easily and quickly. The first bikes to use the technique were two 250 prototypes built in 2001. The advantages were no different in MotoGP, specially machined CNC beam sections of different thicknesses and new designs could be executed very quickly. The accuracy of the machining was very high, with good repeatability should it be decided that the parts needed to be put into more regular production.

The first year of MotoGP saw Aprilia rider Regis Laconi fighting the bike all the way round each circuit. The centre of gravity was progressively raised, with the chassis setup, and particularly the swing-arm angle, becoming quite badly distorted as the team tried to get the bike to turn properly. The bike was significantly over its minimum weight limit because of the widespread use of aluminium, instead of magnesium, for castings, and it was going to require a substantial increase in funding to get it down. Tyres during the first year were Dunlops, and the combination of the Aprilia chassis' characteristics and the Dunlops gave the bike a reputation for suffering badly from chatter.

During 2003, Superbike refugees, Colin Edwards and Noriyuki Haga, took over the riding duties. The engine's peak power was slowly reduced, and the mid-range was improved to make it more rideable; the bike was down

to a peak of around 240bhp, but with a much smoother power delivery and enhanced mid-range. During the year, several different exhaust systems were tried, including one open megaphone; all were unbelievably loud.

Colin Edwards' reputation as a good superbike tyre tester for Michelin meant that Michelin tyres were used. To try to balance the needs for a higher centre of gravity and the right swingarm angle, the chassis was redesigned, raising the front of the engine and rolling the engine backwards. For real progress, though, the bike now needed a new gearbox casting to allow for a more conventional chassis to match its new-found, more conventional, power output. Unfortunately, Aprilia's financial problems saw that this would remain a dream for the time being.

Weight was still an issue. The bike is now claimed to be only 8kg over its class limit, but the whole point of using a triple was supposed to be the 10kg lower weight limit it was allowed. Lighter engine cases were made, with substantial sections machined away to lower the weight, and several side-covers and the sump were recast in magnesium. A number of different swingarms were used; first the old ones were tried with longer chain adjusters welded in, then new parts were introduced with varying degrees of stiffness. Noriyuki Haga's bike was consistently one

FAR LEFT: Several different exhausts and swingarms were tried, this swingarm had a cutaway section intended for the never raced evolution version of the bike.

LEFT: McWilliams special Mugello fairing complete with winglets designed to keep the front wheel on the ground at the end of the main straight.

generation behind Edwards, but that didn't stop him continuing to push hard.

Aprilia's 2004 was very different. The development slowed as the financial crisis in the parent company worsened. The riders were Jeremy McWilliams and Shane Byrne, both using chassis that were developments of the chassis Edwards had finished the previous year on. Several of the senior MotoGP engineers had left the project in the winter, leaving Jan Witteveen, Aprilia's long-term race director, to run the team. A believer in the philosophy that 'first we get a good motorcycle and then we add the trick stuff', he turned to basic engineering solutions for some of the bike's complex problems.

Over the course of the year, quite a few new parts were fitted, but they were all relatively simple items – a higher inertia crankshaft to further calm down throttle response, a new fairing for some easy speed (with winglets for better front-end grip at Mugello), and halfway through the year another revised swingarm. All these parts were being prepared for use on the new bike. The redesign was nearly ready and it needed more and more as time went on. There was no doubt that the Aprilia Cube made sufficient power; it was just that it seemed impossible to put it down when the bike was not completely upright.

The Aprilia Cube chassis was one of the first to be built using CNC manufactured sections welded together. You can see the welds used to internally brace the chassis.

Witteveen admitted earlier in the year that they had not used most of the fly-by-wire systems that had given Colin Edwards such an adventurous year in 2003. Instead, the system had been programmed to provide a simple one-to-one relationship in the top three gears, and an adjustable, but linear, throttle system giving say 50% of butterfly movement for all 90° of twistgrip travel in each of the first three gears. Michelin's new super grippy tyres did not work well on this chassis, however, with both riders complaining regularly of really bad chatter problems; both tyres off the ground in some corners. It seems the increased grip levels of the new tyres triggered chatter all over the place, and Aprilia's already compromised chassis made it more difficult than usual to dial out.

The long-term solution was a new chassis and a revised engine, with the balance shaft set high between the engine and the gearbox as opposed to the now three-year-old layout with the balance shaft set under the crank. This required a completely new gearbox and primary drive arrangement, together with a new chassis. The bike was tested many times during 2004 by McWilliams and veteran Aprilia test-rider Marcellino Lucchi. At the end of the season it was tested in public at Valencia, but within two weeks the new owners, Piaggio, had pulled the plug on the whole project.

As this book is being written, the new post-Piaggio-takeover chief of racing in Aprilia is Luigi Dall'Igna; previously the engineer in charge of the Cube project. We also know there is a four-cylinder superbike engine in the works, so even though the Cube never did win a race, it may yet have a big influence on the future of four-stroke racing in Aprilia.

OPPOSITE: Shakey Byrne's crew watch the race from the garage after his massive practice crash at Brno. This bike has the later frame, and note the different engine and seat mounting points. You can also see the 3-into-2-into-1 pipe.

LEFT AND BELOW LEFT: The evolution Aprilia was never raced, it was only seen in public once at a test after the end of the 2004 season. This bike had a redesigned engine with the clutch lowered, the balance shaft moved up the back of the engine and finally the correct swingarm angle and swingarm pivot to countershaft relationship is established.

BELOW: Aprilia were the first to use carbon outer tube Ohlins forks, something they had tried before in their 250 programme.

OVER THE COURSE OF THE YEAR, QUITE A FEW NEW PARTS WERE FITTED, BUT THEY WERE ALL RELATIVELY SIMPLE ITEMS – A HIGHER INERTIA CRANKSHAFT TO FURTHER CALM DOWN THROTTLE RESPONSE, A NEW FAIRING FOR SOME EASY SPEED (WITH WINGLETS FOR BETTER FRONT-END GRIP AT MUGELLO).

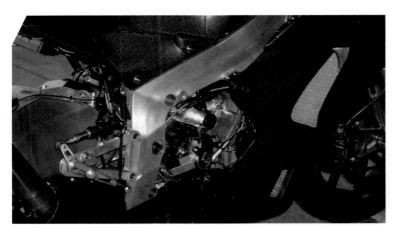

MORIWAKI

**The MD211VF
Dream Fighter**

ENGINE: Liquid-cooled 75.5° four-stroke V5, 3 cylinders front, 2 rear [Honda customer engine]

CAPACITY: 990cc

POWER: Over 240bhp

TOP SPEED: Over 200mph

TRANSMISSION: Six-speed cassette

IGNITION: Programmable CDI

CHASSIS: Tubular steel

SUSPENSION: Ohlins, inverted type telescopic front, link type rear

WHEELS: Marchesini

TYRES: Michelin 16.5" front and rear

BRAKES: Nissin, two carbon front discs, single steel rear disc

WEIGHT: 148kg

Famed tuner, Mamoru Moriwaki, the man responsible for the remarkable rise of Graeme Crosby to world level on a high-barred Kawasaki Superbike back in the late-'70s, still had a few dreams to live – to have his own MotoGP team. Unlike many, however, Moriwaki also had connections and the drive to get a team onto the track. The project started in the second year of the series, using RC211V engines provided by Honda, and the bike continued through to 2005 with several wildcard entries a year for the best 'shop project' in the world.

Using a team made up of his tuning shop employees, Moriwaki built two Honda RC211V-engined specials. Both had Moriwaki's own tubular-steel chassis and bodywork, using Ohlins suspension and, initially at least, Dunlop tyres.

All through his experiment, Moriwaki stressed the input into the project from the people in his shop, and the way in which they were encouraged to look for new solutions. Riders in the first year included Andrew Pitt and Olivier Jacque, and the second year included Japanese rider Matsudo and Honda test-rider Ukawa.

By the second year, Moriwaki had really got serious. New fairing and seat were obvious, but underneath it all was a new chassis and swingarm. The engine was higher and the swingarms were a lot stronger. For Motegi the bikes were different again, with a new chassis using thicker wall tube.

Honda supplied the same early model V5s all through the project, easily spotted with their muffled Mk1 exhaust systems. For the second year, however, Ohlins supplied then top-of-the-range TT25 forks. Michelin tyres and Nissin brakes showed their support as well, all with factory technicians in attendance.

USING A TEAM MADE UP OF HIS TUNING SHOP EMPLOYEES, MORIWAKI BUILT TWO HONDA RC211V-ENGINED SPECIALS. BOTH HAD MORIWAKI'S OWN TUBULAR-STEEL CHASSIS AND BODYWORK, USING OHLINS SUSPENSION AND, INITIALLY AT LEAST, DUNLOP TYRES.

Olly Jaque has his MotoGP comeback as a Moriwaki rider at Motegi; 11th place and five points were the result.

© GOLD AND GOOSE

ABOVE: The last version of the Moriwaki steel tube chassis. The bike always had the first version of the Honda RC211V motor and always ran with the early muffled exhausts.

LEFT: Even the first versions had class suspension, seen here with the then new Ohlins TT25 forks.

BELOW: Moriwaki kept the class with custom built tie-wrap holders on the workbench.

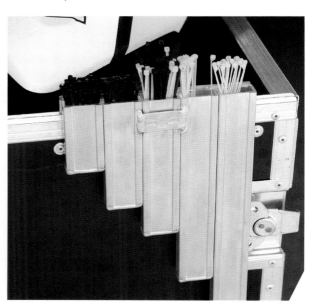

THE TECHNOLOGY

Uncovering the complexity of a MotoGP bike

Hell freezes over. Honda fitted proper return springs to their race bike rear brakes in 2006.

A successful performance motorcycle is far more than the sum of its parts. The challenge is to achieve the best and most competitive solution to the packaging constraints, and this inevitably means that significant compromises have to be made. The bike that has the most effective compromises is the one that will win, and the design of a Grand Prix bike is as pure a test of evolutionary theory as you could hope for. If something is seen to work on one machine then the chances are that something very similar will work on all of the bikes; and usually the teams or factories will have their own versions on track within weeks.

Let's consider the evolution of the current bikes. Honda debuted a 75.5° V5 990cc engine right at the start of the series. It was neat – the front bank of three cylinders was wide at the front and narrow at the back, and the V-angle was wide yet narrow enough to fit behind the front tyre and radiator. In one piece of design, Honda had got five cylinders on the bike (initially by using RC45 technology), they got the frame as narrow as possible and allowed the rider to tuck right in.

Then things get tricky. Five cylinders are fine, but how do you balance them? According to Honda's patents, the most important thing is to have four cylinders working as if they were a normal four, and offset the fifth cylinder by 180° minus the angle of the V. This means that the power pulses leave the engine in two closely-bunched groups and, funnily enough, that style of power delivery is exactly what you need for good traction.

So, Honda not only initially saved money on their budget by using the basic power production parts of a previous design, but the basic architecture of the motor gave them power effects that would take the others some time to discover they even needed.

It was Yamaha that finally realised the benefit of Honda's 'long bang'. First they redesigned their crank and modified their jack-shaft to double up as a balancer, but it was with their second version that they got it all together – the M1-B motor incorporated gear drive cams, a four-valve head, the revised firing order and, crucially, a slew of chassis modifications only achievable with a very short in-line four engine using a stacked gearbox.

Once the Yamaha started winning, the rest of the pit lane decided that it was the irregular firing order that was the key. This made the bike sound like it had a particular type of V4 engine and clearly gave traction benefits. Roberts and Ducati all had their own versions within a few weeks.

The chassis modifications centred around a long swingarm, which allowed the Yamaha to be very stable going into corners, and that is where most overtaking takes place. The bike wasn't the fastest (although it was an improvement on the previous bikes) but it had good traction and stability where it mattered.

Over at Honda they realised that, as Yamaha had finally understood the importance of the V-firing order and used it, they were going to have to find a way to counteract Rossi's advantage into the corners. The 'Brno bike', the New Generation RC211V, was the result. With a shorter engine – not easy if you have already built the best packaged V5 you can – and a longer swingarm, what came to be called 'Nicky's bike' could match the Yamaha where the Yamaha was strongest. In a lot of ways it was slower than the older versions of the bike, but it was better where it mattered.

The point here is that both Yamaha and Honda had to build new engines to allow them to use certain chassis features. The engine repackaging didn't automatically give them more power – in some ways it gave less – but it allowed them to build a bike that could counteract a perceived racing benefit enjoyed by the other.

Ducati's 2003 Desmosedici stripped right down to the last nut and bolt. By 2006 just about the only part not redesigned is the crankcase.

© DUCATI CORSE

PACKAGING

Fitting 260bhp into a motorcycle fairing

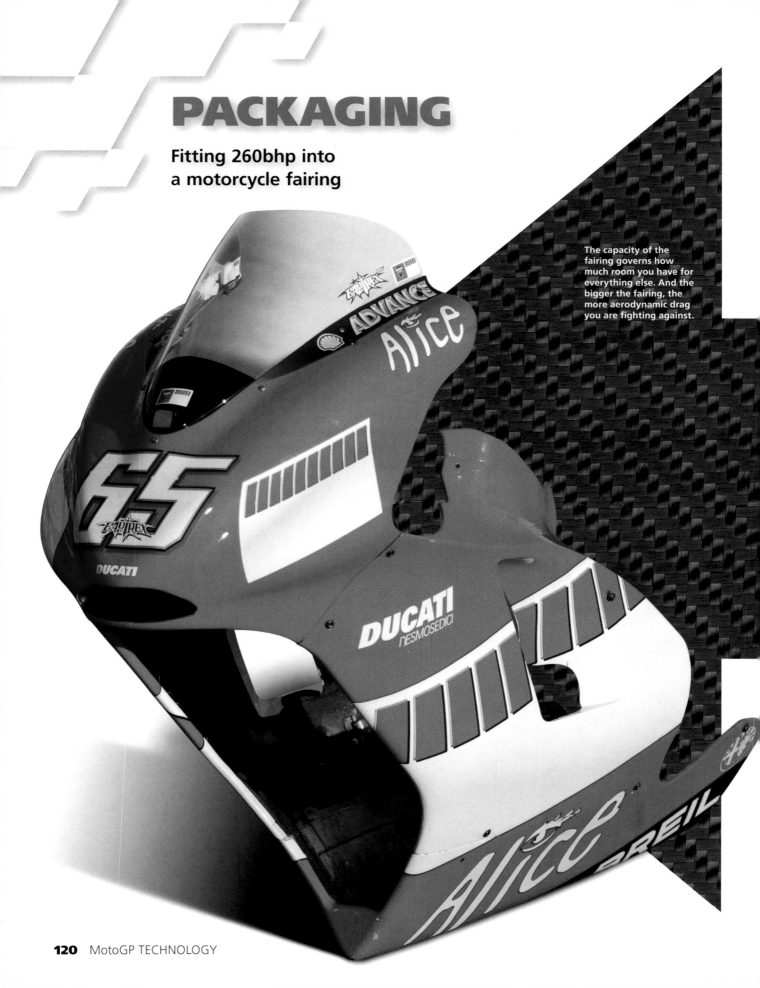

The capacity of the fairing governs how much room you have for everything else. And the bigger the fairing, the more aerodynamic drag you are fighting against.

Essentially, the main limitation on a racing motorcycle is the fairing. Operating within the rather restrictive rules, you want the smallest and most efficient fairing you can get away with. Whatever the size and shape you choose, you have to find room inside (or behind, if you prefer) for the rider, the engine, the airbox, the fuel, the electronics and, of course, the frame. All of this has to be arranged so that the weight is in the right place for the best handling, that the radiator can flow enough air to cool the engine, that the hot exhaust pipes can find a way out without touching anything not considered disposable and that the gearbox output sprocket is in the right place to get the right chain pull effects into the chassis. This very complex and crowded situation means that every design decision taken will affect several other parts of the bike, not always positively, and that the final decision has to be considered the best compromise between all the possible solutions.

The nature of that compromise is constantly evolving. Another 10bhp will mean more heat is generated, so you may need a bigger radiator, or perhaps a revisit to the wind tunnel to improve the efficiency of the radiator exhaust ducts. Better tyres may require different flexibilities to be built into the chassis components; and that trick has to be accomplished without setting off chatter.

Most of the factories involved during the five-year history of the class have repackaged engines and bikes to change the focus of the original design compromise. The changes are not automatically just to make the motorcycle faster, they can just be to get a small advantage in one area of the bike's operation sufficient to get bike and rider into a position to spoil a competing bike's performance. But, to achieve those small changes in performance, entire bikes have been repackaged. The final iteration of the RC211V was just such a bike, everything except the engine internals and forks was new, just to get in a longer swingarm to help match the Yamaha's corner entry stability.

All the motorcycles in this book are examples of packaging efficiency. Making 260bhp engines work in an overall package no bigger than a 500cc street bike is a tremendous achievement. The ongoing problem is to keep finding space for the systems we keep adding. Improvements in electronic controls have helped traction and feel, but these systems have posed their own problems in terms of power supply and a place to put the computer and its electronics. The same with power levels, it's all very nice having 260bhp, but once you have it you need a different chassis to work well with it and a newly designed cooling system.

ENGINES

**Fast forwarding
the future**

It is easy to say that the major difference between the old 500cc two-strokes and the new four-stroke class was just the engines, and that was indeed the prime difference between the two motorcycles, but, as we have seen from the other chapters of this book, a change of engine from 500cc two-stroke to 990cc four-stroke meant that everything else changed as well.

Each factory addressed the new formula in a completely different way. The choices appeared simple: you could be adventurous and overtly be seen to learn something new while trying out designs with no obvious link to your company's streetbike range, or you could decide for marketing reasons to stay as close as possible to the streetbikes you already made. The first engine we actually saw was Honda's V5, which was unique insofar as it was the first motorcycle with an engine of this configuration built (although not the first seen on paper as various design studies released by the old BSA Triumph group in the UK had included this configuration).

Other designs came forward. Yamaha chose an across-the-frame four-cylinder which, as long as you didn't look too close, was like their streetbikes. In actual fact the only thing that was the same as their streetbikes was the number and layout of the cylinders. Suzuki have used a V4 design – actually they used three different V4 designs, with ever widening Vs.

Kawasaki were initially the least adventurous, making a very simple across-the-frame four, but by the last few races of the 990cc formula they had irregular firing order cranks and even a racing prototype with a reverse rotation crank.

The Italians were more adventurous from the start. Aprilia contracted Cosworth to help them out with a stroked version of three cylinders off a Formula One engine; this was nothing like the rest of their range and gave them plenty to think about when it strayed into a motorcycle chassis.

Ducati also moved out of the box, and straight into the world of Formula One, using ex-Ferrari engineers to create a 90° four-cylinder, parts of which bore an uncanny likeness to the last of the racing V12 Ferraris, the 1995 3-litre 044/1. Once fitted with a motorcycle gearbox and desmodromic valve gear, this immediately took the fight to Honda and Yamaha.

On track these engines have done nothing but change, with more power, more revs, different firing sequences, different crank rotations and different layouts, and that's before we get to the throttle and clutch systems. The last five years have seen one of the most concentrated periods of motorcycle engine development ever.

VALVES

How to
move them

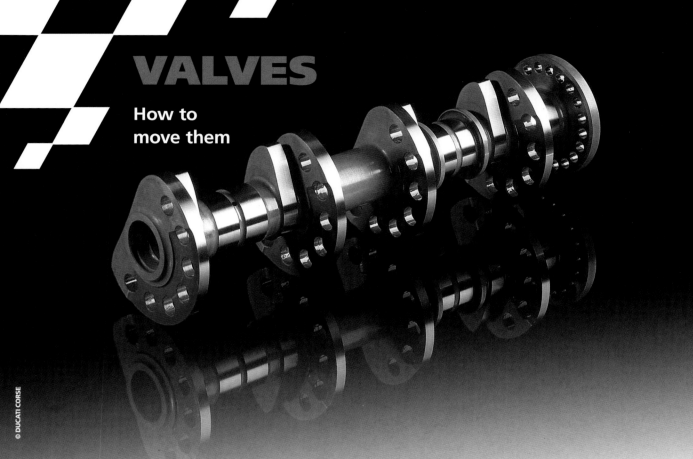

The Desmosedici runs a classic Ducati desmo cam, looking like a cam from a Testastretta twin, only with twice the normal number of lobes. The opening and closing profiles are offset by 90° because the closing rockers have a 90° L-bend in them (see the schematic on the next page).

Given that all the engines in MotoGP are four-stroke, you might think that there wouldn't be much to say about different methods of valve operation. Cylinder head design, however, has seen some variation over the last few years, with several factories using different systems at different stages of their engines' evolution.

As well as the various methods of operating the valve gear, there have been substantial advances in the technology of the valves themselves. It is only in the last few decades that titanium has been used in valve manufacture. The metal's light weight is its major advantage, allowing the cams to be designed for more abrupt operation, and permitting the engine to rev higher. Titanium has also been used for valve spring retainers and their collets.

As the class has progressed, however, the need for more power and torque has meant that conventional materials, including 'normal' titanium, are beginning to prove insufficient. For more power, engine designers need to get the engine to breathe better, and more often. Bigger ports and valves help the breathing but, to maintain the mid-range power, the overlap between the inlet and exhaust phases has to be minimised. Despite the larger, heavier valves that the larger ports dictate, the valve opening period has to be as short as possible. That

means the speed with which the valve is lifted from its seat to full lift and then back again has to be as high as possible.

New cam profile designs are helping, but the high rates of valve acceleration have focused attention back on valve materials. This isn't something the constructors are going to talk about, but there are several materials that could be used – most now banned from Formula 1 as part of that sport's desire to dramatically cut costs – that could be used in certain parts of the engine. For valve gear, titanium aluminide is the material. It can be used both in valve manufacture, where its ability to maintain strength at high temperature is prized, and for buckets, spring retainers and gudgeon pins, where its 15% weight advantage over normal titanium is the main selling point. Given this material's Formula 1 provenance, the MotoGP bikes that may use it are likely to be from constructors who already have cross-fertilization with Formula 1.

VALVE SPRINGS
Most engines use conventional valve springs, and this certainly seems to be the case with the top-line factories. But normal springs approach their limit around the 17,000rpm mark, and there's always been at least one bike on the grid

124   MotoGP TECHNOLOGY

with Formula 1-derived technology, such as pneumatic valve control. None of the bikes using pneumatics have been major successes, yet (to be fair) that is unlikely to be the fault of the chosen method of valve operation. Many argue that anything more than the conventional spring is unnecessary and would merely add further complications, and just as many see valve springs as a simple solution in terms of space within the cylinder head.

While the following figures are undoubtedly exceeded under extreme conditions, peak MotoGP revs seem to be around 16,500rpm – the Desmosedici four-cylinder, we know, is fuelled for at least another 1,000rpm, as was the KTM. Ducati, in recent years, have concentrated on corner exit speeds, and sheer top-end power and revs is not now quite so important to them. Sheer revs wasn't the original aim of Honda or Yamaha, but they have been steadily brought up to 16,500rpm over three years of effort, with both major factories getting to around 16,500rpm at sometime during the 2005 season. It was at these revs that Honda, and then Yamaha, first reported valve failures (this is, of course, different from when they first actually suffered valve train failures – in racing the announced reason for a failure is rarely the actual cause).

Japanese steel springs have a reputation for being the best in the world. Several different grades, or qualities, are available – each grade being progressively (and significantly) more expensive than the last. It is safe to say that, with the demands now being made on the springs, the highest quality, and therefore most expensive, steel springs will be being used.

PNEUMATIC VALVE SPRINGS

Aprilia was the first company to use pneumatic valve operation with their Cosworth-designed Cube three-cylinder. With only three cylinders, the individual pistons and cylinders were proportionally larger, meaning the valves also had to be larger and, therefore, heavier. That, in turn, meant that more effort was going to be needed to control them.

Pneumatic valve springs were considered the logical solution, especially as Cosworth had had a lot of very positive experience with them over the previous ten years. Aprilia's pneumatic valve springs used an industry-standard 11 to 14bar of nitrogen as the actual spring pressure. The design consisted of a single cam lobe pressing down on a bucket, just as you would find in most sports bikes of the last 30 years, only in this case, instead of there being a coil spring secreted underneath the bucket, there was a seal and high-pressure nitrogen. Of course, any system

like this can leak, and to compensate for this, one hour's worth of 'top up' gas was held at 200bar in a small canister hidden on the bike – in Aprilia's case just above the gearbox – to get it through the race.

In the event of a greater than normal leakage of gas, the engine management unit – programmed to ensure that the engine never reaches a point where it loses its 'springs' – automatically shuts it down if the depletion rate exceeds a certain figure. We are not aware that this ever happened to the Aprilia, but it did most probably stop the Suzukis several times during the disastrous Qatar MotoGP in 2006.

Suzuki's system was sourced from consultants previously operating in Formula 1, and it made a great difference to the reliability of the bikes as, even though it had its birth pangs, it was more reliable than the atrocious valve springs previously used by the Suzuki factory.

Pneumatic valves were also used by KTM in their 70° V-4, and the inclusion of a large bottle of nitrogen in the corner of the Roberts garage made for a rather space age look once Roberts preferred water-warmer device was also attached. KTM considered the after-market Del West system but, in the end, designed and built their own. With pressure between 10 and 14bar, this system used finger followers to actuate the valves.

Pneumatic valve return systems and valve springs aren't actually that different in principle, but there is a lot of devil in the detail of both.

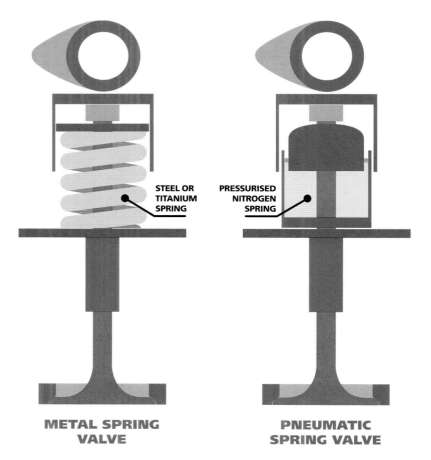

STEEL OR TITANIUM SPRING

PRESSURISED NITROGEN SPRING

METAL SPRING VALVE

PNEUMATIC SPRING VALVE

DESMODROMIC VALVE OPERATION

Ducati are unique in their choice of mechanical valve operation – called desmodromic valve control. They sought outside assistance in the design of their MotoGP engine, with engineers from Piero Ferrari's HPE organisation joining Ducati Corse to help in the original layout. While unsubstantiated, there were many rumours that the engineers brought in would have preferred to stay with pneumatic valve operation, but the desmodromic valve system was a unique selling point in Ducati's range of road bikes and they wanted to stay with it. The system both mechanically opens and closes the valves. It is very similar to that developed by Mercedes for their 1955 M196 Le Mans car. Ducati adopted the system on their racing singles in the late '50s, and for many years it has been a mainstay of their competition bikes. From the mid-'70s, all Ducatis have had desmodromic valve operation directly from the factory. All the World Superbike bikes used desmodromic valve actuation, and the advantages and disadvantages of the system were well understood from this sustained period of development.

The inlet valves are opened by a conventional rocker, the cam acts on the back of the rocker and its tip simply depresses the valve just as you would

have on a normal rocker type valve system. A small hair spring is used to provide a little valve seating pressure for a reasonable low rpm tickover. The closing system is a bit different; a second rocker is used, on the four-valve engines it is L-shaped and runs on a D-shaped lobe ground alongside the opening lobe on the camshaft. One tip of the rocker runs on the cam and the other opens into a fork, its tip sitting underneath a top-hat-shaped shim placed around the valve. With this many levers operating, shimming is quite critical. While all the Ducati engines have proved to be very reliable in MotoGP, it can be assumed that reshimming the valve gear is one of the major operations when the engines are taken out.

From a design perspective, it's one thing to have a straight rocker with the cam pressing against it in the centre and the end pushing down the valve; computer modelling would show the sort of flex that would occur in the back of the rocker and how this would affect operation and valve life. What is new is to have an L-shaped rocker undergoing the same pressures.

One of the major advances in the last ten years in high performance engineering has been the maximising of the speed with which valves are opened and closed. The aggressiveness of a cam lobe can be measured by what is called the jerk – jerk is the speed with which acceleration is

Ducati's desmodromic valve system in all its glory. With sixteen different rockers for each of the cylinder heads, each one requiring a shim, this is not exactly a low maintenance design. In use it has proved to be extremely reliable, even at 17,000rpm plus.

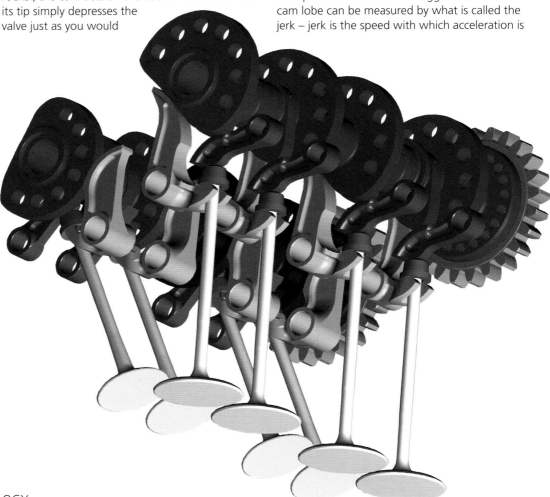

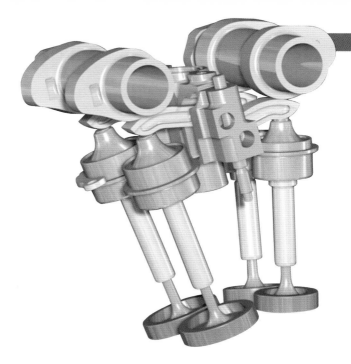
© KTM

applied to the valve in order to open it, or shut it, very quickly. Modern port and cam design uses high valve accelerations to obtain the maximum breathing from a given set of specifications, while maintaining the shortest possible periods of overlap to maintain power band width.

Ducati have in recent years used their mechanical valve system to maximise valve jerk to get the best possible breathing allied to the best possible power band width. We can only imagine the amount of computer modelling that was required to build the lightest possible L-shaped rocker capable of taking the highest levels of jerk in opening and closing the valves of the Desmosedici at revs in excess of 16,500rpm.

DIRECT VALVE OPERATION

Having the cams act directly on a bucket covering the valve is a classic high-performance solution to valve operation. The shims can be carefully placed on top of the valve, and under the bucket, so ensuring that, regardless of how high-performance the cams are, the shim cannot be spat off the top of the bucket. The system has the disadvantage of not increasing the work done by the cam, the valve's lift will be the same as the lift that is built into the camshaft, and the large surface area of the bucket does seem to cause some drag. As a system, however, it's bulletproof, simple and hard to beat.

ROCKER VALVE OPERATION

Using a rocker to amplify the effects of the cam brings with it many advantages in terms of space, packaging and weight. Unlike buckets, however, rockers are more difficult to lubricate – to minimise wear they depend on a regular supply of fresh oil forced into the camshaft/rocker meeting point as soon as possible after the engine has been started. The beauty of the design, though, is that the camshaft lift is magnified by the geometry of the rocker. This means that not only can the camshaft be placed closer to the centreline of the engine, it can also be smaller in size. Suzuki had notably used rockers for several years in MotoGP and, whether it was a weakness of the valve springs or the rockers themselves, all we know is that the engines had a healthy appetite for cylinder head parts each weekend.

CAM DRIVES

Just as there have been several different types of valve spring operation, there have also been several different methods of driving the cams in the first place. Most street four-strokes use a simple chain to turn the cams – most, indeed, have a sprocket on the crankshaft end and one on each of the camshafts that also provides the half-speed reduction the camshafts require.

Most of the bikes in the pit lane use gear-driven cams. A series of gears up the side of the engine, or each cylinder bank in the case of the Vs, has proved to provide the most accurate and reliable form of cam operation. This was not always the case, however, with the Yamaha in particular using a cam chain for the first three years of MotoGP, but even then their system was not entirely conventional. The Yamaha's crankshaft rotates backwards, and early photographs of the engine clearly showed the cam chain adjuster on the front of the cylinder block. Rather than drive the cams directly, however, the chain turned a gear at the bottom of the cylinder head which, in turn, rotated two gears on the end of the camshafts. This system is used on street bikes, but it is not exactly common. The old Suzuki TL1000 was one bike that used it, however.

Yamaha changed their system from an 'end of crank' chain to a gear-driven system at the start of 2005. During Valentino Rossi's championship year in 2004, the chain drive showed itself to be at its limit, becoming increasingly unreliable over 14,000rpm and needing replacement after each day's operation. To take the design of the engine forward, Yamaha knew they would have to increase revs and, in all likelihood, the severity of the cam profiles, and the additional load of each cam banging open its valves would only make the system more unreliable.

In a packaging tour de force, the gear train starts at the jackshaft that takes the power from the centre of the crank and takes the cam drive up the back of the centre of the engine. The gears don't go between the cylinders themselves, but they are as close as possible to the cylinder liners. Yamaha effectively cut the width of the top part of their engine by 20mm, this redesign allowing valuable extra room for their bike's radiator exhaust ducts.

KTM eschewed proprietary pneumatic valve systems, instead choosing to build their own from scratch. This schematic doesn't show the series of valves and gas reservoirs necessary to make the system work. Typical pressures in the 'spring' would be between 11 and 14bar.

CRANKSHAFT

The effects of motorcycle crank rotation

Honda's RC211V crank is notable for its thin full circle flywheels and removable flywheel. The fifth cylinder crankpin lags the main pairs by 104.5° and allows Honda to balance the 75.5° V5.

The first two years of the MotoGP Championship were won with a Honda that has its crankshaft turning forwards – the same way as the wheels – then Rossi jumped ship to Yamaha and took the championship on a bike that has its crank turning the other way round. So, does it make a difference and, if it does, why?

On most street bike engines the crank turns forwards, but there have been in the past some notable models with backward-turning cranks – the original Ducati 750 bevel drive is one. However, of the bikes that have been on the MotoGP grid, fully one quarter of the engine designs, including Rossi's Yamaha, have cranks that turn backwards. To turn an engine backwards calls for an extra shaft in the power train, a shaft that soaks up as much as 5bhp; and racers don't give up 5bhp to anyone without a very good reason – so what's the reason?

It all has to do with stability. When revolving at speed, the wheels on a motorcycle act like gyroscopes, and they don't want to change direction. This helps to keep the motorcycle vertical and stable. It takes effort to make them change direction, and more effort to get them to stop doing it once you have started; and when you do change direction some interesting things happen. If you take a spinning wheel and turn it to the left, in exactly the same way as a

motorcycle wheel is turned when you move the handlebars, you will find the wheel will want to twist on its axis over to the right. The opposite is also true – turn the spinning wheel right and it will roll to the left.

Gyroscopic stability is quite a strong force. If you hit, in a forwards direction, one of the handlebars on a bike travelling at 60mph, there will be a very brief shake, after which the bike will regain its stability and continue in a straight line. The problem with this is that, on a racetrack, you don't want too much stability. Indeed, you want a motorcycle that will turn accurately and, it is hoped, quicker than the one you're trying to beat.

It's possible to build a lot of instability into the chassis set-up; the more vertical the forks are, and the bigger the offset of the forks (i.e. less 'trail'), the quicker the bike will turn – but you still have to deal with the gyroscopic effects. These effects become stronger as the revs rise (the speed the wheels are turning); and the weight of the wheels (and where the weight is) also makes a difference.

There are also gyroscopes on the bike other than the wheels – all the shafts and gears in the gearbox, the cams and the crankshaft. Of these, the crankshaft is heavy enough to significantly add to the overall gyroscopic effect felt by the motorcycle, although all the smaller shafts will have some effect as well. The crankshaft, however, operates at different revs from the wheels, and it changes revs at different points on the circuit – the greater gyroscopic effect being when the engine revs are high.

The effects of gyroscopic precession are felt mostly through the front wheel. When you turn the handlebars, the front wheel turns the most. Working back along the bike, the crank moves a little less and the rear wheel moves the least, so the effects of trying to turn a gyroscope are felt less as you go back along the bike. Once you have put effort into moving the 'gyro', though, it reacts by changing direction. As you turn the handlebars slightly to the left (i.e. the initial 'counter-steer' in a turn to the right), the wheel, and therefore the bike, rolls to the right. In one manoeuvre you have created a force tipping the wheel over to the right, and moved the front wheel out to the left. The bike's and your mass is still charging forwards at the same speed, however, and topples over to the right. Put another way, the bike effectively trips over itself.

Then a second gyroscopic precession kicks in, as the bike is snapped over onto its right-hand side, the wheels turn 'into' the corner. You have gone from a vehicle that just wants to go straight, to one that now wants to oversteer. Again, this is speed-related – the faster you are going, and the faster you tip the bike over, the stronger the reaction.

So, gyroscopes don't really want to turn, but once you have turned them you get some immediate, and quite strong, reactions. Kawasaki have tried to use the benefits of a short wheelbase to overcome the not inconsiderable effect of having not only both wheels, but also the long four-cylinder in-line crankshaft, turning in the same direction. It still didn't want to change direction and was too stable, so revised weight distribution with a raised engine was tried.

So, if we normally have three (or more) big forward-spinning gyroscopes, what would happen if we turned one of them round? Depending on how you design the engine, its primary drive and the gearbox, it is possible to run the crankshaft in the opposite direction to the wheels. Depending on the revs of the crankshaft, this would negate some of the gyroscopic effect of the wheels and make the bike less stable – that is, less difficult to both make a turn and then to stop it turning.

There are other things to consider as well, when do you get the most gyroscopic effect from the crank? When happily over revving on downshifts into a corner, and at top speed, so it reduces the overall stability just when you need it to. For instance, a bike that is trying to go through a series of very high-speed flicks,

GYROSCOPIC PRECESSION

If you consider the three main units that act as gyroscopes – and remember that the front wheel has the most effect – we can try to apportion gyroscopic effect around the bike. Given the relative sizes and weights, it is reasonable to assume that the proportions would be: front wheel 5; crank 2; rear wheel 3. If we then decide that our engine's crankshaft will turn backwards, we can see that the overall gyroscopic effect is greatly reduced, or rather that a significant part of the wheel's gyroscopic effect is cancelled out by the reverse rotation of the crank.

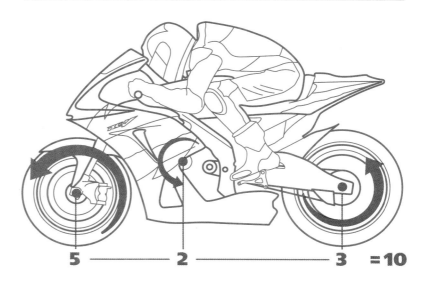

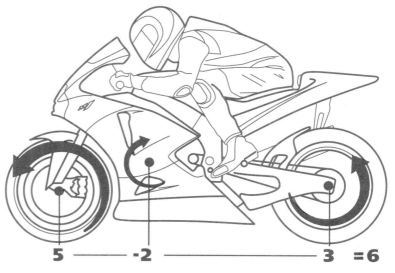

These graphics are purely descriptive, the gyroscopic effects of the crank and wheels vary at different revs and wheel speeds.

TORQUE REACTION

If you start a motorcycle on the centre-stand, the front will typically lift or fall as you blip the throttle. If the crankshaft is turning forwards, you will notice that the bike rises slightly on its front suspension – this is a torque reaction which is increased or decreased by the rev rate of the crankshaft. Literally, as the crank turns one way, the crankcase, which is bolted to the rest of the bike, is trying to turn the other way.

This torque reaction is very small, but the question is whether it is significant on something like a MotoGP bike where the fine balance of weight distribution is critical. An additional force on the front wheel, either lifting or pushing down depending on whether the crank is being accelerated or decelerated and turning backwards or forwards, could have an effect similar to the addition or subtraction of something like two kilograms.

This may not seem much but, when considered against the overall mass of the bike, it can make a one to two per cent difference. When you are fully leaned over, given the very important part the correct weight distribution has on grip, the question is whether the direction the crank is turning causes a benevolent change or not. If the bike is set up with slightly too much weight on the front wheel, then an accelerating forward-rotating crank might lift it slightly and make it grip better. Conversely, if the bike has insufficient weight on the front wheel, a backward-rotating crank, being accelerated, will have the effect of adding a little weight and improving grip.

The same torque reaction is evident in wheelie mode. Typically, a forward-rotating crank will slightly enhance the bike's desire to wheelie, and a backward-rotating crank should help keep things down.

Rossi has got the throttle pinned, the electronics won't let the bike wheelie by limiting the power, and with his backwards-rotating-crank the point at which his bike gets its front wheel airborne is very slightly higher.

Hayden's Honda crank rotates forward. Under hard acceleration the front has a slightly greater tendency to lift than on the Yamaha. The bike will have been set up slightly differently to counteract this, but there will be side effects.

© GOLD AND GOOSE

like the back 'straight' at Assen, or down Craner Curves at Donington, can be difficult to turn. A bike that has less of a stability increase at high engine speeds will be easier to turn, and therefore quicker.

There are other benefits from this design strategy too, a four-cylinder engine is a lot harder to flip onto its side than a narrower V4 because there is a lot more crankshaft sticking out from the centre line, the ends of the crank have to accelerate from parallel with the ground to 45° to the ground as near instantaneously as the rider can make it do so. This isn't such a problem with the narrower V4 designs. If we were designing an in-line four from scratch and wanted to make it easier to start a turn and easier to get to full lean, then turning the crank round would make the bike feel more agile, with less stability from the gyroscopes to help make up for the extra effort of swinging that long crankshaft around.

And there are secondary effects from the choice of direction of crank rotation. The torque reactions felt through the crankcase (and, therefore, the rest of the bike) are sufficient to change the weight felt on each wheel – enough to make a wheel slide or not – and it can change the bike from understeer to oversteer in a corner and, to cap it all, it can change the way the bike wants to wheelie out of a corner.

Gyroscopic precession is one of the major reasons that motorcycles work; the stability it imparts to the wheels and the way in which the wheels react to forced changes of attitude are fundamental.

STEERING A MOTORCYCLE

Several different forces act on a bike when you steer it into a turn. There are those that derive from the gyroscopic effects, from the shape of the tyres, and from the twisting of the tyre carcase. There is the angle of the rim and the grip of the tarmac. There are the forces generated by the changing angle of the forks and the length of the trail, the height of the centre of gravity, and the radius of the turn itself. There are also a number of other effects brought on by chassis and fork rigidity. Everything works together to produce the feel we get when we initiate a turn, and makes isolating the gyroscopic effects rather difficult! However, let's have a go. We want to turn right and, as this is about racing bikes, we want to turn right fast. So what happens and when?

Spinning wheels want to continue in a straight line, and if you force a change in direction they react strangely. The higher the revs of the wheel, and the heavier that wheel is, the harder it will be to initiate a turn. Equally, you will get a stronger response from a faster-spinning, heavier wheel once you have turned it.

To change direction on a motorcycle, you use gyroscopic precession to help initiate the roll into the corner. When you steer into a right-hand corner, you actually twitch the handlebars sharply to the left. This has the effect of starting to roll the wheel to the right. As this happens, the bike starts to trip over into the corner with the front wheel now being driven out from under the bike's centre of gravity.

As the front wheel and the other spinning gyroscopes on the bike are rolled over to full lean for a right turn, the gyroscopic effect now steers the bike to the right, into the turn. To stop the roll, you use throttle and handlebar position to increase centrifugal force to hold the bike in a constant turn. The faster you roll in the wheel, the stronger the gyroscopic reaction. To get out of the corner you merely increase power, and centrifugal force brings the bike up to vertical, with gyroscopic precession helping to straighten the front wheel.

The best way to feel the force yourself is to take the front wheel out of your mountain-bike and, with a little help from some friends, spin it while holding it by the axle away from you. Imagining your arms to be the front forks, turn the wheel to the right and you will discover that it will want to roll to the left. Conversely, if you turn the wheel to the left you will find that it wants to roll to the right. Now hold the mountain-bike wheel right out in front of you and quickly roll the wheel over to the right, just as would happen as a motorcycle rolls over to full lean. You will find quite a strong gyroscopic effect turning the wheel into the corner; the faster you roll the wheel over, and the faster it is turning, the faster it 'turns in' to the corner. The reasons for this reaction are quite complex, but suffice to say that all spinning objects have this tendency.

CRANK LAYOUTS

What we are seeing in MotoGP is an evolutionary process where the various possible layouts of engine are competing against each other, with the layout containing the best set of compromises coming to the fore.

Most of the field has opted for V-configuration engines, but it is noticeable that Yamaha, Kawasaki and Aprilia have not. Motorcycle design is very much led by compromise, and the choices made by these companies show that they are far more concerned with packaging – the ability to place the engine where they want – over pure mass centralisation. It might also show, in the case of Kawasaki and Yamaha, a certain allegiance to their road configurations.

Crankshafts are quite heavy. In MotoGP they are probably between 4kg and 8kg. In a motorcycle weighing only 148kg, that's a significant part of the bike's weight. The V-engine will typically have a very short crankshaft, whereas an in-line four has weight sticking out further from the centre-line. The effect of this is that, for a given steering input (assuming everything else is the same), an in-line four will require more effort to turn or, more accurately, roll over, than a V4, simply because the ends of the crankshaft have to be moved further.

For a quick experiment in feeling this, grab a 2kg steel ball and a 2kg dumbbell. Although both are the same weight, the dumbbell requires more effort to twist than the ball, simply because its weight is further from its centre. If you think of the crankshaft as a dumbbell, you can imagine that the same effect as a racer snaps the bike over to full lean. Even if the four-cylinder crank is virtually the same weight as the shorter V-version, it requires more effort to roll.

So, if you have an across-the-frame three or four and you have both the 'dumbbell effect' and a lot of gyroscopic forces working against you when you want to make a motorcycle turn really fast, then it's quite possible that one of the things you can do to reduce the combined effect is to turn the crank backwards.

The additional width of an across-the-frame four-cylinder crankshaft means that it rotates further when the bike is leaned over. If the bike has less gyroscopic stability in the first place, the chassis setup doesn't need to be as radical to make quick changes of direction possible.

IN-LINE FOUR-CYLINDER CRANKSHAFT

DISTANCE TRAVELLED

V-CONFIGURATION FOUR-CYLINDER CRANKSHAFT

DISTANCE TRAVELLED

GREAT BACKWARDS CRANKERS OF OUR TIME
- **Honda RC166** six-cylinder across the frame four-stroke.
- **Ducati 750/860/1000** bevel-drive cam twin.
- **Yamaha TZ700/750** four-cylinder across the frame two-stroke.
- **Yamaha YZR500 OW35** four-cylinder across the frame two-stroke.
- **Suzuki RG500** (1978 onwards) four-cylinder square two-stroke (both of them!).
- **Suzuki RE-5 Rotary.**
- **Honda NSR500** (1988 onwards) four-cylinder across the frame two-stroke.
- **Aprilia Cube** three-cylinder across the frame four-stroke.
- **Foggy Petronas FPR-1** three-cylinder across the frame four-stroke.
- **Yamaha M-1** four-cylinder across the frame four-stroke.

QUOTES FROM THOSE WHO SHOULD KNOW

Tom O'Kane has been a crew chief at KR Proton, and is currently with Chris Vermeulen at Suzuki. He recalls a Roberts team experiment in 1999 at the Brazil GP (Saturday free practice, in case anyone is counting): 'We tried a back-to-back test. We ran a three-cylinder two-stroke then, and we had a primary drive made with a chain and one with gears. The rider was Mike Hale. He went out with the engine turning forwards, then – same tyres and same settings on everything – he went out again with the crankshaft turning backwards. Turning backwards it certainly made the bike less stable, but it also reduced its tendency to wheelie. With the crank running the same way as the wheels, it has less tendency to understeer – backwards, it understeers more.'

Jerry Burgess spent years at Honda, then moved to Yamaha with Rossi: 'There's nowhere near the effect on a four-stroke. You blip the throttle and, if the crank rolls forwards, the forks come up and, if the crank rolls backwards, the forks go down. But, the way these things (four-strokes) spin you never see an effect. This is not a Yamaha thing, it's a Honda thing. They just said it has nowhere near the same effect on a four-stroke as on a two-stroke.

'To me, they are all tools and you just go out and find the right setting. If I try to be the engineer, I tread on their toes. At the end the day I just take what they make and I try to make it work.'

Kenny Roberts has been there and done that: 'The Yamaha TZs turned backwards and gave a certain characteristic, and you had to get the best out of that characteristic on the racetrack. If it turns backwards it does one thing; if it turns forwards it does another thing. You know, Honda would have won the races whichever way the crank turned – they would have just done it through engineering. I understand the Aprilia turns backwards, and that has certain characteristics built into it that you have to counter by engineering.'

Eskil Suter was in charge of redesigning the FP-1 engine from a MotoGP engine into a superbike power plant, and is currently in charge of Kawasaki's MotoGP chassis programme. One of the main differences between the two bikes is that the FP-1 crank turns backwards and the Kawasaki he is currently working on turns forwards:

'I took a long hard look at Honda's NSR 500 before considering which way a crank should turn.

You have to consider there are two effects, one is the gyroscopic precession and the other is the torque reaction from the crank. When you have the crank turning forwards, you have the precession from the wheels and the crank all turning the same way, keeping the bike stable. In addition, when the crank turns forwards, as you accelerate the crank you get a change of as much as two kilograms at the front wheel, lifting the wheel off the ground. This is not such a problem in corners, but if you have a motorcycle that wants to wheelie, this will help it do so. If you have a crank turning backwards, then that same two kilos will provide an anti-wheelie effect, but I have never actually back-to-back tested the two directions and would like to do so.'

Jan Witteveen, racing boss at Aprilia until the end of 2004: 'The gyroscopic effect is different; if the wheels are turning forwards and the crankshaft is turning backwards, you need a different chassis with a different balance for the bike. For me the effect is better if you run the crankshaft backwards, gyroscopically the bike is more neutral. We think our solution is better for high-speed corners. It is a better compromise, there is little gyroscopic effect and you can compensate with trail and everything.

'The torque from the crank is not worth worrying about; if you put it in the forces, a couple of kilos is negligible.'

Shogo Kanaumi was the project leader for the RC211V in 2003: 'Both ways have advantages and disadvantages. I think the RC211V way is better for 'rider feeling' (the RC211V has a forwards-turning crank).'

Claudio Domenicali: 'We know the Yamaha is turning backwards. I think there is no real reason to turn it backwards – we try to understand by calculation what could be the effect, but it is very little. To turn it backwards you need an extra shaft, which will lose power. They are just losing two per cent of the power – which is five horsepower that you are just giving away.'

Masao Furusawa is the boss of Yamaha's MotoGP effort: 'Our crankshaft turns backwards. Sure, we have a small balancer that eliminates some of the effect, but predominantly the backwards torque is higher. The chassis geometry makes a difference too, but I would say our engine design helps stability and agility as well.'

CLUTCH

The use of slipper clutches in MotoGP

1

2

1 The Ducati MotoGP clutch uses plain ramps, better for putting up with 260bhp but a high maintenance operation with the clutch being stripped and serviced several times per GP.

2 The clutch back plate locates the centre and contains the opposite side of the ramp mechanism.

OPPOSITE TOP: Yamaha's clutch pack and basket. The plates are sintered and use what looks like a 48 tooth basket.

OPPOSITE BOTTOM: Yamaha's Motegi 2006-onwards pressure plate. Designed to pull in additional cooling air, this clutch was debuted at Motegi, a circuit that is notoriously hard on clutches.

Racing is about far more than power down the straights; well-controlled high corner-entry speeds are just as important to a quick lap as sheer grunt. The two-strokes previously used in top-flight GP racing simply didn't generate enough compression under shut throttles to really destabilise their rear suspension, but the new four-strokes of the MotoGP generation most certainly do.

Engine braking is the result of shutting the throttle on a high-compression four-stroke. There may not be much air going in past the throttle, but the piston has to compress what is there in any event. This wouldn't be a problem if the engine wasn't connected, via the gearbox, to the rear chain and thence to the rear wheel and tyre. The chain-drive system to the rear wheel plays a critical part in the way a motorcycle works on track. Motorcycle designers use the positioning of the gearbox output sprocket and the swing-arm pivot to create a pull on the swing-arm that pushes the rear tyre into the ground under power. Conversely, if the rear wheel is driving the engine, the reverse happens and the chain tries to hop the rear tyre off the ground, especially when it is fighting a lot of compression. As far as the rider is concerned, as soon as he shuts the throttle, the rear end of the bike starts to feel different and 'unstable'. The problem becomes much worse if he is changing down through the box and braking

hard; each gear change makes the problem worse and, if the rider is being very aggressive (as you would expect on a race track) the engine's revs increase to the point that they are pushed up through the rev limit. The forward pitch of the bike under heavy braking lifts weight from the rear wheel, further exacerbating the problem.

Riding fast on a circuit, or for that matter on the road, is all about smoothness – it is about loading up the tyres to their limit of grip (or controlled slide) and holding them there at that fine margin of grip; just before they really 'let go'. All the suspension and chassis set-up effort goes into helping this situation to be predictable and accurate. What you do not want is the big pistons at the other end of the chain jerking the swing arm about, either while floating into a high-speed corner or coming into a slow, hard-braking corner. To go fast and maintain grip, you need smooth progressive deceleration as you roll off the throttle, and no jerks that would result in a movement in the swing-arm.

There are two ways to try to eliminate these effects. One is to attack the root cause of the problem and try to set the throttle to a point where there is little or no engine braking in the first place – the problem with this is that different 'levels' of throttle, depending on the situation (the engine revs, the gear and the throttle opening) are required to get the right effect. The other is to fit a slipper clutch to allow the engine to automatically disengage the clutch whenever too much resistance is felt. Obviously, that resistance is much reduced by a higher throttle position, so slipper clutch activity can be much reduced. The combination of the two solutions lets the bike's suspension work much better coming into (and going through) corners, and also allows the engine to take the abuses of racetrack use without the constant threat of over-revving.

There are several types of slipper clutch. Various designs have been tried over the years, but all those on the MotoGP grid are basically ramp types. In these, most of the clutches have a separate centre section that has a ramp system built into its base. The clutch is a purely mechanical device. When the throttle is closed and the rear wheel starts to turn over the engine (let's call it reverse torque), a simple system of angled ramps (with or without ball bearings, depending on manufacturer) inside the central drum forces the drum up against the outer pressure plate, so forcing the clutch plates apart. As soon as the clutch starts to slip, the forces holding the clutch apart are controlled, and the clutch is held in perfect slipping mode – just enough power is transmitted to maintain the equilibrium. In a normal riding situation the clutch

A BIT OF HISTORY

Listening to the wonderful, drawn-out, chest-pounding boom and roar of Read and Bonera on the two works MV Agustas going into the final two turns of the Assen GP track is an abiding memory of my first GP at Assen in 1976. Never mind that the race was a brilliant duel between Sheene and Agostini, both two-stroke mounted.

What I had not appreciated was that I was listening to the four-stroke 500GP endgame. In 1975, the once all-powerful MV Agusta GP squad was struggling. The main enemy was the big 500 two-stroke – light and quick. The Japanese engineers were using their small-bike knowledge to great effect. The two-strokes had power aplenty as well as their unsung advantage – minimal engine braking. They were faster into the corners as well.

The MV Agustas we were watching were making beautiful emotive noises, like hollow rolling thunder – noises that came from the rear wheel turning over the engine; engine braking. The noise was fantastic, but the effect was for the chain to jerk the rear suspension around; the bigger the pistons and the higher the compression, the worse the problem. It was bad enough to be a significant disadvantage with a 500 four like the MV, and with the lumpy great 247cc pulses from a 990 MotoGP bike it is sheer poison. It's the same with all big fours; as soon as there is any decent engine compression there is going to be a lot of engine braking interference with the rear suspension. Even worse; in an attempt to control the pulsing, the rear suspension damping is normally set very stiff, which compromises the suspension's ability to float over bumps elsewhere on the circuit.

In 1979 Honda debuted the NR500. This was their re-entry into racing after a 12-year hiatus. The bike was designed by the youngest and brightest of their engineers. It was a deliberate attempt to look for alternative solutions to existing designs. As a bike it wasn't a success, but its unique oval-piston, twin con-rod per piston, design had a lot of engine braking, and one of the solutions developed was a 'back torque limiter', otherwise known as a slipper clutch. Just three years later, the FWS1000 turned up at Daytona. Their biggest pure motorcycle-racing engine ever, it was a four-stroke V-4 prototype designed solely to win Daytona. It failed, because the clever new idea to eliminate rear wheel hop wore out the clutch. An inauspicious start, but the anti-hop slipper clutch was born.

The same year, these clutches were also used on Honda's 750 Interceptor factory superbikes. Rob Muzzy had several different versions to get his Kawasaki superbikes into corners easily. It became apparent that, while a slipper clutch was handy on a four-cylinder 750, it was absolutely crucial to have one on a big 1000. Development has continued, and now no self-respecting four-stroke race bike, be it superbike or MotoGP bike, would attempt to race without something to stop the engine braking forces messing up the rear suspension and tyre grip.

ENGINE DRIVING THE REAR WHEEL [NORMAL TORQUE]

As the engine drives the chain, the clutch operates normally, and the clutch plates are held together by the normal springs.

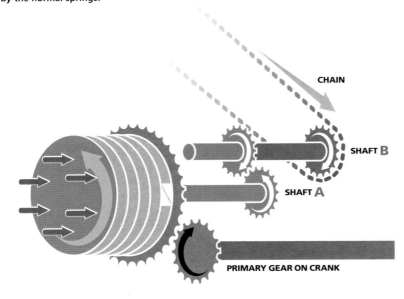

CHAIN

SHAFT B

SHAFT A

PRIMARY GEAR ON CRANK

REAR WHEEL DRIVING THE ENGINE [REVERSE TORQUE]

As soon as the rear wheel tries to turn over the engine, the clutch centre rises up on its ramps and pokes the pressure plate off; and that simply disengages the engine.

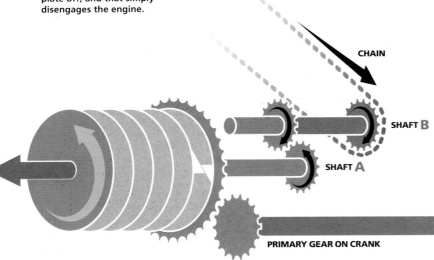

CHAIN

SHAFT B

SHAFT A

PRIMARY GEAR ON CRANK

operates just like any other. The point at which the clutch releases, and the way it does it, makes a real difference to the way the engine braking affects handling, and to the suspension set-up.

Yamaha, Ducati and Suzuki use the simplest, with coil springs and ramps. Honda used a large-diameter diaphragm spring design for most of the life of the RC211V but changed over to a coil-spring variation on the final version for the works team to provide a lighter feel for Dani Pedrosa. The previous diaphragm design used two different pressure-plates in its five year tenure, with a 'turbine' cover added to provide additional cooling in mid 2003.

WCM, Aprilia, Roberts and Kawasaki used some interesting designs over the course of the 990 years. WCM first used a carbon AP clutch. This was a small-diameter unit that was very light and which came with a staggering range of choices for ramp angles. The carbon plates were its ultimate downfall, however, as carbon is very temperature-sensitive and it proved to be very 'grabby' at low temperatures. This caused great difficulties in setting the bike up to be able to launch off the line and also provide predictable levels of slip during the race. WCM eventually changed over to a conventional STM clutch.

Aprilia also initially used an AP carbon item, but claimed to have developed it so that most of its temperature sensitivity had been removed. Colin Edwards still managed some seriously jumpy starts, though – on one occasion shooting across the grid and nearly taking out several riders. Kawasaki initially used a Suter item, a natural progression from their use of the same design on their superbikes. This used a small series of ramps situated next to the primary gear, and drove the clutch pressure-plate up via a series of pins operating through an oil seal. In the last year, after Suter had all but left the project, an FCC clutch was used. Team Roberts used clutches manufactured by their Japanese sponsor FCC at first. This was a diaphragm clutch, and the speed with which it went out of adjustment through pack wear in the early laps of the race caused much angst. For the KTM engine, an STM diaphragm clutch was used most of the time, with a KTM coil-spring unit used occasionally. For their Honda year the engine came with a standard Honda diaphragm unit.

SO HOW DOES A SLIPPER CLUTCH WORK?

When the engine power is driving the bike forwards in the normal direction, the little ramps lock solid, and the clutch acts completely normally. The diagram shows what occurs when the power is shut off and the engine is being turned over by the rear wheel. As gearshaft B is turned over by the rear wheel, the clutch (attached to gearshaft A) is forced to take the load in the opposite direction. This forces the centre of the clutch up the ramps; thus starting to force the clutch pack apart.

As soon as the clutch pack stops gripping (i.e. when the centre has risen slightly on its ramps) most of the force to hold the pack apart is lost and, theoretically, clutch grip is re-established as the pack tries to come back together. In practice, the clutch establishes an equilibrium position where there is just enough force being transmitted to hold the clutch apart (i.e. to hold the centre partially up the ramps), yet just enough to stop the engine being revved up.

AND HOW DO YOU ADJUST IT?

The main adjustment is the ramp angle. Most bikes in pit lane have 45° ramps as standard. This angle is preferred because most of the teams can simply start their bikes with some form of powered roller operating on the rear wheel. On an engine as large as a 990cc four, a slipper clutch ramp angle much lower than this would slip the clutch during starting. Ducati obviously use a lower angle on their clutches as part of the way they deal with their very-high-compression engines – a lower angle is typically needed to allow smooth clutch operation when the ramps are working against very stiff springs, themselves needed to deal with very high engine torque outputs. Again, this is easy to observe in pit lane, with the Ducati mechanics pinning the clutch solid for each rear-wheel start. Most teams have several different clutches available to them, all using different ramp angles so that easier or stiffer clutch action can be selected, depending on conditions and available grip. Lower ramp angles would be used in conditions with less surface grip – in the wet, for instance.

Slipper clutches can, and are, adjusted in other ways too. The speed with which the actuation mechanism (in most cases the clutch centre) can rise can be controlled with different 'secondary springs', be they coil or diaphragm. A stiffer secondary spring will mean the clutch needs more reverse torque before the centre reaches, and pushes off, the pressure plate. With more reverse torque required, the clutch will typically work later into the corner, and on some occasions not at all. A very similar adjustment is to set the pressure plate nearer the centre using thinner clutch plates. In this case, the distance the centre has to travel before it connects with the pressure plate means that a closer clearance will require less reverse torque before the clutch starts to operate, and a wider clearance means more torque is required for the centre to get to the pressure plate and start to lift it.

Once you have adjusted the speed with which the centre of the clutch can climb to the pressure plate (or the distance it has to do it) you will find the amount of work the centre has to do to hold the clutch open (i.e. disengage) can be adjusted by varying the main springs. These main springs have to be strong enough to hold the clutch together under acceleration; once they are, normal slipper clutch practice is to have them as light as possible to minimise pack wear. If, however, the main-spring rate is further increased, then the centre has a harder job in lifting the pressure plate off. The increased effort translates into an increased amount of engine braking getting through the clutch. This increases clutch plate wear, but may provide a 'feel' the rider might prefer. On a six-spring clutch you might only strengthen two of the six main springs; the Suzukis ran like this most of the time.

BELOW: Suzuki use a six-coil spring clutch. The different spring colours signify differing spring rates. This is one method of adjusting the amount of engine braking.

BOTTOM: Honda's turbine cover with the outer face plate removed. You can see the scoops that pull air into the centre of the clutch to keep it cool.

BIG BANG

Big bang, long bang or smooth bang. What's it all about?

Bike leaned over, throttle open, Valentino Rossi demonstrates the Yamaha's exceptional traction out of corners.

Something changed in MotoGP when Valentino Rossi rolled out for his first Grand Prix on the Yamaha. The deep, gruff exhaust note was something new, and it was to influence the engines of most of the bikes in pit lane.

Vibration specialist, Masao Furasawa – the Yamaha engineer who built the vibration-reducing mountings of the original RD350LC – had a theory as to why the in-line fours were having more difficulty than the V-engined bikes in getting nearly 250hp onto the ground.

He has an innate understanding of the way small vibrations can cause big differences to the way things work, and what he saw in an in-line four's power output was a series of small fluctuations. Every 180° of crank movement, the crank slowed down a little as the piston got close to full compression up at TDC, and then sped up again as combustion occurred. He understood that those small fluctuations in crankshaft speed would be felt all the way through at the contact patch of the tyre. And those fluctuations going into the contact patch would make it far easier for the tyre to break traction and slide sideways. The closest analogy in normal life is the vibrating plate that construction workers use to finish the surface of a new concrete floor, floating easily over the new surface as it is pushed around.

Back in the early '90s, when the four-cylinder

500cc two-strokes were king, a system called 'big bang' gave them additional traction. Big bang typically involved pairs of pistons firing together, or within a few degrees of each other – the theory being that the longer space between each power pulse would allow the tyre time to regain its grip. One of the benefits of having two pistons fire together is that the initial pulse of power is very large and, in a lot of ways, that helps the tyre get a grip. It literally drives the rubber into the surface of the tarmac, the subsequent long space before the next big pulse arrives allows the tyre to roll forward and present a new 'fresh' section of rubber to the road.

The modifications Yamaha made to their M1 in 2004, revising the combustion timing sequence, appeared to make the bike more usable. The Flammini brothers, owners of the World Superbike series, were so concerned about the potential upset to the formbook from this idea that they, together with the FIM, rushed through a new rule banning 'big bang conversions' from World Superbike. But, as we will see, they probably didn't have too much to worry about.

There is still no definitive answer as to what exactly happens when you change the combustion order of an engine, but the various theories do seem to fit quite nicely together. This, then, is the current understanding.

THE YAMAHA VIEW

Furusawa had very different views on the sort of power that would allow the Yamaha to get up to the front. In early 2004 he explained, 'We took a long look at the problem and optimised the combustion timing – no two cylinders fire together. In Japan the Shinkansen (very fast) trains run on steel wheels and there is very little traction, but the power still gets through. This is because the torque from an electric motor is very smooth. Just go and ask Valentino or Carlos, the engine they have is very smooth and that is what they need to have speed in the corners.'

With his optimised firing order engine, Furusawa had basically reinvented the in-line four as a GP motorcycle power plant. A classic in-line four has a crank that provides four firing pulses every four-stroke cycle, and creates equally-sized power pulses every 180° of crank rotation. It seems that, at 250bhp, the tyres find the regular arrival of these pulses a real problem. Just down the pit lane, Honda were clearly getting their power to the ground without too much difficulty, and Furusawa surmised that it was a side-effect of their 75.5° V-configuration engine. The RC211V has four of its cylinders on a conventional 360° crank, and the fifth slightly offset for balancing purposes. With a firing order of 0–75.5–104.5–180–75.5–284.5 Honda ensured that the tyres received two 'long pushes' followed by a rest period for the tyre to recover and regain grip. Not only was the Honda slightly more powerful, but the way it delivered the power to the tyre clearly achieved better grip.

In a 'normal' in-line engine the crankshaft doesn't rotate at a constant rate, during each revolution it slows down and speeds up a little depending on what's going on above the piston. As the piston comes up on the compression stroke, first it has to compress the basic mixture and then, before it gets to top dead centre (TDC), it also suffers the initial effects of the spark plug setting off the mixture. At this point the rate of crank rotation slows slightly. But, as the piston goes over TDC, the full force of the combustion hits and it accelerates down again, speeding the crank back up. On a 180° crank there are four 'slow down, speed up' sessions in every two rev cycles. If, however, the crankshaft is rephased so that the second piston arrives at TDC just 45° to 90° after the first, its 'slow down' session is effectively cancelled out by the first of the close running pair shooting away from TDC after its mixture has been ignited. From the tyre's point of view, it gets a series of long pushes without grip-damaging torque peaks, and a much smaller number of crank-speed fluctuations overall. So, rather than describing the engine as 'big bang' we should consider 'long bang' or 'smooth bang' or, most accurately, 'biggish bang with a long smooth bang afterwards'! All these benefits seem to allow a tyre to maintain grip and, in the RC211V, Honda had a simple version of it all along.

However, once you have decided to rephase the combustion timing, an in-line four has advantages over a V. With four individual cylinders and a balancer shaft (or shafts) the in-line four can be modified to even more adventurous specifications than the V. Furusawa and his team were fortunate that the original design team had decided to both take the power from the centre of the crank and reverse its rotation. To do this they added a shaft just behind and above the crankshaft. In the original engines it just reversed the direction of rotation and drove the alternator; from the 2004 engines onwards it also worked as a balance shaft. This has enabled Yamaha to design a crankshaft that optimises the effect.

POWER PULSES AT THE TYRE

Four-stroke engines get their name because every two revolutions of the crankshaft, or every four strokes of the piston, they fire the combustion mixture trapped above the piston.

Furusawa brought a new approach to the racing department at Yamaha; he binned the five-valve heads, so long a Yamaha feature, and introduced an irregular fire crankshaft for grip.

'THE COMBUSTION SIGNAL IS IMPORTANT, TOO. YOU WANT THE TYRE TO FEEL THE INITIAL COMBUSTION. BIG BANG HAS THIS, BUT IN STEADY STATE WE NEED TO DESTROY THE NOISE AS WELL. WE ARE BANG-BANG-----BANG-----BANG; SOMETHING LIKE THAT – OUR CRANKSHAFT IS NOT 180° ANY MORE. WITH AN IN-LINE FOUR AND A BALANCE SHAFT WE CAN HAVE A NEW COMBUSTION TIMING SEQUENCE.'
MASAO FURUSAWA [YAMAHA]

The subsequent explosion fires the piston back down the bore creating a pulse of power. With the old 'across the frame' four-cylinder engines there was an even space between each pulse, four individual cylinders and each one firing every four strokes or two revolutions of the crank. So let's just consider what happens as those power pulses get down to tyre level.

At 14,000rpm, the crankshaft is rotating at 233 revs per second. If the bike is travelling at 150kph (93mph) the rear tyre is rotating at nearly 24 turns per second. That means that there are nearly ten crank turns per wheel revolution, and with two bangs per crank revolution there are 20 power pulses per wheel revolution. The rolling circumference of a race tyre is currently about 1.7m, so if there are about 20 pulses per wheel revolution at 150kph, at that speed the rear tyre gets a new pulse every 8cm to 9cm.

So what is different if we have a big or long bang engine? Well, if we redesign the crankshaft so that all the bangs happen closer together, using our example above, instead of a load of little pulses pushing the tyre once every 8cm the pulses would be all crammed together, all four in one long push of 16 –18cm of tyre rotation and then a big gap of around 16–18cm before the next long push starts. Five long

pushes and five long spaces per tyre revolution.

Bear in mind that these figures are deliberately not peak revolution figures. They are examples that assume the time this effect is best needed is the period where the bike is on its side, either accelerating out of a corner or diving into it.

SO WHY WOULD THE TYRE CARE ABOUT WHEN THE PULSES TURN UP?

The theory holds that as the tyre receives each power pulse it gets wound up, it distorts and twists under the force, then it receives another one, then another. As a result it starts to move, slide even, across the track surface. In a conventional in-line four-cylinder engine the tyre never gets the opportunity to unwind and regrip the surface. For good traction we want the tyre to have a really good grip on the surface before thumping it with a series of power pulses totalling 250bhp. The long bang theory is that there is a combination of effects, when all the 'bangs' are rearranged to be close together, they arrive as one long firm push, with no vibration and without an increased peak load. The tyre then has a long gap, with no power pulses, for it to regain its grip on the track before the next long push.

The big bang theory is slightly different; if all

STANDARD FIRING PATTERN

BIG-BANG FIRING PATTERN

IRREGULAR FIRING PATTERN

the combustion effects happen together then the really violent initial power thrust buries the rubber of the tyre into the surface of the track, the shorter length of the power pulse then allows the tyre a longer undisturbed period of grip. The best analogy so far is to consider the relationship between the tyre and the road surface as being similar to a heavy box that you have got to push along a rough floor. If the box is really heavy it requires a lot of initial effort to move it. You need to really put your back into getting it moving, but once it is moving it is relatively easy to keep shoving it along.

In the same way, the tyre needs a lot of effort to break traction and slide sideways, but once it is sliding sideways all those little regular bangs from the crankshaft keep it sliding. By grouping all the bangs closer together we give the tyre time to sort itself out and get a real grip on the surface of the track before the next big push appears. It is just like moving that box one pace, stopping completely, and then starting the big initial push again.

Furusawa won't be drawn too far, but he gives more credence to the long bang theory than to that of the big bang, 'The combustion signal is important, too. You want the tyre to feel the initial combustion. Big bang has this, but in steady state we need to destroy the noise as well. We are bang-bang-----bang------- bang; something like that – our crankshaft is not 180° any more. With an in-line four and a balance shaft we can have a new combustion timing sequence.'

The Yamaha is, therefore, very likely to have a completely irregular firing sequence – two combustion events close together, followed by the other two spaced out more, then a long gap – all to get the benefits of an initial shove followed by a gentle, but firm, long smooth push with no vibration at the contact patch.

SO HOW DOES ALL THIS TURN INTO QUICKER LAP TIMES?

Corner exit speed is critical on the race track because every advantage gained is kept the whole way down the next straight, and corner entry is important because that'll always be where some irritant will try to stuff his front wheel under yours. Without long bang, the rider used to have to deal with a tyre that was trying to slide sideways when he hit the throttle. Now that same tyre has been given the time to recreate its grip on the surface, it is able to make sure that the bike fires forwards under power, and doesn't spin sideways. Because the effect is felt at each corner exit, and there is a similar off-throttle effect going into the corner as well, the bike holds its line better and can take a bunch more grief before it slides.

BIG TWINS HAVE ALWAYS BEEN BIG BANG

It is worth noting that Ducati ruled superbike racing for years with a 90° V-twin, revving to around 12,000-13,000rpm. Its power pulses hit the tyre only twice every four-stroke cycle, on the figures above, and at the same 150kph (93mph), that would be one pulse, a wait of 15.6cm, and then a second pulse and a wait of 25.99cm. On that basis, it seems fair to say that V-twins have always had the big bang effect.

It is also fair to say that you may need to change the firing sequence to maximise the positive effects of a big bang engine if you are operating in a different rev zone. With Kawasaki's BB2 engine, the 540° of crank rotation would give a space in power delivery at the tyre of 31.2cm at the same 12,000rpm and 150kph, but if the Kawasaki had an engine turning at 14,400rpm at the same speed, as you would expect with a higher-revving four-cylinder, the tyre would also get a rest space of 25.99cm!

Even though the Ducati firing sequence was called 'Twin Pulse', it didn't consist of two cylinders firing together. Instead it used a crankshaft phased to mimic as close as possible the Honda V5's firing sequence.

© GOLD AND GOOSE

Kawasaki redesigned their firing sequence very quickly after Ichiro Yoda joined them from Yamaha. The firing sequence they used for the next 18 months was a big bang sequence rather than Yamaha's long bang.

REDESIGNING THE ENGINE

So, if we want to get a break in the delivery of the power, the trick appears to be to re-time the firing intervals governed by the crank to get the best effect at the tyre and, at the same time, keep the internal stresses of having irregular firing pulses as low as possible. In MotoGP, where the prototype rules mean you can change things to your heart's content, the cranks are being redesigned.

Honda's genius RC211V engine had a version of this type of power delivery all along. They appear to have tried several variations, but the one now in use is the same as the original. Yamaha initially appeared to have redesigned their in-line four as a 'virtual V', but now it is looking more as if they built an irregular-phased-fire engine. Ducati, Suzuki and Proton all tried different crankshafts in their V engines, all firing in such a way as to get the longest possible gap, somewhere in their engine's power flow, as well as the most effective push.

In most cases, the big or long bang version of an engine makes a little less peak power than the unmodified version. This is usually because the exhaust system and airboxes are designed specifically for each application. A new firing sequence needs different exhausts and usually a different airbox too; all manufacturers fit new pipes but it took until the second year for most of them to change their airboxes.

WHAT IF WE HAVEN'T GOT THE TIME TO REDESIGN THE ENGINE?

Kawasaki MotoGP didn't have the option of retiming their crankshaft to create a long bang power delivery, but there was a quick way to get the big bang effect. An in-line four has, as it says on the box, four pistons, and each piston has a set of cam lobes to open and close its valves at the right time. The pistons usually operate in pairs, two rising and falling together, one on the exhaust stroke and one on the compression stroke. Kawasaki redesigned the camshafts and made one of the pairs of pistons act together, just by giving them identically phased cam lobes and ignition timing. This gives three unequal power pulses and then 360° of crankshaft rotation where no power is delivered. Obviously this does cause some problems, the gearbox and primary gears were all originally designed to take, shall we say, regular 247cc-size power pulses. By doubling up two of the pistons' firing strokes, one of the resulting pulses gives nearly 500cc worth of pulse through parts not designed for that sort of abuse.

Kawasaki tried the one-big-bang-and-two-little-ones approach, unsurprisingly called the BB3, but their riders initially preferred the BB2 version, the so-called 'double twin'. This version simply has each pair of cylinders firing together, 180° apart. This gives one massive 540° break in the power flow every pair of revolutions, and two thumping great bangs.

Olly Jacque obviously liked it in China in 2005, but Nakano destroyed at least one set of primary gears in testing, and all the time the engines used this sequence the team changed the primary gears each day. Once Kawasaki sorted their electronic throttle bodies, the riders tried the BB3 version again, and this seemed to be favoured.

Kawasaki had a new engine for 2006 – still an across-the-frame four, but it had a balance shaft. The existence of the balance shaft gives the team the ability to change the firing order as much as they like.

Similar experimentation went on in the British Superbike Championship, where the Virgin Yamaha BSB team seemed to have made one of their pairs of pistons act together.

A BIT OF DOUBT

You would think that the tyre companies would notice a different type of wear when riders report big grip improvements, but none of that. Bridgestone say they cannot see a difference in the tyre wear, and neither can Michelin. In Michelin's case, both the Yamaha and the Honda are said to like similar tyres. In the case of Bridgestone, though, all their bike tyres get different constructions; but it seemed for a long while that the Kawasaki could live with softer compounds than the Suzuki. That was frustrating for Suzuki, and they are trying to find out why, even to the point of testing a full big bang engine. So, maybe we still need a little more research before we can certainly say that we have understood what is going on.

On the engine side there is no doubt that, unless the airbox and exhaust systems are redesigned, the bike is going to lose some power when the firing sequence is changed. All these parts help focus the power of the engine, and changing one thing means you have to change another to keep the focus. One view is that the changes soften the power output just enough for the rider to feel more comfortable opening the throttle on a 250bhp motorcycle, but as we get bikes with redesigned airboxes, this effect is lost.

Other doubts centre on the flex and damping within the drive train. Proponents of this view argue that natural damping within the chain and rear tyre would eliminate most of the vibrations that are supposedly damaging grip. Perhaps one day Yamaha will let us have a crankshaft so we can at least confirm what they did!

BANGING ON ABOUT DIFFERENT BANGS

Kyochi Yoshii – Honda RCV Project Leader (March 2005): 'The effect on the tyre is like one of those big balls you used to ride as a kid. You know, a 'space hopper' – just a series of big, soft pushes on the tyre!'

Ichiro Yoda – Ex Yamaha Project Leader, now Kawasaki MotoGP Technical Director (November 2005): 'One reason I can see is the time that big bang gives the tyre to recover, on a four-cylinder you have 10 or 12 times combustion in a circle, so you have a 15cm or 20cm gap that the tyre can recover. Also, another thing, if you choose the firing order properly you can have a bike that's a little bit smoother. Although there is more stress the way we have done it, it is not a problem at the moment.'

Masao Furusawa, Executive Officer, Engineering Operations, Motorcycle Headquarters, Yamaha Motor Co. Ltd. (March 2006): 'We have stayed with the same concept as the 2004 M1. We have experimented with many changes, but we have found that the basic design of the 2004 bike was about right. From my analysis of the others, I think Honda is using the same idea they started with. For a while they tried a big bang, two cylinders together (when Barros had the special exhausts-NS), but they are now back where they started. Ducati are trying four combustions in a straight group, and Kawasaki use a system like the old Laverda, with one cylinder missing. The Suzuki is a V4 engine. They tried two different things, but now they are back with the original. The important thing is making the engine smoother on the crankshaft. With the current system there are four fluctuations, that makes a big "noise", and that is key. As long as Kawasaki is using the 180° crank, then I don't think Kawasaki is the best. I don't believe the big bang theory. The smoothness is more important.'

'THE EFFECT ON THE TYRE IS LIKE ONE OF THOSE BIG BALLS YOU USED TO RIDE AS A KID. YOU KNOW, A 'SPACE HOPPER' – JUST A SERIES OF BIG, SOFT PUSHES ON THE TYRE!'
KYOCHI YOSHII [HONDA]

ELECTRONICS

How to keep 250bhp in check

Designers have always tried to keep motorcycles simple. An ignition system and some lights have got us through the first 100 years and many would like to keep it that way.

The world is changing though and new demands are being made of all forms of technology, so while complex electronics have not really been part of the motorcycle experience until now, it is something we are going to see a lot more of.

A class of racing motorcycles that develop 250-plus bhp was always going to be difficult to control. Some things had already been tried. The two-stroke 500s of the previous generation had ignition-based traction control of sorts to soften their power when the rear wheel started to spin too much. There had been some investigation into electronic throttles in Superbike too, but that class had lost its attraction when rules designed to minimise costs rather than encourage experimentation were introduced.

Once MotoGP was announced, Aprilia started the ball rolling with the use of a full ride-by-wire system on their Cube. This was full of potential, but its benefits were masked by an engine that was simply too unruly. Yamaha then introduced an electronically controlled clutch to try and defeat rear wheel hop on corner entry, a particular problem for them in the first few races of the first season. Very quickly it was realised that a simple slipper clutch backed up by an adjustable engine tickover device was the simple way to go. Honda then upped the ante with a separate air-bleed system to the inlet ports. Within two years all the major factories had full ride-by-wire in one shape or another.

Against a backdrop of ongoing emissions legislation and the need for improved fuel economy in our day to day lives, motorcycling needs to address these concerns at source. Properly developed electronic throttles can help achieve these aims, as they have with cars, but motorcycles require more sensitive solutions and that's where racing can help. Legislation might have achieved similar results, but that wouldn't have been as much fun nor given the technology the all important performance tag necessary to gain customer acceptance in the motorcycle market.

We now have several variations of electronic throttles that work and the first systems are popping up on streetbikes. Better still, having been developed on the racetrack, they have the benefit of being considered a 'must have' addition to any new sporting bike.

RIDE BY WIRE

The history of electronic throttles

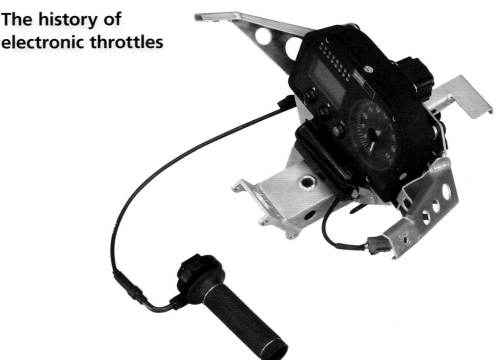

Electronic throttle controls on MotoGP bikes have come a long way in a very short time. When the class started in 2002, all the bikes used conventional superbike-style cable-controlled throttles – exactly as you would find on most street bikes.

EARLY ELECTRONIC THROTTLE CONTROL

The primary objective of the designers of the first generation of MotoGP bikes was to control the damaging effects of engine braking. In normal use, as a motorcycle enters a corner and the rider shuts the throttle, the rear wheel has to turn over the engine and, as it does so, the chain tries to move the swingarm and unsettles the rear suspension. The problem was worse in MotoGP than in superbike because all the riders were used to two-strokes, and on two-strokes you simply didn't have the level of engine braking the new 1,000cc four-strokes were generating.

The first layer of defence was a slipper clutch, exactly the same as used on superbikes – the 'back torque limiter' is a mechanical clutch that automatically disengages the engine when the rear wheel tries to rev-up the crankshaft – but it was soon found that, with the higher outputs and increased compression of the MotoGP bikes, the slipper clutches were getting quite

hot and bothered by the amount of work they were required to do. At this point development seemed to move in different directions. Some factories, notably Yamaha and Suzuki, tried electronically-powered clutches – clutches that didn't rely on a simple mechanical setup but which were activated by a computer-controlled motor.

During the second year of MotoGP, Honda admitted to using a secondary throttle system. This was a computer-controlled air bleed, allowing air and fuel mixture into the inlet tract when the computer systems on the bike detected excessive engine braking. Kawasaki, in their first year of MotoGP competition, had a small stepper motor driven from their ECU to increase effective tickover, and Yamaha had a revised set of throttles that made the bike sound like it had morphed into a blubbering CB500 twin at the end of the straights. At the time, Yamaha wouldn't say what they were doing, but we now know that they were tuning in a kicker system on a guillotine-style (flat slide) fuel injection system.

2003 was also the first year of MotoGP competition for Ducati. Over the course of the year most of the Ducati's parts had been seen and analysed, but one piece remained permanently under cover, or behind the fairing, and that was a small stepper motor mounted up on the dash which essentially increased the tickover level as and when the engine control computer decided it was required. It's difficult to confirm it, but it seemed that a standard Yamaha EXUP power valve actuation motor had been given a new role in life. The motor certainly looked remarkably similar.

Over at Aprilia, however, things were decidedly more adventurous. Aprilia's engine had been designed with a lot of help from Cosworth in the UK, and Aprilia knew that they would need some form of electronic throttle system to produce a power band and style of delivery that would be acceptable to the rider. They chose not to use Cosworth's system and decided to develop their own. This was to be the first true ride-by-wire system on a MotoGP bike, with all of the throttle butterflies controlled electronically the whole time. The main difficulty was that the underlying engine was a particularly challenging one on which to get the correct throttle response. The ride-by-wire system could be tuned to change the response the rider got from any given degree of throttle movement, but Aprilia found it impossible, using electronics alone, to damp down the lightweight crankshaft's desire to rev up very quickly. When combined with some quite experimental chassis-design decisions, Aprilia were right up against it from the start.

EARLY TRACTION CONTROL

This is not the first time that electronics have been involved in actively changing the way the engine works during a race. Over the last 15 years the big two-strokes in 500 Grand Prix softened and civilised their power output by careful use and manipulation of ignition timing.

The point at which a spark plug fires is carefully set, when the engine is first developed, to maximise power output and minimise any detonation. Typically, the point at which a spark plug will fire is somewhere between 30° and 45° before top-dead-centre (TDC) when the engine is pulling hard. Firing the spark plug before TDC is needed to ensure that full combustion can be achieved – typically the spark ignites the mixture as early as is necessary to get the most economical burn and to develop maximum pressure from the mixture. Clearly, to achieve the best possible burn at a set time, the start point has to vary depending on revs and cylinder design. The bigger the bore, the longer the flame front has to travel; and the higher the revs, the less time it has in which to do it.

Modern computers allow the actual ignition point to be varied tremendously, based on the amount of throttle being applied and the revs the engine is running at. A typical street bike, for instance, will have its ignition timing at 10°

Aprilia's engine supplier, Cosworth developed an engine that was always going to need electronics to calm it down. In this picture you can see the high pressure injectors in the airbox.

The settings on the basic systems are all adjustable. Where do you want the anti-spin to start and how much spin do you want? Suzuki's Mitsubishi system used a small dedicated flashload device.

the rotation speed of the rear wheel could merely have been caused by the bike being pulled over to 45° of lean and a consequent sudden decrease in the rolling radius of the rear tyre. So, the system that has been developed is based on a comparison between front and rear wheel speeds. Wheel speed sensors are fitted on both wheels, and if the rear wheel speeds up more than the front then it's fairly safe to assume that it is spinning.

The real trick would be to be able to set up different strategies – different rates of allowable spin, if you like – for different corners. In the Formula 1 world this is quite common, with GPS providing an active feed to the car's computer systems so the ECU knows where the vehicle is on the circuit and has time to access the particular strategy for that section of track before it starts. It's difficult to see whether this is actually happening in MotoGP yet, but most of the bikes have GPS sensors on their tails. GPS is increasingly quick and accurate, and certainly these sensors will be sufficient to give the data-logging engineer a map of the lap the bike has followed. But whether the GPS is accurate enough yet to control an active function of the bike is another matter.

STARTING TO MOVE THROTTLES AS WELL

So, if we have systems that tinker with an engine's ignition curve and the tickover speed, seemingly quite automatically, why do we need more? We need it because a properly developed ride-by-wire system will allow the factory to modify an engine's throttle responses, either for maximum economy on the road or for the best possible emissions control. In the world we live in, such a technology has a very high commercial value – sufficient, in some ways, to make the cost of MotoGP quite acceptable. The staged limitation on allowed fuel capacity has brought the need for fuel economy, as well as power, to the racetrack; indeed, some teams regard the fuel limit as more restrictive to engine performance than the capacity limit.

The first time there was any evidence that something was changing was Barros's first sensational ride on the RC211V at the end of 2003. Alex stepped straight off his two-stroke, then beat Rossi in a straight race. What was noticeable about the races was that Barros's bike looked really stable going into corners, whereas Rossi's was jumping and sliding all over the place – it was as though Barros's win was assisted by a motorcycle that was electronically simulating the engine braking of his old two-stroke. Barros crashed in one of the sessions, and a large brown box (with a substantial number of Bowden cables coming out) could be seen through the smashed fairing. To this day, Honda will not confirm what the unit was, but they have acknowledged that it was around this time

before TDC, or maybe a little less, with 1° of twistgrip throttle movement and at 1,000rpm. Full advance is typically reached somewhere around full throttle and the engine's torque peak. The full advance point is logically the point at which the most power is developed.

If the bike was fitted with a sensor that detected wheelspin in excess of a given measurement, it would be fairly simple (and extremely quick) to reduce power by reducing the ignition advance. Let's say that, at 12,000rpm and half-throttle, Mick Doohan's Honda 500 required 25° of advance for the best power. Suddenly changing the timing to 5° or 10° before TDC would remove a substantial amount of horsepower, possibly a third or more, and that is exactly what you would need to do to slow down a spinning rear tyre. With modern computers, changes like this can be made within one crankshaft revolution – it is a seriously quick-reacting system. The difficult bit is deciding how much you want to adjust and under what circumstances – Mr Doohan would not have thanked you if you had retarded his ignition just sufficient for the tyre to get maximum grip and promptly dispatched him over the high side.

One of the biggest difficulties with any form of traction-control system is to know when a rear tyre is actually spinning – an acceleration in

that they started experimenting with ride-by-wire throttles.

Suzuki's 2003 bike was almost fully automatic and, judging by the team's pit lane reaction when the bikes were first unpacked, most of the features were also unexpected. It took a year of ups and downs (literally!) before the system was simplified for 2004. In that year, though, a lot was learned. We heard many riders' criticisms about throttles that wouldn't react accurately to rider input, leading to comparisons with video games. In some cases the system was blamed for collisions caused by an increase in speed when the rider had just shut the throttle.

The first two years of the formula had taught everyone that the top priority in MotoGP was for a well-sorted engine and chassis, and a good connection from the rider's hand to what was happening at the tyre. Only after you had those basics could you start to increase engine output and introduce systems to deal with that additional power.

Aprilia announced a retrenchment, with a new heavyweight crankshaft to slow response and a ride-by-wire system set on a one-to-one basis – this would get the engine calmed down sufficiently to be a good base level from which to start. At about the same time, Ducati and then Kawasaki discovered Weber Marelli's

missing spark traction control system. The old two-stroke method of controlling excess spin was particularly quick and effective (simply retarding the ignition would take away power and reduce the tendency to spin) and most four-strokes had this from the first day. Weber Marelli went a stage further for the four-strokes, cutting sparks from selected cylinders on the Ducati, reducing power even further. By mid-season it was not uncommon to hear the bike coming out of a corner accompanied by a noise not dissimilar to a burst of machine-gun fire. The Kawasakis were suffering severe traction problems and were using the same system by the end of the year, but on their bike it seemed to kick-in almost every corner.

We now know that Yamaha had swapped from a flat-slide fuel-injection system to a butterfly system, along with their other changes for Rossi in early 2004. By the test after the Le Mans MotoGP they were ready to adjust two throttle butterflies automatically, the control of the other two remaining with the rider. This was combined with an irregular firing order that endowed the M1 with an improbable level of grip. During the course of the year, Honda admitted to using a throttle system that geared

Kawasaki introduced their ride-by-wire at Shanghai in 2004, based on Marelli software. New settings can be flashloaded straight in from a PC.

the throttle response, allowing the riders different throttle gearing in different gear ratios. In first gear it was suggested that a full 90° of throttle movement at the handlebar would only result in 50% at the throttle butterfly, 60% in second; 80% in third. The important thing was that, although the overall movement of the throttle has been reduced, the throttle reacted to the slightest movement of the rider's hand – rider feel is very important. Since then, Kyoichi Yoshii, who took over as the Chief Engineer of the RC211V project in late 2004, has confirmed that the system operated in all six gears pretty much from day one.

Yamaha were staying very quiet at this time. It was obvious they had made an advance, and there were many (still unsubstantiated) rumours of a connection with Toyota's Formula One team (Toyota and Yamaha have a cross shareholding) to help out in the design of a new throttle system. Yamaha were clearly changing something; their bikes behaved very strangely at the Le Mans round, with all of them suddenly proving difficult to start and Rossi stalling his bike on the line. The only comment we got was that the fueling system had now become fully Weber Marelli, replacing the previous system which used parts from three different manufacturers. At Suzuki, a great deal of automation was being removed so that the riders were back in control of the bike, but the

throttle stayed. Ducati were clearly also aware that, while their throttle system might help control wheelspin, they needed to have an engine that helped produce grip as well as the Yamaha did. Ducati's major effort went into providing a good basic engine, the 'twin pulse', that was usable, rather than develop a throttle system designed to control the uncontrollable.

So, where were we? By the end of 2004 the rules of the game were pretty much defined. If you had an engine that produced enough power to be competitive, you needed to control the wheelspin and the engine-braking using electronics and modifying the throttle position to give the desired effect. But the engine had to be at least vaguely correct before electronics would be able to control it sufficiently. Those bikes with very light crankshafts ended up with substantially more weight, and those bikes with regular firing orders were redesigned to allow an irregular power delivery.

For 2005 a new fuel restriction came into force. Until 2004 the maximum fuel allowed on the bike was 24 litres but, for 2005, 22 litres was the new limit. On a bike with a high-revving 990cc engine, which had to go the full distance in a GP, that was going to be difficult. The improvement of fuel consumption to enable each bike to finish the race became the new prime objective in everybody's preparations.

Yamaha's throttle system initially had two cable operated throttles and two electronically controlled ones. By 2006 all the butterflies were electronically controlled, but it was still a 50:50 split between ECU and rider control.

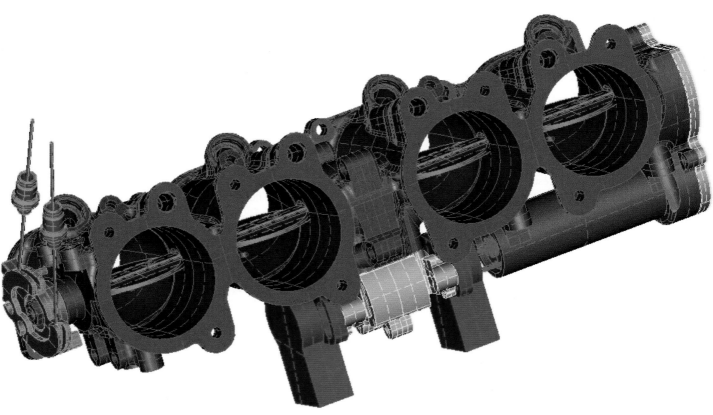

MECHANICAL

ELECTRONIC

RIDER'S INPUT AT GRIP

ECU

ENGINE DATA

POTENTIOMETER

THROTTLE BUTTERFLY

POTENTIOMETER

ELECTRIC MOTOR

REAL PROGRESS

2004's electronic systems included the wasted spark traction control. This effectively takes an engine that makes too much power, and deliberately misfires a cylinder or two in order to dramatically reduce power when excessive wheelspin is detected. That waste of fuel became very difficult to deal with in the new 22-litre limit situation. Revised ideas were needed, especially on the higher-revving engines, to ensure that there was enough fuel for the duration.

The most spectacular results were at Ducati. They debuted not only a new electronic throttle system but also a computer-controlled automatic clutch. This system was designed to disengage fully on the entrance to a corner and then re-engage smoothly as the bike accelerated back out again. The systems were tested in the weeks leading up to the season, but only got on to Capirossi's and Checa's bikes at the final tests before the start of the racing year. It was clear from the start that the riders were not particularly keen, but they persevered despite being deposited on the ground on several occasions. The system made it through to final qualifying at the first Grand Prix at Jerez, but an accident that broke a bone in Capirossi's foot signalled the end, and the system was taken off. Ducati soldiered on, fine-tuning their electronic throttle system while they waited for Bridgestone

to develop a family of tyres that would suit their chassis and also provide durable stable grip for the duration of the Grand Prix.

While all this was going on, Yamaha's 2005 M1 got an uprated engine-control computer to help it deal more accurately and quickly with the demands being placed on it. All of the systems work on the basic premise that the engines can easily make too much power pretty much all the time. It's a question of managing that power and delivering it smoothly and accurately – and without any lag.

Yamaha's system used a pair of throttle butterflies controlled by the rider – he has a 495cc twin, if you like – and an electric motor operates the other two (the second 495cc). By having one pair of throttles directly under the rider's control, all the sensitivity you need to deal with the limited amount of grip available on a MotoGP bike is kept. The second pair smooth the power delivery using the very accurate data, held in the computer, of the engine's performance at any particular rev and throttle opening. Using the pairs of throttles independently, Yamaha constructed a group of settings that delivered a consistent supply of torque to the rear wheel. An example would be the point at which the engine suddenly hits its power band; the rider would be holding constant throttle on his pair of butterflies, but the automatic pair would be shutting down at a rate designed to keep the

TOP LEFT: Ducati's 2006 system used a cable and potentiometer system; the development bike was seen several times with a full electronic throttle, the only cables leaving the handlebar being electrical.

ABOVE LEFT: The main ECU on the Ducati was a Marelli Marvel 4 computer. This had significantly more processing power than the early versions.

ABOVE: A schematic of the Ducati throttle system as it was at the end of 2005. Note the two potentiometers, one to detect the rider's preferred throttle setting and the second to tell the fuel injection system what position has been chosen by the ECU.

crew chief, was even more frank, 'When I first saw the readings, I thought this is crazy, this is all bullshit. You can have a situation where the rider shuts the throttles just as the computer is opening its throttles, but it works – the rider just can't feel it, and the whole bike worked better.'

Kawasaki first fitted their system in Shanghai to Olivier Jacque's (subbing for an injured Hofmann) bike. After just two practice sessions it was obvious that it was a quantum leap forward, and Nakano's bike was also equipped. It certainly didn't hurt Jacque's performance in the race, although a mechanical malfunction in the system appeared to have stopped Nakano in the same race. The combination of improved grip and improved throttle control made the Kawasaki pretty competitive for a while. We now have full-blown torque by wire. All riders feel the torque of an engine through the seat of their pants but, while they are used to feeling it, they can ride faster if the supply of torque is linear – the perfect world is where a rider turns the throttle 25% and gets 25% more torque. It assumes that there is always more power available than can be used, but that's usually about right with a 990cc MotoGP engine.

Ducati released details of their throttle system at the end of 2005. Similar to Yamaha's, they have all their throttles moved by stepper motors. Nevertheless, two follow the rider's inputs directly and two act as torque-curve smoothing devices. Both systems take their instructions from a Marelli Marvel 4 ECU. Ducati's race system uses a pair of push-pull throttle cables to a potentiometer mounted to the left-hand side of the bike. That potentiometer signals the rider's intentions to the ECU. The stepper motors then adjust their relevant pairs of throttles as appropriate. To ensure that each pair of cylinders fuels correctly, each pair of throttles also has a potentiometer to control fuelling and to signal back to the ECU exactly how much throttle is being applied. The basic rule is that the actual throttle applied cannot exceed the rider's demand at any time, except when he has shut the throttle fully and the system opens up to say 3° maximum to try to deliver minimal back torque. Although the other teams have not released details, we can expect all the throttle butterflies to be being moved by stepper motors now and increasingly, as the factories develop more accurate and sensitive systems for all of the throttles to work together.

A measure of how important this technology is to the future of motorcycling can be gleaned from the fact that Yamaha, within two years of first fitting an active ride-by-wire system to Valentino Rossi's M1, launched the 2006 R6. This bike has a fully-developed Mikuni ride-by-wire throttle, controlled by one of Yamaha's own computers. In standard road form, the throttle settings allow the high-performance engine to maintain reasonable

'as delivered to the rear wheel' torque constant – exactly what the rider's hand is asking for. Colin Edwards, who has more experience than most of the differing systems, conceded that the bike would be completely unrideable without the throttle system, 'You can dial in the throttles to give you exactly what torque you want for any corner.' Once they have a good basic setting, the rider and his crew chief have to fine-tune it for any given circuit. This throttle has allowed the Yamaha to be tuned for more and more top-end power.

Over at Kawasaki, the arrival of Ichiro Yoda from Yamaha caused a few changes. The first task was to get an irregular firing order, which transformed the grip levels of the ZXRR. The second was to obtain an electronic throttle system – Kawasaki's was developed by Danilo Casonato, their Italian electronics engineer, and, like the Yamaha, has two butterflies controlled by the rider and two by a Weber Marelli developed computer and software. Casonato said, 'What matters is the zone. There is a certain group of settings where a rider is comfortable. We can change the butterflies, the ignition advance, or miss ignition on the cylinder – all these things can be adjusted to get the bike into the most effective zone to be competitive on the track, and it's up to the rider and his crew chief to perfect that zone.' Christian Bourguignon, then Hofmann's

economy and excellent emissions. Yamaha has trumped the rest of the motorcycling world, however, with their super sport kit replacement computer. Using a special race-only wiring loom, this setup discards most of the careful road settings that Yamaha put into the standard R6 and allows the tuner to set the bike up from scratch.

As a race system, you can easily change the fuelling and ignition timing, plus or minus 30% – more than enough for tuning the 600 engine. You can also play with the 'normal' trims: barometric pressure, air temp, coolant temp and redline. Some slightly more unusual features are the adjustable duration ignition cut-out of between 0 to 150m/sec for quick shifting; a ram air compensation of up to 10% and a pit lane speed limiter. But the real trick is the programmable ETV (electronic throttle valve). With a different throttle correction ratio for each gear, the system allows a choice of no correction up to 100% correction (i.e. moves the butterfly up to twice, or half, the amount of the handlebar throttle-grip movement), and another option is an acceleration correction, the ability to shut down the throttle by up to 20% in a throttle zone where the torque is overpowering the tyre grip – just the sort of thing you need when exiting fast corners, leaned right over and hard on the throttle.

In a mere two years we have gone from virtually no electronic throttles in bikes, at even the highest level, to providing club racers with inexpensive programmable systems from the original factory.

EMISSIONS LEGISLATION

The timing of MotoGP has also been very advantageous. Over the last ten years motorcycles have enjoyed substantial leeway on emissions legislation. On the bases that there were not many motorcycles and that it is difficult to store emissions control devices on the typical motorcycle, we have been allowed emission standards that have hardly affected the sport we love. Over the same ten years, however, cars and other forms of motorised transport have had their emissions standards continuously upgraded, and they are now so rigorous that the allowances for motorcycles can be seen to be ludicrously generous. We all associate heavy and hot catalytic converters with emissions legislation, but that is only part of the story.

The efficient burning of fuel and the careful control of the use of fuel through an electronic throttle system is the other half of the story, and when MotoGP started we had absolutely no idea how to make such a system work safely on motorcycles. The technologies couldn't be transferred straight over from the car world because they are built for car use, and the simple act of balancing a powerful engine on two wheels means that we have a requirement for far more subtlety and precision. MotoGP has allowed the development of systems that will work in the real world and will allow us to keep motorcycling a valid form of transport, and at the same time retaining the fun element.

Yamaha's R6 was the first true mass produced ride-by-wire streetbike. Race versions of the computer allowed the whole system to be fully adjustable.

© YAMAHA

DATALOGGING

To develop a motorcycle, you need to know what's happening to it

It's not just the engines, chassis and tyres that have raised their game for MotoGP, the whole business of analysing what is going on and helping the teams build the best possible setups has grown too. More actions and operations can be recorded and used, more can be read from the data collected and now the electronic controls on the bike rely on some of the sensors too.

Datalogging is used to help the rider and his team understand exactly what all the major components of the motorcycle are doing at any given point in a lap. The technology isn't in itself new, but there is no doubt that the MotoGP class has seen its sophistication increase dramatically. When MotoGP started, datalogging was a simple recording exercise. Now, as the 990cc era comes to a close, those same sensors are used as a fundamental part of the engine management system.

One of the important things to understand is that any datalogging system is intended as an aid to the crew and the rider. With current technology levels it is not used to automatically change suspension settings in any way, but the system does provide an accurate factual recording of the movement of several variables at various points on the circuit. Things have developed over the last five years to the extent that even basic systems use GPS for locating themselves on the circuit.

In 2002, most MotoGP motorcycles had two wiring systems, one for the ECU (Engine Control Unit) and one for the datalogging system. It quickly became apparent that this involved a lot of excess weight. Yamaha, in particular, had very untidy wiring in the early years, but as part of the 2004 rebuild it became very neat and well laid out. At about the same time, the datalogging system started to provide active engine management data. Bikes, where the two systems are combined, typically send data straight from the sensors to the ECU and from there to a recording unit.

So, what sort of thing can be recorded? And what data can be used to improve the control of the bike in an active manner? The answer is anything that happens on the motorcycle can be recorded, it's just a question of how much trouble it is to record it and what benefit the data gathered might bring. You have to be aware of the problem of simply having too much data, and then there is always the possibility of not being able to deal with the important issues (you only have 4 hours and 20 minutes of practice for each event remember) because you cannnot discern the information that will make a difference.

At all times you have to be aware of the limitations of the data-gathering process, you have to be aware of the manner in which the data is recorded, the precise situation of the sensor, and you need a decent software package so that you can analyse the data and make some sense of it.

A basic datalogging setup at MotoGP level would include the following sensors:

- Brake pressure, front brake.
- Brake pressure, rear brake.
- Front wheel speed.
- Rear wheel speed.
- Front suspension travel, and the ability to calculate the rate of change.
- Rear suspension travel, and the ability to calculate the rate of change.
- GPS, so you can monitor the bike's position, and as a comparator on speed to the wheel-speed sensors, so wheelspin can be recorded.

In addition to these chassis parameters you would have the basic engine sensors:

- Throttle position – in the case of ride-by-wire bikes this would be throttle opening requested by rider and throttle opening as delivered by system.
- Water temperature.
- Air temperature.
- Air pressure.
- Airbox pressure (usually instead of air pressure).
- Lambda sensor.
- Oil temperature.
- Oil pressure.
- Gear selected.

ABOVE: This long strut is actually a potentiometer to measure the fork movement. It is used as part of the 2D datalogging system.

BELOW: A Yamaha dashboard during warm up. The readout includes WT (Water Temp) 63.0; FP (Fuel Pressure) 3.1 bar; TH (Throttle) 0 degrees; OP (Oil Pressure) 3.8 bar and BT (Battery) 14.6 volts.

Then there are the 'specials', the sensors that collect the information the particular manufacturer is interested in. Honda's practice is to monitor fuel usage carefully and to change the fuel map to ensure the most power possible is available for as long as possible. Honda also, uniquely, monitors the rider's clutch lever pull. Other factories put different sensors on the bike as and when there are specific problems to resolve, or when specific data is needed.

It is not unusual to see a series of three heat sensors on the swing-arm to monitor tyre temperature. Modern slicks have three different compounds on their surface and specific data can be very helpful in getting the right ones.

When the Yamahas were having chatter problems, vibration sensors were fitted to the forks and swingarm to obtain accurate records as to exactly when the chatter started and, more importantly, exactly where all the other parts of the motorcycle were at that point. Everything that could affect the onset of the chatter was logged. The data gathered wouldn't solve the problem – far from it – but you would at least have a good record of exactly how much trouble you were in.

Other factories' additional sensors on their bikes would include brake temperature sensors; slip angle sensors on the steering head (data for the tyre companies) and three axis sensors to detect the rate of acceleration, braking and side-to-side movement.

Given the sheer amount of data now gathered, the logging system has to be set up in a way that provides the data in usable forms. In these days of relatively cheap data storage, it's not the storage that matters but the presentation.

So if you have all this data, how do you actually use it? To a data analyst there are five main zones of the operation of a bike that

you have to be able to record. These are the operations where the most accurate settings will get the best results in terms of lap times; they are, therefore, the areas of a bike's performance where accurate datalogging is the most important. It also means that for each zone there is a group of sensor readings that work well together in a display of relevant data for that part of the bike's use. They are:

■ **Main straight** (WFO!). The main points of interest are on the engine side: throttle, lambda, airbox pressure and then oil temperature, water temperature, oil pressure and air temperature, and finally GPS so you can monitor rear wheel spin.

■ **Braking in a straight line** (including anti-hop strategies). Here the focus is on the throttle, suspension, brakes and an accurate comparison of wheel speeds to decide on the anti-hop strategy.

■ **Braking into a corner** (including anti-hop strategies). Again, the focus is on the throttle, suspension, brakes and an accurate comparison of wheel speeds for the anti-hop strategy.

■ **Rolling through the corner** (just a little throttle). Wheel speeds and throttle position are important, as are the two suspension travel indicators.

■ **Accelerating out of the corner:** suspension, wheel speeds, throttle, lambda and GPS.

Bringing specific segments of data together for easy analysis means that the important points are easy to see and the correlation between the various sensors can be more easily judged.

Most things can be recorded, from lap-times to wheel-speeds, tyre surface temperatures to brake pressures. The trick is how to interpret them...

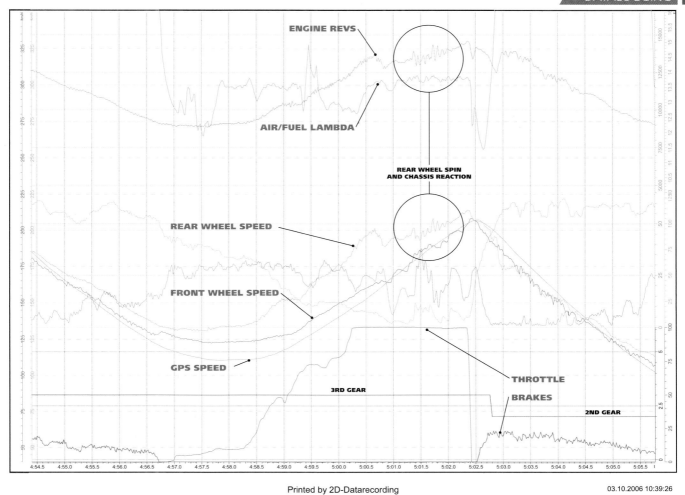

ENGINE REVS

AIR/FUEL LAMBDA

REAR WHEEL SPIN
AND CHASSIS REACTION

REAR WHEEL SPEED

FRONT WHEEL SPEED

GPS SPEED

THROTTLE

BRAKES

3RD GEAR

2ND GEAR

Printed by 2D-Datarecording

03.10.2006 10:39:26

These data traces are a typical cornering sequence from two corners at the Sachsenring.

In the 11 seconds the bike we are following travels though corner 10 at the bottom of the hill and up towards the last turn.

As the bike comes in to turn 10 you can see the brake pressure at the bottom of the display. As the bike apexes the rider then opens the throttle, again you can see the throttle opening trace edging up to 100% open. Immediately above the throttle trace you can see the two red wheel speed sensors and the GPS speed sensor showing the rear wheel spinning up, as it does so there is a sequence of irregularities in the trace showing some chassis reaction to the ensuing slide. Once crew chiefs see this they know they have a problem to resolve...

Of interest at the top of the display is a log of the engine revs and the Lambda (air fuel mixture) readout.

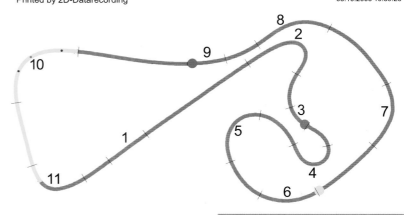

	2FH303	
Lap	△	2
	⊟	1:25.65 min
Time tot.		4:57.31 min
m total		10443
Time Lap		1:11.08 min
m Lap/Track		3101/3101
Fspeed [km/h]		124.8
Rspeed [km/h]		131.8
F_Susp [mm]		79.3
R_Susp [mm]		23.5
RPM_ECU [1/min]		8987
GEAR_POS [Gear]		3.0
THROTTLE% [%]		4.8
AF1		13.2
F_Brake [Bar]		-0.1
V_GPS [km/h]		113.7

CHASSIS

The backbone of
the motorcycle

In an aluminium frame world, Ducati stands alone with their steel tube trellis frame. While outwardly seeming unchanged, there have been modifications each year of the MotoGP championship, and that was for a company who sat out the first year of development!

When MotoGP started, chassis design was considered a fairly mature science. So you wouldn't think that you would see that much change over the ensuing five years. There has, however, been a lot of change, a good deal of it in one particular direction – a direction that has improved lap times tremendously. As usual, it hasn't happened in one fell swoop, but with each factory having to address similar problems that typically means that over time similar solutions are found.

At the beginning Honda launched their RC211V, a bike with a quite complex chassis. Of note were the beams that came down the side of the front bank of cylinders to engine mounts on top of the crankcase proper, a rear shock absorber location that located the bottom of the shock on a linkage and the top eye on the underside of the swingarm.

It was quite interesting in other ways. Most of it was made from pressings welded together, as was the initial swingarm. Later versions of the swingarm had sections machined from solid aluminium and then welded together – much better for accuracy of build and for accurate wall thicknesses. The design had a very long swingarm and long wheelbase compared to the 500 GP bikes it replaced.

Most of the bikes in the pit lane, however, initially used identical specification chassis to the 500 GP bikes that each factory's MotoGP machines were replacing. The teams understood their old chassis and knew the differences certain adjustments would make. So, rather than lose all connection with their previous two-stroke experience, the old chassis dimensions seemed the logical place to start.

It didn't last long, though. Honda, again, was one stage ahead.

The 2005 Ducati frame was modified for Capirossi to include the detachable long bracing bars at the bottom of the chassis, giving additional support to the swingarm.

CONSTRUCTION

Utilise material properties and manufacturing techniques

One of Team Roberts' chassis from late 2006. Debuted at Sachsenring, this has the longer side beams and uses normal construction techniques.

Most of the bikes in MotoGP use aluminium beam frames as the basic chassis design but, while all the chassis may look quite similar to those that rolled onto the grid in 2002, methods of construction have changed since the class started and significant development has taken place.

Let's look first at the basic construction. Aluminium beam frames were initially made by welding together pressings, but with a better understanding of the technology, and in the quest for simpler manufacturing processes, aluminium extrusions began to be used for the beam sections. The difference here, of course, is that the pressing is a custom-designed piece, whereas an extrusion implies an element of mass-production. It had been discovered quite quickly that the pressing method had its faults. With bikes' new-found sensitivity to deflection when leaned right over, chassis made from welded pressings were found wanting in that there was a lack of adjustability, and factories couldn't guarantee to exactly repeat levels of flexibility in their chassis and swing-arms. The solution, first tried by Aprilia and now in general practice, was to machine all the pieces of the chassis out of solid aluminium before welding. Using modern-day CNC processes, this is quite a simple operation, and it allows a very

accurate wall thickness to be maintained and, more important, very small changes can easily and accurately be made to individual parts to enable experimentation with the flexibility of any given component. The main beams on most bikes are now constructed in this way, as are their swing-arms.

However, the Roberts chassis, from 2004 onwards, was created using techniques introduced to Roberts by noted Formula 1 designer John Barnard. He decided that the irregularities that could occur when welding two pieces of metal together were such that it wasn't worth persevering with. His preferred method of construction was to take a solid beam of aluminium, prepare the outside in accordance with his finished specifications and then very accurately spark-erode the centre away down the length of the beam. With this method, webbing and wall thickness can be designed exactly as you wish. Other than cost, which was significant, the only major drawback to this process is the length of the beam – there being limits to the depth the current technology of spark-erosion can go in something as small as a chassis beam. Indeed, during the second half of 2006, Roberts actually reverted to their original method of construction, which was the hand-building of beams welded together, simply so they could make a beam long enough to reach right to the steering head.

Ducati are notable for staying with their corporate signature steel lattice frame chassis. Again, over the four years that Ducati competed in the 990cc category of MotoGP, this structure changed as they learnt and understood more of the requirements. The first version was a very simple latticework steel tube chassis, linking the top of the crankcases to the steering head. The tube layout was almost identical to the chassis of the Supermono that Claudio Domenicali had helped design nearly nine years previously. To cope with the somewhat higher power output, however, the tubes were of a substantially larger diameter. With a relatively long distance from the rear cylinder head to the steering head Ducati never did have a problem getting enough steering head deflection. The fact that their chassis works particularly well when leaned right over has been a Ducati trademark for many years, and it is quite possible that the steering head deflection aspect of that design had not been fully understood by the other manufacturers. With their chassis merely being a connection between the cylinder heads and the steering head, the rear suspension and swingarm were

Ducati finally decided to stop their chassis bending backwards under braking. Have a look at the different design of this 2006 chassis, especially around the steering head, and compare it with the 2005 one on page 159.

HONDA RC211V NEW GENERATION FRAME

HONDA RC211V CUSTOMER FRAME

The 'New Generation' chassis. This is the early 2006 chassis using the central shock absorber position. You can see how complex the modifications to the main frame have been; now imagine having to make a number exactly the same!

The standard 2006 customer chassis. By the end of the year only Tamada and Elias were on this version. A revised version that allowed more steering head deflection was given to the rest of the Honda riders as the year went on.

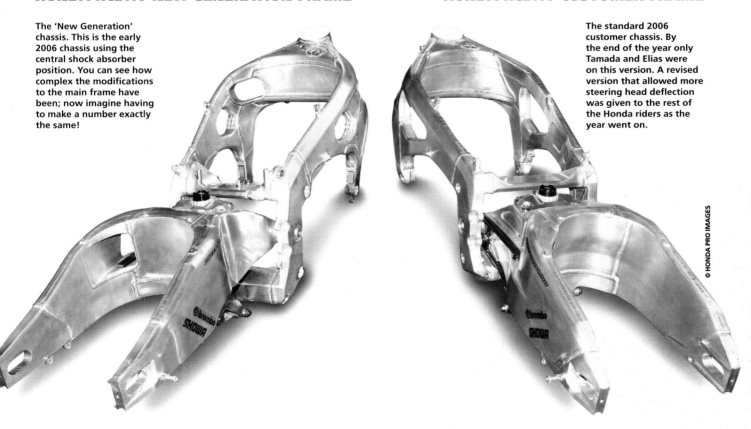

© HONDA PRO IMAGES

© YAMAHA

© HENK KEULEMANS

1 Suspension travel in the corners is limited to the combined flex of the tyre, wheel, forks and headstock.

2 The long front engine mounts, added when Rossi first came to Yamaha, allow the headstock to move a very small amount, helping grip in corners.

3 The area of the frame at the front of the swingarm is heavily reinforced to withstand the efforts of the chain carrying 250bhp to crush it.

both bolted to the back of the crankcases. It used a shock absorber design that crushed the shock from both ends, one end from a linkage attached to the crankcase and one from the underside of the swing-arm. A rear subframe was required merely to support the rider and the exhausts.

While the inherent flexibility of the Ducati chassis has helped the bike at full lean, the sideways deflection appearing beneficial, the same flexibility has not helped under braking. This has caused some difficulty with the set-up of the Desmosedici. Since the bike was first launched, the chassis set-up has been raised at the rear and dropped at the front. In the garage, the bike could have as much as 5 to 10mm between the back of the tyre and the radiator at full fork compression. Once set up like this, however, the front tyre could move back under braking and actually hit the radiator. The temporary solution was to leave off the 'bib' (the part of the fairing that stopped air flowing straight through the bike) at a high cost to the bike's aerodynamic efficiency. For 2006, the chassis was, therefore, redesigned using more of a 'birdcage' construction. In this design a series of small additional tubes are welded into the chassis to make it more rigid under braking but still allowing it to deflect sideways in corners as previously.

The Ducati is also unique in using the crankcases as the sole mount for the swing-arms. The bearings and crankcases are in board of the swing arm. While most of the engineers involved in the project were quite certain that this was more than strong enough, Loris Capirossi needed to see an outside support on the chassis to be reassured of its strength. This required a redesign of all the parts between the two engine mounts, on both sides of the engine at chassis level. It involved cutting away large lumps, all the alternator, and adding perhaps 2kg of steel tube to support the swingarm on the outside. Capirossi liked the modification, but his team-mate at the time, Troy Bayliss, seemed less convinced, as was Checa who followed him. However, once Bridgestone had found a tyre construction that the Ducati liked, one of the first modifications was to change the swing-arm pivot position in order to place slightly more pressure on the tyre under acceleration. This called for new outer supports, so Capirossi went to the Japanese GP in 2005 without his preferred exterior support struts. Having won there without them he didn't seem to feel the need to refit them.

One other construction technique was tried in the early years, and that was sand-casting. Kawasaki's initial chassis were strong, but in all the wrong ways. Large cast sections of aluminium can easily be used to make chassis, and in some ways casting allows otherwise complex shapes to be made relatively easily. The latest mass-production techniques are very good at precision manufacture. Unfortunately, the Kawasaki variant was unable to take into account the need for flexibility, seemingly in any direction. The result was a bike that could not find grip, either accelerating or through a corner. The joint Kawasaki/SRT chassis used in 2004 and 2005 was made entirely of machined and welded parts.

Once you are away from the basic chassis, you get to the ancillaries – carbon fibre, magnesium and titanium are the usual suspects here. Carbon is used for all the bodyworks and most of the support structures; carbon fibre airboxes, seat units, electronics supports and fairing supports are fairly de rigueur now. The seat units and fairing supports are the only parts that are in carbon and structural, with the exception of the carbon outer upper tube fork legs on the Ducati.

Magnesium and titanium are commonplace on the bike. Ignoring the engine itself, magnesium is used a lot for the fork clamps and wheels; titanium tends to be on exhausts and exhaust mounts, but the Roberts bike has lower triple clamps made of several different titanium machinings.

The 2006 Ducati swingarm was lighter and used a stiffener welded into the beam, effectively moving the start of any flex nearer to the tip of the arm.

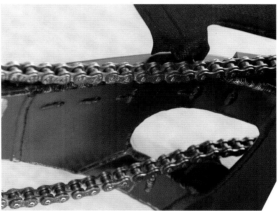

Rossi's Yamaha swingarm shows the amount of effort that goes into keeping the swingarm rigid under the compression that 250bhp can bring.

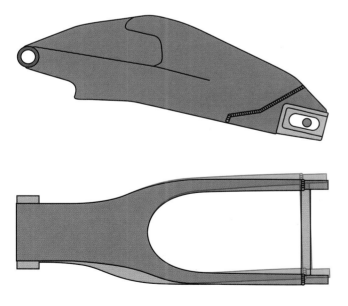

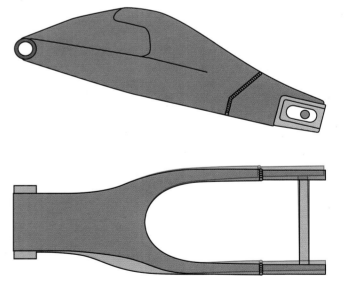

HONDA RC211V STANDARD SWINGARM [PEDROSA AND CUSTOMER RIDERS]

The standard swingarm for the Honda RC211V is much deeper in section with a shorter machined section around the chain adjuster block. We have exaggerated the likely flex for illustration purposes.

HONDA RC211V NEW GENERATION SWINGARM [HAYDEN]

Hayden's swingarm is of a different section and has a longer machined section around the chain adjuster block. Actual flex will depend on the thicknesses of the materials used and any internal webs. Like the Ducati above, however, Honda appear to be trying to control not only the amount of flex but where it might occur.

PACKAGING

The influence of the engine on chassis design

This swingarm is an early 2006 Roberts-Honda piece. The special bracket that holds the top of the shock absorber also allows the ride height to be changed. By Le Mans the team were experimenting with a chassis that attached the shock to the main frame, mostly to speed up the amount of time it takes to change shocks during practice.

Given that most of the chassis in MotoGP are aluminium beam frames you would think that something as simple as the rear shock absorber and its link would be a standard design. The whole purpose of the rear linkage is to allow crew chiefs to change the rate at which the shock absorber affects the chassis. The typical design has a basic setting with a very slight rising rate, and the aim with all suspension is to get a workable balance between front and rear set-ups. Given that the fork legs have air trapped within them, and that it increases the spring rate as it compresses, the rear linkage has to be set to mimic the effect. This isn't necessarily the final position, however; it is just another variable. The final choice of linkage – how fast it increases the suspension rate and at what point in the stroke it changes the suspension rate – is part of the set-up for each individual circuit.

There are three main types of rear suspension design within MotoGP, and all use a single shock attached to the bike via a system with a virtually infinite number of linkage permutations. Let's have a look at them.

Honda, Ducati and Roberts all use a system whereby the top mount of the shock absorber attaches to the bottom of the top of the swing-arm. The other end of the shock absorber is attached to a linkage connecting both the swing-

arm and the crankcases. The major advantage here is that the shock absorber doesn't require a cross-member at the back of the chassis to mount to.

The rear exhaust routing of any V-engine is quite critical to the overall packaging of the engine, in that at the front of the bike, in order to get the engine as far forwards as possible, you have two options. One is that the front cylinder head is presented to the front wheel top-of-cylinder-head first (a Ducati is a classic example of this), and the other option is that the front cylinder bank is parallel to the radiator, sitting just behind the front wheel. Clearly, it is quite difficult to have a 90° V-engine with the rear cylinders parallel with the back of the radiator and still have room for a gearbox, let alone room to get the exhaust pipes from the rear cylinder out above the gearbox.

Moving the top shock mounting to the bottom of the top of the swing-arm, however, has given the Ducati designers the freedom to have a vertically stacked gearbox, shortening the back of the engine considerably. For Honda it has allowed a 75.5° V-engine with the front cylinder bank running parallel to the back of the radiator. The Roberts team hasn't been quite so slavishly supportive of this concept, however. There has been some difficulty with its design of swing-arm bracket, which has to be both strong enough to transfer the suspension movement accurately and simple enough to enable the shock absorber to be extracted in the 30 seconds or so that allows you to continue through a practice session without losing time. For most of the 990cc MotoGP era, the Roberts team stuck with the same basic swing-arm mounting, but the last few chassis have reverted to a cross-member design because it reduced the time of shock absorber extraction from almost 10 minutes to 15 seconds.

Kawasaki, Suzuki and WCM stayed with a cross-member design. Suzuki clearly thought they could get away with it, as their initial engine designs were 60° and 65° V's. This made the routing of the exhaust pipes sufficiently high for the existence of a cross-member not to be a big problem. Now, of course, their engine is a 75° V and it is obvious that the exhaust plumbing is becoming quite convoluted in order that the pipes can get round the top shock position. If, when we get to 800cc, Suzuki sticks with a 75° format (which, given its success, seems quite likely), it's possible they will reconsider this point. Kawasaki have kept most things conventional. Unlike Suzuki, they have used an across-the-frame-four design, so they do not have a rear cylinder routing issue. Nevertheless, they do have to get their fuel load as low as possible. The same can be said for WCM.

The only other major factory, not yet mentioned, is Yamaha. In the first few years, Yamaha were quite conventional with a cross-member holding the shock absorber in a classic deltabox chassis. The M1-B models in 2005 and 2006, however, had redesigned crankcases, and the shock was always mounted to the back of the engine. This has proved to be a quite effective middle position. Extraction of the shock is extremely easy, yet Yamaha can run a slightly larger airbox and they have taken their fuel level right down close to the top of the crankcases. One possible side-effect, however, that might need some examination is the introduction of the engine into the suspension package. The top mount of the shock is always going to be quite hot and, as the engine is bolted to the shock and then the chassis is bolted to the engine, there are additional opportunities for chatter-related issues. Given the problems the Yamaha had in 2006 with chatter, perhaps this is worth a second look.

2004 YAMAHA M1 CHASSIS

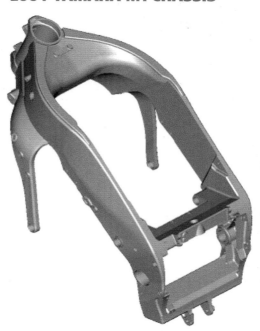

The Yamaha chassis is an evolutionary design; the 2004 version was effectively the 2003 chassis modified with the long front engine spars. The new spars blocked off some of the radiator exhaust ducting causing some cooling difficulties. The shock was mounted to a crossmember at the back of the chassis.

2005/06 YAMAHA M1 CHASSIS

Yamaha's new chassis was able to be narrower because of a redesigned engine. It also had new mounting brackets linking the back of the cylinders to the small beams connecting the main spars to the drop down engine mounting spars. This replaced some of the rigidity lost because the crossmember at the back of the engine was no longer incorporated.

FAR LEFT: The latest Suzuki used a 75° V together with a shock mounted to the rear cross member.

LEFT: The Yamaha attaches its shock absorber to the rear of the crankcases, saving space and allowing the fuel load to be dropped lower down.

SUSPENSION

Less about cushioning, more about control

The first five years of the MotoGP class have seen quite a change in suspension design. Apart from the development of the internals of the forks and shocks, the bikes themselves are changing the way the suspension units are mounted; from the space-saving rear swing-arms, with the rear shock mounted on the swing-arm on the Hondas and Ducatis to the engine-mounted units on the Yamaha. Advances in shock absorber technology have led to smaller units and will, in the long-term, lead to further advances in shock placement.

Before the advent of MotoGP, 500 GP racing had been almost in stasis for the previous ten years. Little or no real changes had occurred to spur technological development. All that changed, however, when four-stroke MotoGP started. Ohlins, at least, had started towards a different front fork design – their first gas fork was being tested by their own in-house test team as far back as 1998. Yamaha used a prototype set in the 8-Hour race at Suzuka in 2000, but it wasn't until 2002 that Yamaha was sufficiently convinced of the design's advantages to fit them full-time on the Grand Prix machinery. That decision coincided with the start of MotoGP. Ohlins' gas forks were, at the start of 2002, the most advanced suspension unit on the front of any conventionally forked motorcycle.

There are only two suspension suppliers currently on pit lane, Ohlins and Showa. Showa are fitted to all the Honda works and customer bikes, and Ohlins are fitted to all the rest. The Ohlins story is a little complicated in that they are owned by Yamaha, and since Valentino Rossi joined the team, Yamaha has had slightly different suspension from the rest of the Ohlins runners. This, undoubtedly, was intended to help Yamaha win the MotoGP championship on their 50th anniversary, but it also gives them a small psychological, if not technological, advantage over the other teams.

During the first years of MotoGP, the experimentation was with different diameter forks. Ohlins produced 42mm, 46mm and 50mm forks as a stab in the dark to see how teams and riders reacted to fundamentally different stiffness rates, rather than any specific idea that a particular fork size would be a good idea. The 50mm forks, in particular, were an experiment to find the limits of the need for fork stiffness. Yamaha tried them but, because they did not feel any immediate race-winning advantage, they did not get

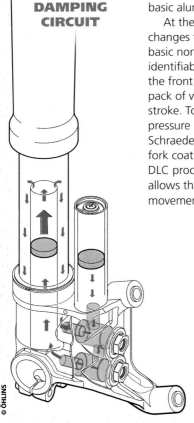

COMPRESSION DAMPING CIRCUIT

© ÖHLINS

REBOUND DAMPING CIRCUIT

© ÖHLINS

substantial testing. Ohlins were quite aware of the downsides implicit in the design – restricted air to the radiator, increased drag and the sheer bulk of the fork around the steering head, but it seemed on the Yamaha chassis that it had no other advantages to offset these downsides.

Ducati had different problems, however. Their steel-tube chassis design was not as rigid as the riders seemed to want. Ducati tested the 50mm forks before the Brno GP in 2003, and the riders found that the combination of the very stiff forks and the slightly weaker steel-tube chassis gave an overall flexibility they found comforting. The downsides to the design remained, and it was noticeable that, from the moment that Ducati fitted 50mm forks, they failed to get to the top of the top speed charts in each GP – something that up to then they'd managed to do since they arrived in the class earlier that year.

While Ducati was experimenting with the 50mm Ohlins gas forks, Aprilia were using carbon-fibre outer tube 42mm forks – their experience from 250s had shown them that they could get most of the rigidity increase they needed once the forks were compressed by simply changing material from the aluminium outer tube to the carbon-fibre versions. The 2004 Ducati also used carbon-fibre outer tube 42mm forks, with Capirossi using them all the time, but Checa, then his team-mate, preferring the more basic aluminium versions.

At the same time, Showa were making changes too. The early fork on the RC211V was a basic non-pressurised 47mm fork, easily identifiable by the compression stack holder on the front of the fork leg. This would contain the pack of washers that control the compression stroke. To ensure that both fork legs had the same pressure in them each side the forks had Schraeder valves situated in the fork caps. The fork coating on the sliders used the sophisticated DLC process; black in colour, this is very hard and allows the fork to respond very well to small movements. The design of the Showa fork wasn't

This is the oil circuitry in a TTx20 fork. It is based on a simple 'twin tube' design. The oil is literally forced to move from one side of a piston to the other via passageways around the piston. Two sets of combined check valves and shim stacks, one governing compression, and one rebound, restrict these passages. As the system is sealed, the oil displaced by the rod (not shown) that pushes the main piston in the fork leg up and down finds its way into the small reservoir, to ensure it flows out easily. This reservoir is pressurised at 6 bar.

in any way revolutionary, but it was clearly an extremely high-quality conventional outer upper-tube fork design.

By 2004, both Ohlins and Showa were ready to raise the stakes in the technology game. On the works Yamahas, Ohlins quietly debuted their TT25 front fork, which was a derivation of technology used for some time on their TT44 rear shock. The TT means Twin Tube and refers to a damping system that is almost a constant volume system. Not unlike a steering damper in concept, the piston in the middle of the shock absorber moves oil through two adjustable bleed valves into small orifices down the length of the tube wall from one side of the piston to the other. Because the design does not use high gas pressures, stiction from seals being forced hard against shafts by gas pressure is much reduced, and the fork's ability to follow small ripples in a surface is much improved. The TT bleed valves had much improved adjustment capabilities. Instead of the usual adjusters, with tapered needles into fixed diameter holes (a system that gives different degrees of adjustment depending on where you are in the stroke of the adjuster), these give a more precise and predictable adjustment for every click of the adjuster.

Down at Honda, Showa also revised their fork in 2004, and small external architectural changes in the fork were obvious, with the compression stack holder moved around the fork and inserted through the caliper mount. Showa insist that this was as much to lower crash damage as for any technical gain, but it would seem to improve the aerodynamics slightly, with a smooth mudguard replacing the old reservoir on the front. The top of the fork was also revised, and the air valves were dispensed with. Fork diameter remained unchanged during this redesign.

By 2005, Ohlins were at it again. Secretly tested by Rossi at Valencia at the end of 2004, the new forks were called TTx25TR (the designation means twin-tube, experimental, 25mm piston, through-rod). This is a 'through shock' design. With this the shock absorber rod passes right through the shock absorber unit in the centre of the fork. The damping is provided by shim stacks placed in the passageway that routes the oil from one side of the solid piston to the other. By routing all the oil through the twin walls of the shock, Ohlins have a constant volume of oil and a damping action that is both far more accurate and much quicker reacting, as the oil is both pushed and pulled through the damping orifices. The same basic design was built into the rear shock version of the design tested on Rossi's Yamaha M1 after Le Mans. That's why you can't see a big gas reservoir on Rossi's TTx40TR rear damper. Edwards tested the new design in practice at Mugello that year, with both factory riders switching over full time at Mugello.

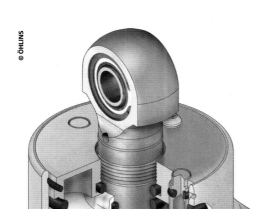

© ÖHLINS

LEFT: An Ohlins TTx shock using a similar internal design as the TTx36 shocks used by Kawasaki, Suzuki and Ducati in 2006. Again, in a simple twin tube design oil is forced from one side of a solid piston to the other via passageways in the outer tube. The effect is to both simultaneously push and pull oil through the various passages and valves.

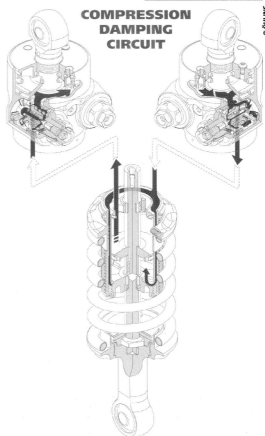

© ÖHLINS

COMPRESSION DAMPING CIRCUIT

TOP RIGHT: Compression damping circuitry shows the flow of oil up through the valving and shim stack and then around to the other side of the solid piston.

RIGHT: Rebound damping circuitry is simply the opposite to the compression side, but when the oil comes from the opposite direction the compression check valve remains shut and the oil is routed through the rebound valve and its shim stack.

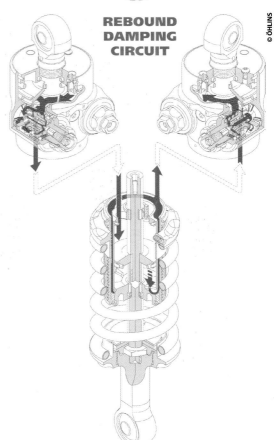

© ÖHLINS

REBOUND DAMPING CIRCUIT

RIGHT: For speed of suspension adjustment, Showa have spring changing vices on each side of the Repsol Honda Garage.

BELOW RIGHT: Showa forks are individually numbered. These are on a Repsol Honda and are the later type with the compression stack set into the rear of the caliper mount.

LEFT: Rossi's Yamaha is being given a quick increase in oil level towards the end of a session. This raises the effective spring rate in the last few millimetres of fork travel, helping to prevent bottoming.

OHLINS' CUSTOMER TT SUSPENSION

Both the new customer forks and the new customer shocks operate on the same basis as the current (2005/6) works TTx25TR forks and TTx40TR shocks used first in 2005 by Rossi, but have a simplified design. The shock absorbers are also physically a lot smaller and almost half a kilo lighter. As far as the rider is concerned, it is in the quality of the damping action where there is an improvement. The actual damping curves of any of the old TT44 shocks, the Works TTx40TR and the new 'customer' TTx36 shock will look very similar, but the speed of damping reaction will be much faster with the newer designs.

With the new customer shocks, Ohlins have taken the opportunity to shrink the whole shock absorber package. In MotoGP, smaller is better, and with the new 800cc category coming, being small is only going to get more important. A shock 50mm (2in) shorter allows the whole rear section of a bike to be redesigned with a lower section of swing-arm and more room for fuel and exhausts (on V-engines).

Unlike the TTx40TR works Yamaha items, the new TTx36 is not a true 'through-shock' but it uses the same damping technology in a design that has a damper rod that stops at the piston. To accommodate the extra oil displaced by the rod, there is a small reservoir at the top of the shock.

The circuits remain very simple, with oil simultaneously pushed out by the piston coming through the shock and the damping control circuit, and then being sucked in behind it. This results in a very immediate damping response.

The size of any shock absorber is rather governed by the size of its spring. Ohlins has now fitted smaller 50mm shock springs, replacing the previous 56mm ones. These springs are also shorter, typically around 130mm long rather than the old 150mm to 160mm ones fitted to most bikes. The whole shock is shorter, though the first ones being used in 2006 have 50mm, or thereabouts, extensions so they will fit the current mountings.

To make a smaller diameter and shorter spring provide the same quality of suspension as before, Ohlins has turned to springs made from cold drawn steel. This material is more expensive, but it allows the spring designer to reduce both size and weight by providing the same springing action in a smaller package. The weight of the new small steel springs is very similar to the much more expensive normally-sized titanium ones used by Yamaha for the last few years. Similar designs were first used in Indycars about 17 years ago, but it has taken a while for the technology to get to bikes.

In 2006, all the Ohlins 'non-Yamaha'

LEFT: A set of TTx25TR Ohlins forks on a Fortuna Yamaha in 2005. Because of their internal 'through rod' design, these forks did not require a gas reservoir.

BELOW: A works Yamaha TTx40TR rear shock. The minimal reservoir is only there to deal with oil expansion due to heat.

INSET: A customer-spec TTx36 shock showing the different construction and reservoir size. In this design some oil is displaced because the shock rod does not go right through the shock.

customers used these units, and all did so with up to 50mm extensions added to the end eyes. On the 800s for 2007, the whole shock absorber packaging will be very different, with the extended eyes removed, and the frame around the shock brought closer in.

BRAKES

How to stop a 200mph projectile, and its rider

MotoGP is unique in motorcycle racing because it is the only class that is allowed to run brakes other than 'standard' steel items. As a result, in the dry, the bikes are equipped with carbon discs which are substantially lighter than their steel counterparts, but they are not without their foibles.

Disc brakes took over from drum brakes in the late '70s – they were lighter, easier to cool and, most important, they were much more progressive. Some aspects of disc brake technology took a while to sort out, but the technology is now quite mature. Cast iron was initially found to have the best properties for good braking, but the discs rusted badly, and on road bikes the cast iron was first replaced by stainless steel. Early versions of these steel discs didn't work very well in the wet, and it took several years to develop a combination of the right specification steel and the right type and material of pad to give reliable, progressive braking in both the wet and the dry.

Most road race motorcycles now use a special austenitic steel. In operation it combines most of the best attributes of the old cast iron and stainless steel discs. Meanwhile, considerable development work continues to be done on the various forms of sintered material in the pads. These brakes are very powerful, and it is no longer the size of the brake, or the amount of braking that is available, that is the limiting factor on a racing motorcycle. Front tyre grip is now so good that, with the height of the centre of gravity and the quality of the front tyre and suspension, with most brakes it is possible to flip the bike over in a giant stoppie if too much brake is applied. As a result, the focus has moved from simply improving the amount of braking to getting the right quality and feel, then to eliminating as much as possible the side effects caused by having a pair of large steel discs added to the unsprung weight at the front of the motorcycle.

You will remember, from the chapter on crankshaft rotation, how gyroscopic effects influence the stability of a motorcycle, and you will also remember that a race bike with too much stability is as unsatisfactory as one with too little. The two steel discs add substantially to the gyroscopic effect. With its carrier, a steel disc weighs about 1.7kg, so two attached to the front wheel amount to a not inconsiderable 3.4kg. The discs are now nearly 320mm in diameter, so the weight is distributed in the worst possible place, out towards the rim. To try to reduce the stability,

© YAMAHA

To get extra grip when braking, the tyres are designed to flatten out as the bikes weight transfers forwards. This increases the size of the contact patch and hence the amount of braking force that can then be applied, and so on.

This strategy has been so successful that the limiting factor now is a motorcycle's propensity to trip over the front tyre, and flip over, if the brakes are applied too savagely. This 'hit the brakes hard then modulate them' grip strategy means that it is very difficult to use one of these bikes at anything less than full intensity.

The front discs therefore tend to be as large as can be accommodated within the currently most popular 16.5in rim. Yamaha use 320mm discs, but Honda have limited themselves to 314mm because they have a slightly different rim design that includes a small 3mm reinforcing ridge immediately outboard of the disc caliper, giving them a 6mm smaller wheel rim internal diameter. Both brakes are more than sufficient to stop the bikes. 16.5in rims have been standard equipment since early 2004 when the additional sidewall depth became Michelin's main front tyre design aim. Before that, wheel rim sizes had been 17in, and it had been quite easy to get the calipers onto the discs without dismounting the calipers every time the front wheel was pulled out. The advent of the 16.5in rim complicated the front wheel change procedure and, initially, it meant that the calipers had to be hauled off every time.

The strategy for the rear brake is not about pure stopping power, it's more to allow the rider to control the way the rear end behaves during corner entry. As soon as the front brakes are applied, most of the bike's weight is transferred to the front tyre – as much as 90%, in fact – with only 10% on the rear tyre. Only a very small amount of brake can be used before the rear end loses traction altogether. Most riders seem to use the very small brake at the rear to either start the bike stepping out going into a corner or to bring the back down slightly in order to stop it stepping out. These seemingly contradictory instructions merely depend upon when and how hard the rider uses the brake. Again, some riders find that using a foot actuated rear brake is the best, but a small minority prefer a thumb brake under the left handlebar. In any event, the very small amount of work that the small-diameter rear brake does makes it simpler for the team to fit a single steel disc that can stay wet or dry.

One of the issues dealt with in the last few years has been how the teams respond to changes in the weather during practice sessions. Each team obviously wants to give their riders as much time as possible on track, and, with each GP allowing a maximum of only 4 hours and 20 minutes of practice, that time is very precious. And once that time is up, whatever set-up is on the bike is going to have to do for the race. As a result of this, the teams have put a lot of effort has gone into making the wheels, tyres and brakes easy to change.

which will simply make the bike difficult to turn (especially at higher speeds), the chassis geometry is usually moved towards a more unstable position – the centre of gravity might be slightly higher, the fork angle slightly steeper or the trail slightly reduced. The problem is that all of these changes have other side effects that may not help the bike be as fast as it could be around the rest of the track. The solution, then, is to try to find a way to make the brakes as light as possible yet still be capable of providing more than enough braking for the motorcycle.

And this is where carbon brakes come in. Carbon discs weigh 750g to 800g for the same diameter disc as the 1,200g steel discs (just the annular part). As brakes, they don't have to be any more efficient than steel ones, but what does matter is that they are much lighter and, more to the point, they are lighter out near the rim of the wheel.

In MotoGP, the work of the brakes has increased as the tyres have evolved. It used to be that tyre grip was the limiting factor, but now tyres have developed so much that the only way to achieve maximum braking is to slam the brakes on hard in order to squash the tyre hard against the track, effectively increasing the area in contact with the track and, in turn, increasing the amount of stopping force that can be applied.

Carbon discs, although they are very light, are quite temperature-sensitive. If the weather is dry but cold, special heat shrouds are fitted to help them maintain heat levels. The addition of water is a lot more serious – the carbon discs will not reach their operating temperature and, without that temperature, they simply don't work as brakes. The solution is to revert to old-fashioned normal steel discs if the conditions are deemed wet. If steel discs are fitted then different calipers are also required, both because they carry different brake pads and because the internal tolerances of the calipers are different (to accommodate the thicker carbon discs and their higher heat capacity).

There's a need to be able to change discs quickly, anyway, because the most efficient braking comes from a matched set of pads and discs. If a rider is testing different front tyres during a practice session, then it is quite common to see the discs being taken off the wheel that is coming out of the bike and being attached to the new wheel, with its new tyre, before a rider goes out again.

This need to change calipers, discs and caliper disc systems quickly has led to a whole new science in quick-change componentry around the front wheel. A recent innovation for GP has been the use of endurance-racing style dry breaks in

the brake lines. These small units allow the caliper to be dismounted and replaced with another, without the hydraulic fluid having to be released or bled. It is only in 2006 that these units have become common throughout the pit lane. Before that, most teams had replacement master cylinder, brake line and caliper sets ready to be bolted on should the need arise to change from carbon to steel discs during a session.

The discs also have to be quickly detachable. It used to be that most teams used a six-bolt fixing to hold the disc in place, but Yamaha have for many years only used three on their race bikes. Some teams, such as Kawasaki, have changed

ABOVE: Carbon discs only operate well in a certain temperature band. If the air is too cold then these shrouds are added to maintain temperature.

BELOW: The calipers for carbon discs have slightly different internal specifications to cope with the heat. To help the team swap over to the right calipers and pads for steel discs, 'dry breaks' are used, which allow the caliper to be unplugged without any fluid leakage.

over the years, with three of their six mounting bolts now replaced by thread pins, so that the disc has six locating points, but only three actually bolting the disc to the wheel. Honda have always stayed with a five-bolt system for their discs, and they have been one of the last to adopt dry breaks in the brake lines.

Being fussy on the number of bolts holding the front disc in place might seem a very small matter, but it can easily make a difference to the number of tyres a rider can try during a crowded practice session. Even with only three bolts holding a disc in place, it is not uncommon to see a rider waiting for mechanics to finish a wheel and disc change.

The benefit of the dry breaks in the front calipers is a bit more subtle, as it has a far lesser effect than the speed of front disc changes. At the start of 2005, Brembo issued a new caliper design with different (stiffer) materials and different cutaways on its top and back to help the teams change wheels without removing the caliper from the fork leg each time. This has helped speed-up changes, but was initially intended to help under the then-proposed rules of having pit stops to change wheels and tyres in the event of a race becoming wet. Before the season started, however, the rules were changed and the concept of an entire wet bike that the rider could climb onto, in the event of the weather changing, was brought in.

ABOVE: Carbon discs and their pads are kept as pairs. Every time the front wheel is swapped over, the brakes are swapped too. Ducati use a five-bolt mounting system.

BELOW: Kawasaki use six-bolt-hole discs, but three of the mounting holes have been converted to studs with just three bolts holding the disc on to the wheel.

CARBON – THE BEST DISC MATERIAL?

We know that the advantage of carbon brakes is that they are lighter, and we know they can work just as well as steel discs – in fact, within their optimum temperature range they can work better than steel discs. But we can't look upon carbon as a straight substitute for steel. Carbon discs are far more complex to make, they are not cheap and they are difficult to maintain – and there are some restrictions on where, and under what conditions, they will work best.

The discs used on bikes are made slightly differently from the ones on cars, and they operate at slightly lower temperatures. Carbon discs for bike racing are made from carbon-fibre blanks originally intended for the aerospace industry. Using a process called carbon vapour infiltration (CVI), the carbon-fibre blanks are cooked in a high-temperature oven for a period of between three and six months, during which the graphite (carbon) matrix is deposited on and around the fibres, creating a solid disc. It's pretty clear that keeping an oven going for this length of time, with just one batch of material in it, is not going to be a cheap process. This is, though, the most expensive part of making these discs. Once they are out of the oven, they are fairly easily machined using normal CNC machinery. After all this, the cost to the teams is around €3,500 per disc. They do last quite well, however, with each bike only needing six to eight for a season.

In operation, carbon brakes are quite temperature-sensitive in their current form, and are at their most efficient between 300°C and 600°C. Some work needs to be done by the rider on the warming-up lap to make sure that the discs are fully up to temperature for the first few corners. The peak temperature can get a lot higher than this on initial brake application. With a first hit on the brakes designed to squash the front tyre, it is possible to see temperature spikes of over 750°C at the disc surface. Regular, sustained temperatures in excess of 750°C, though, will actually damage the disc – the surface charring, just like charcoal.

At some circuits – particularly Donington and Motegi – the track includes a sequence of slow corners in quick succession, and this causes a problem with the standard type of carbon disc as there is insufficient distance from corner to corner in which to lose the heat created during braking. Normally, the airflow from the straights between each application is relied on to get temperatures back under control. Because, under such circumstances, the discs could start to overheat, brake manufacturers have developed high-mass versions which can sustain more heat. These are slightly heavier, and consequently impart a little bit more gyroscopic stability, thereby detracting to some extent the unsprung weight advantage that using carbon discs had given in the first place.

At the moment, all the discs used in MotoGP are produced by Brembo or Nissin, they are all made of carbon-carbon which is the lightest currently available material. There is one option which is possibly 80g heavier per disc, but which is not nearly so sensitive to high temperatures. Commonly called carbon ceramic discs, these are now becoming available on ultra-high-spec performance cars, such as Porsches and Ferraris, because of their lightness and ability to provide consistent braking at all temperatures. They are made slightly differently, with the carbon-carbon material being infused with silicon before the disc is put in the oven. An advantage of this method is that the materials take less time to 'resin char' in the oven. Different materials can also be used to tailor the braking performance and control the disc temperature.

ABOVE: To keep an eye on temperatures, heat sensitive paints are added to the edge of the discs. Each colour turns white at a different temperature.

RIGHT: For circuits where there isn't much opportunity for the brakes to cool between hard applications, special high-mass discs are used.

TYRES

There's far more to it
than rubber rings

Michelin have a very fine-tuned racing department. They have dedicated production facilities for the limited production runs special racing tyres need. Michelin developed a new method of building tyres a few years ago, and they haven't looked back since. Make no mistake, Michelin have ruled MotoGP since it started. They have the knowledge, the resources and the desire to win and stay winning. They regularly try new technologies – some we can see, like their annual test of 16in rears and now occasional tests of 16in fronts, and undoubtedly a lot of things we cannot see. The other tyre companies are starting to catch up, however.

At the start of MotoGP, Dunlop were slipping behind. Their last big GP win (and don't forget that they still completely rule the smaller classes) was at Donington when Simon Crafar took his 500 Yamaha past Mick Doohan and won, but that was back in 1998. Dunlop have suffered since then. Their MotoGP performance failed to keep up with Michelin and as Bridgestone came up to speed they provided the tyres for the smaller factories; Dunlop became the supplier to the privateer teams.

Bridgestone decided to come back into racing's top class back in 2000. After a year running a test team with Erv Kanemoto and Nobuatsu Aoki, with a Honda NSR500, they went racing, and the first time the tyres went onto four-strokes was in 2003 with Makoto Tamada. Tamada's time on Bridgestones saw a great improvement in their performance, culminating in a couple of wins. Progress was not without its problems, though, with Nakano in particular suffering a massive crash at Mugello when his rear tyre burst while he was going flat out past the pit lane.

Bridgestone came out with some superb qualifiers at the end of the 2004 season, and Ducati used them during closed season testing to set some particularly fast laps. Allowing those times to be published may well have backfired on both Ducati and Bridgestone, because it clearly stimulated Michelin to come up with some new ideas. Michelin completely dominated MotoGP in 2005 until the Motegi round. Bridgestone has been very successful in other motorsports, but it always takes a while to understand all the fine detail that makes your product good enough to get the good guys to use it. Bridgestone's capture of Ducati at the end of the 2004 season certainly gave them the opportunity to compete against Michelin at the highest level, but Ducati itself also needed an edge in order to match Honda and Yamaha.

By 2006, Dunlop had started to make progress. In MotoGP they have sponsored the Tech3 and D'Antin teams with works Yamahas and year-old Desmosedici bikes respectively. Michelin and Bridgestone were still the top dogs, though. New wider tyres took Michelin's grip levels up a stage, and Bridgestone countered with specially tailored tyres for each of their teams. It was rare for there to be three different Bridgestone runners at the top of practice or a race, but the factory seems to get their tyre specs right for at least one of Kawasaki, Suzuki or Ducati at each MotoGP.

PREPARATION

How the game is played

Tyre temperatures and pressures are monitored closely. Each time a bike comes in, the hot pressures are checked and the surface temperature from several different areas is recorded.

The tyre companies are very careful about accidentally giving away their technology. They will talk about their preparations, and they will talk about their problems, but never about the actual leading edge race technology.

Competition between tyre companies spreads well beyond the main manufacturers – there are their suppliers as well. All three major companies will be actively talking to their suppliers, looking for materials or compounds that would have the effects they are looking for on a racing tyre. More grip, more stability, better reaction to stress, more stickiness, and so on.

Each company has its own contracted suppliers, and the race is as much a competition between their entire technical supply chains as one on track. The types of polymers and fabrics that build a tyre for a specific purpose are unique to each factory, and that means you cannot just turn up and compete at the top level, even if you know the construction of your opponent's tyres.

Correct preparation means having a good knowledge of the type and condition of the track surface, how it is wearing and how it reacts with changes in temperature and weather. Bridgestone still don't think they have enough data to predict what the conditions might be at each racetrack before they go.

Moto Kezuka of Bridgestone: 'If we have a new track or a new surface, we will take moulds of the surface of the track so the factory has a record of it. It's not necessary to do that all the time, but it does make a difference if you know the texture when you are designing the tyre.

'The characteristic of the tarmac is different in Europe to what is used in Asia and used to be in Brazil. There are some places where we have caught up drastically. Brno is one where we have made some progress. Some places like Brno have a high Mu [Mu is a measure of friction], and a characteristic of our rubber is that it likes high Mu places. Somewhere like Catalunya we have had to go back to the drawing board. We don't change the main ways we make grip, but if we have something that isn't working we have to reconsider the design.

'We have three different teams. They all have different bikes, so they all need different tyres. Some chassis need different stabilities, and we can build a more stable tyre or a less stable tyre, it all depends on what the bike needs. We allocate a tyre engineer to each team and he has a great deal of say into what should be done for their team. But you really don't know how you are getting on until you have a really fast motorcycle with a really fast rider to test the tyres.'

Michelin, though, have years of data on the racetracks – but what they haven't got is a crystal ball to tell the future. Nicholas Goubert of Michelin:

'Three weeks before the GP, we have a first meeting, but no more than half of the decisions that we need to make are made. We have to consider the track and how it is changing, and how the bikes are changing. Also it is very important to consider the weather. These days that is very difficult, things are changing much more now. After the previous GP, using the best knowledge we have, we decide the other 50% of the things we need to make the tyres.

'The best thing for us is to test before the GP. We still don't know the weather, but you would know enough ten days before to make the best solution for the race meeting. Without the testing we have to gamble on the outcome a lot more.

'The Yamahas and Hondas we have are very similar for tyres, the biggest difference being the riding style. In 2005, only two riders complained about the front, Alex and Nicky, but Max didn't have a problem.'

The location of the three company's factories makes a difference too. Michelin, with its main production facilities in Clermont Ferrand, is in a position to supply additional tyres to any of the circuits in Europe over the race weekend. Sometimes tailor-made tyres are produced during the weekend. Nicholas Goubert again: 'At Valencia last year, we made tyres on the Friday evening from the data taken at the first session. The tyres we had, had three compounds, and we noticed that our choices were working better on one part of the tyre than on another. Another tyre built had other compounds on it, so with this knowledge it was easy to make a tyre that had the best aspects of both, because we knew what had worked we didn't need to test so much. The riders have other issues to deal with. It is not normal for us to do this.'

Dunlop, too, have a lot of information on the tracks. It's just that their technology had fallen behind Michelin. They are getting better, but it will be a while before the top teams would take the risk of running Dunlops; which is frustrating for Dunlop. The teams they have worked with have seen improvements, though, but not as much of an improvement as could have been achieved with more bikes. 'We simply don't have the volume of information we would have if we had half a dozen bikes. In Superbike we run the same stuff we do here, the compounds may be a little different because the races are a bit shorter,' said Jeremy Ferguson.

Dunlop's aim, though, is to deliver the same performance as their opponents. 'The idea is to have the minimum amount of drop-off from the beginning of the race to the end of the race. When you see people setting a lap record on the last lap of the race, then they have done the work on the tyres very well.'

By the middle of 2006, all the manufacturers had test teams. Bridgestone were clearly the most serious with Shinichi Ito and an entire Ducati Corse test team arriving at GP circuits a couple of weeks before each GP to try to find the best compounds and constructions. Michelin had their special operation with Yamaha to try to sort the chatter problem, and Dunlop were also using Sebastian Guintoli, a 250 rider, on one of their M1s to increase the number of tyres they could test at each test session.

This has caused a rapid increase in costs, which each factory wants to control but without affecting what they consider their competitive advantage. By the end of 2006, new rules were in place to try to limit costs. Proposals included a limit on the number of tyres available to each team for each weekend, a restriction on test teams and a requirement that all the tyres to be used at a race event be 'on circuit' by a Thursday afternoon deadline.

Each tyre is balanced and tested for runout by lasers after being fitted to the rim.

Balancing is dynamic and computerised. The old days of marking the light spot with chalk and simply adding lead are long gone.

TYPES OF TYRE

Correct tyre choice is essential, but with so many options it's easy to get it wrong

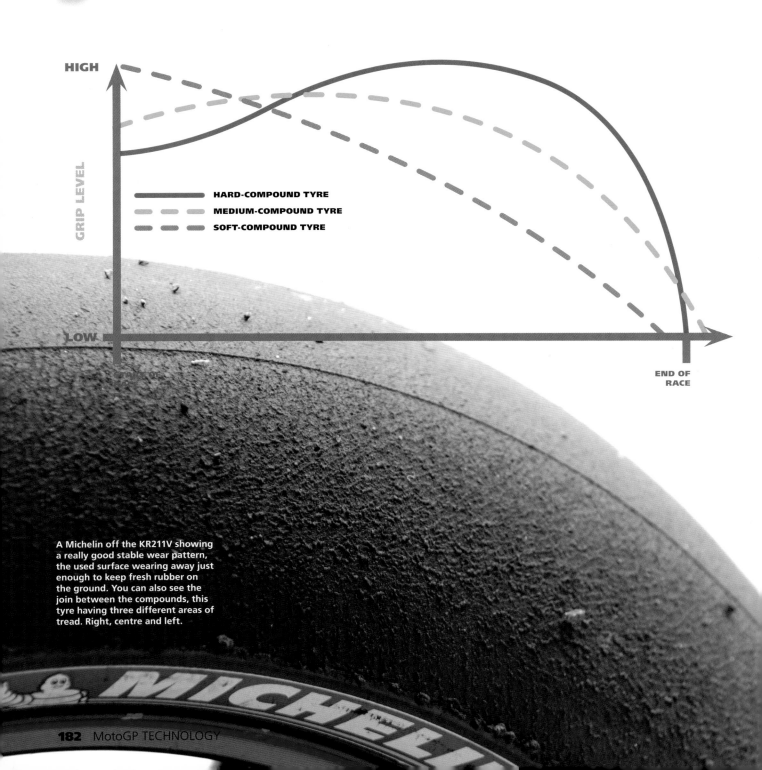

GRIP LEVEL

HIGH

LOW

——— HARD-COMPOUND TYRE

– – – MEDIUM-COMPOUND TYRE

– – – SOFT-COMPOUND TYRE

END OF
RACE

A Michelin off the KR211V showing
a really good stable wear pattern,
the used surface wearing away just
enough to keep fresh rubber on
the ground. You can also see the
join between the compounds, this
tyre having three different areas of
tread. Right, centre and left.

SLICKS

No tread – just rubber. Designed to be used in dry conditions, these can have several different compounds over their footprint. There are as many different compounds as there are chemicals in the factory.

Michelin, in particular, like to make their race-day tyres once they have seen how their initial efforts have faired during Friday's practices. Qualifying tyres are designed to last only two laps, one warm up lap and one at full speed. Once the fast lap is done, so are they.

CUT SLICKS

A few grooves hand-cut into a slick to allow the rubber to move around a little more. It speeds up the generation of heat in the carcase and is typically seen on cold mornings or on circuits where there is one particularly important corner that requires the bike to lean over the opposite way to the rest.

INTERMEDIATES

Partially treaded tyres. These can be created by hand by cutting grooves into a slick, or they can be moulded specially. With each manufacturer running at least four bikes, we are seeing more moulded tyres as the specialist cannot hand-cut enough between sessions to supply all the bikes.

WETS

Treaded tyres. These are designed to shift water out of the way, and fast. Using very soft rubber, they rely on the water to cool them and stop them overheating. They still grip by going soft through heat, so the rider has to ride as fast as possible to get them to work.

TYRE WARMERS

These small electric blankets get the tyres up to their operating temperature prior to the rider going out. Different temperature range heaters are used for wet and slick type tyres.

AERODYNAMICS

Shaping a 200mph torpedo

Aerodynamics are important in trying to go fast, and several times in the history of motorcycling they have been the principal part of the package – remember the 'dustbin' fairings of the mid-1950s and the Norton Commando monocoque in the early-1970s? Even now, full streamlining is still the way to go for top speeds. But one aspect that isn't often considered is the internal airflow, and this becomes ever more important as speeds increase. Through the sheer power of the bikes, we are now seeing 340kph-plus, and all the possible effects need to be managed very carefully.

The four-strokes develop serious amounts of power, and serious amounts of heat to go with it. One solution is to design the engine and radiator to work at higher temperatures. Pressurising the cooling system lets you run at higher temperatures, and if you don't need to cool the engine so much, you can get away with less radiator, and if the radiator is hotter it transfers heat to the passing air more efficiently.

The difficulty is getting any air, hot or cold, past the engine or through the bike. Across-the-frame four-cylinder engines do a good job of blocking airflow behind the radiator, and the long front engine mounts, so necessary for getting corner grip, use the same space as the radiator exhaust ducts.

RIGHT: The long front engine mounts occupy the same space as the radiator exhaust ducts, as shown on this Team Roberts bike with part of the fairing removed.

BASIC THEORY

How to make a motorcycle slippery

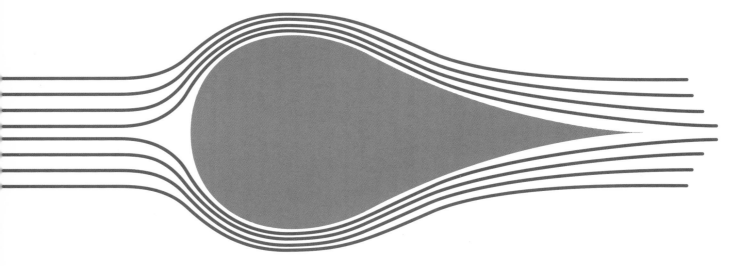

The shape with the best aerodynamic efficiency is the teardrop; it is far more important to close the air behind you than to split it correctly. The difficulty is that a motorcycle isn't long enough to bring the airflows back together smoothly, so we have to make do.

For true aerodynamic efficiency, the perfect shape is a longish teardrop. The narrower the teardrop the less air that has to be displaced in the first place, and the long gently-tapering tail keeps the airflow 'attached' to the sides for as long as possible to minimise any drag-inducing wake.

In motorcycle racing the use of aerodynamic aids – let's call them fairings – is restricted under the rules; they cannot be too long, they cannot cover the wheels and they cannot cover the rider. The smaller the front fairing is, the less air has to be pushed out of the way in the first place, but it does make sense to make the fairing big enough to flow the air smoothly round the rider.

Keeping the flow attached and minimising the wake at the back of the bike is very important, but the rules say the fairing cannot be longer than the back of the rear wheel, which is usually too short for a proper teardrop shape. By making the seat the same width as the rider's backside, and tapering it in gently to a cut-off tail, there's a chance of minimising the wake; but, for practical purposes, most seat tails add very little to the overall aerodynamic package. However, putting the seat in the right place, and at the right height, enables the rider to sit with a very flat back – and that does make a difference. Tests have shown that a rider who can hold a very flat

back can cut the levels of drag quite effectively. This is one area where a taller rider can get better performance than a shorter rider, and it is why you see special seat pads to allow the rider to hold his backside up a little on the straights.

In MotoGP you can see all the teams using aerodynamic aids to a greater or lesser degree. The first RC211V came with minimal fairing designed to allow the motorcycle to turn easily from side to side. Historically, bikes that have very efficient straight-line aerodynamics are prone to be adversely affected by crosswinds and angled airflows. Honda calculated that they had more than enough power to achieve their speed targets, so they designed a fairing that prioritised the ability to turn quickly into corners. The original fairing was so minimal that Rossi had to get it increased in size just to take some of the wind pressure off his shoulders and head.

Once Ducati's speed became more of a threat, Honda morphed their fairing into something slightly better for straight-line efficiency. Changes were being made to Pedrosa's and Hayden's fairings as late as the Catalunya race in 2006.

Ducati's response was to tailor make top cowlings for each rider – last winter putting each rider on the bike in the wind tunnel in the search for the best shape on the edge of each bike's windscreen.

© HONDA

ABOVE: Bikes are wind tunnel tested, with riders on board. It's important to find the best way of attaching the flow to the rider as much as possible, a rider with a longer flatter back will be significantly more aerodynamic than a short rider whose back curves; it's one of the few times in motorcycling where bigger is better.

BELOW: The peak air pressure is right on the nose of the bike; so that's where you put your air inlet if you can. However, this does mean that air has to be taken through or under the steering head to the airbox. To stop it becoming an air dam, the radiator needs to be encouraged to pass air through, so efficient radiator exhaust ducts are needed.

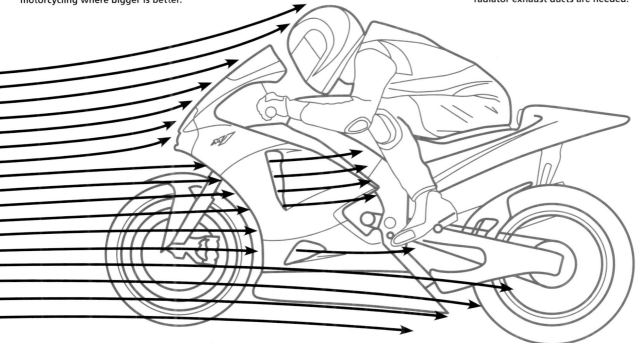

Steering air to minimise drag
and maximise cooling

THE DUCATI EXPERIENCE

Ducati have tried hardest to make their bike aerodynamically effective in a straight line, and they went the wind-tunnel route very early on in their GP project. The initial bike had no radiator exhaust ports in the side of the fairing, and only a simple single air intake at the bottom of the nose. This was done to keep the shapes and sides as clean and slippery as possible – the hot air was supposed to simply flow past the engine and out of the rear of the bike.

Early in testing, in response to some fairly serious problems with heat build-up, Ducati fitted a small radiator exhaust duct to the side of the fairing. The bike still had a reputation for heating everything up, including the rider, and halfway through the 2003 season at Brno a larger fairing radiator exhaust duct was added, along with a pair of additional 'rider-cooling' ducts on the cowling top. But, although this worked, the extra drag created by the additional ducting, along with larger 50mm-diameter forks, kept the bike off the top of the top-speed charts until the last round at Valencia.

At first glance, it appeared that the Ducati bodywork for 2004 was very similar to that fitted at the start of 2003. Closer inspection, however, showed a much larger fairing intake for the radiator, with a redesigned, and now much more aerodynamically efficient, front mudguard, along with a new, smaller but stronger, 42mm-diameter Ohlins fork. Getting the air to the radiator is the easy bit, though. Once there, the air needs to go through, and it will only do so if it has somewhere to go. So the bike was given much larger fairing side radiator exhaust ports. With the new arrangement capable of properly cooling the engine, the bike no longer needed the high drag 'rider cooling ducts'.

But there is a lot more to it than just simple cooling. There is lift. We are all used to hearing designers and manufacturers talk about mass centralisation. Any vehicle has a point which is its centre of mass – on a bike this is typically somewhere below the rider and near the front of his seat. A bike also has a centre of pressure – a point, depending upon the design of the fairing and the positioning of things like the rider's head, shoulders and forearms, where the air-pressure forces act. This is not the point of highest pressure, but the point where all the pressures over the bike's front have their centre – in exactly the same way as a bike's centre of gravity is the middle of all its weight rather than the heaviest bit.

Now, picture the bike from the front and imagine what is going to happen if the centre of the pressure on the front of the bike is above that bike's centre of gravity – and it usually is! The answer is that the bike wants to rotate upwards and backwards; it unloads the front suspension and gives a much lighter feeling to the steering. You will notice it at higher speeds; you'll feel some on a street bike in excess of 130mph. It's not much of a problem in a straight line, but any lift occurring in the really fast corners gives a very strange feeling indeed.

Ducati have Alan Jenkins to help them. Jenkins has been one of the top design engineers in Formula 1 and Indycar over the past 25 years and has had a lot of experience of vehicular aerodynamic design, pretty much all during the time it has been considered a science. Jenkins was reluctant to be drawn too much on the specifics – MotoGP is, after all, a very competitive sport – but he did run through some of the reasons for the Ducati's design.

'Obviously, we needed to check the bike in a wind tunnel – without that we would be just guessing – and we need to use the same tunnel all the time. You just can't get the consistency of approach when you use different ones. You need to see the differences; sometimes it's too subtle to measure. And we need a big tunnel – a bike is far too complicated and the shape and weight of the rider is far too important to use a 40% scale model properly. At the moment we just test straight ahead. We do yaw, but no leaning over. We did try that, but it's just too complicated – you look at the results and think, 'oo-er, we need to just go away and think about that'. The changes we have made are probably just a mid-level stage to where we want to go. It's not easy. Take the subject of lift – if the rider sat up at 200mph-plus there would be enough lift, I imagine, to get his attention. You really, really wouldn't want to do that.

'You have to imagine, we have this big chunk of air trying to get past the front forks, wheel and calipers, but once it does there is probably still far too much coming through for the radiator to deal with effectively at maximum speed. The radiator becomes effectively solid if you haven't got anything behind it to get the air out again. Now, lift is also an issue. It probably doesn't matter to the rider until fairly high speeds, 240-250kph. Then it is something you have to think about, although the one thing we didn't really expect is that riders would get so comfortable with the front wheel off the ground as much as it has been!

'We improved the bike a lot for 2004, and for 2005 the new cowling tailors the aerodynamics to each rider. The testing was done in England in the middle of winter, so the riders had to put up with a fair degree of windchill. You get pretty cold sitting in an 80mph wind for hours in the middle of an English December, and the riders never seem to bring any thermal clothing!'

'OBVIOUSLY, WE NEEDED TO CHECK THE BIKE IN A WIND TUNNEL – WITHOUT THAT WE WOULD BE JUST GUESSING – AND WE NEED TO USE THE SAME TUNNEL ALL THE TIME. YOU JUST CAN'T GET THE CONSISTENCY OF APPROACH WHEN YOU USE DIFFERENT ONES…'
ALAN JENKINS

LEFT: Ex Formula One aerodynamicist Alan Jenkins was responsible for the design of the Ducati Desmosedici's bodywork, seen here at Brno in 2005 giving the 2006 fuel tank design an initial outing.

BELOW: The initial Desmosedici had no radiator exhaust ducts, reflecting the design of the then current 998R superbike. The additional heat shed by the Desmosedici motor unfortunately proved very uncomfortable for the riders.

BOTTOM: The exhaust duct expanded in several stages over the next year.

© DUCATI CORSE

CUSTOMER FAIRING

The standard customer fairing is modified for the top HRC riders. Pedrosa got a special front cowling to improve his aerodynamics at the 2006 Catalunya GP; later he also got a hybrid fairing mimicking the 'New Generation' fairing's lower sections.

NEW GENERATION FAIRING

The New Generation fairing on Nicky Hayden's 2006 bike offers the same frontal air resistance as the standard customer fairing. However a 10% reduction in side area has improved the yaw characteristics to aid handling.

underneath. In order to give Rossi the frame flex he wanted, they fitted long front engine mounts, but unfortunately these took up some of the room previously used to get air out from behind the radiator.

To cool the bike at the very hot Qatar round in 2004, they had to fit additional drag-inducing scoops to get more air through the radiator. The new parts included an angled duct over the small lower fairing, reshaped main fairing edges (with a sharper edge put on the fairing sides to drag more air into the radiator) and small spoilers put on the outside of the radiator exhaust ducts to create more negative pressure behind the radiator, so pulling the additional air though the radiator core. They thought they might need the same fairings for Malaysia, but they were removed after the first practice session.

While not the only reason for the change, the 2005 Yamaha engine was made as narrow as possible by using a new 'behind the block' cam gear drive system to get their long front spars closer to the centre of the bike. This, in turn, allows larger, more efficient air ducts outboard of the spars. Even then, small changes were tried where air management was thought to be a benefit. At Motegi, when Valentino was going for the championship, a small additional duct was added to one of his bikes to direct additional air

TOP RIGHT: The 2004 bike, seen here with is Qatar radiator duct extensions had a quite restricted Radiator exhaust duct thanks to the front engine mount extensions.

BOTTOM RIGHT: The 2005 and 2006 Yamaha fairings had substantially larger radiator exhaust ducts, made possible by the competely redesigned narrower engine.

HONDA

The RC211V was never designed to be particularly clean in an aerodynamic sense, since high manoeuvrability was initially considered to be much more important initially. But that's just as valid a strategy as making a slippery fairing, and requires no less aerodynamic skill. The main point about it, as a strategy, is the balance of wind protection for the rider (as opposed to smooth airflow) and minimising the bike's susceptibility to side winds. It's not a strategy that's been tried before – no motorcycle racing class has had enough surplus power to allow a non 'most efficient through the air forwards' fairing design before.

That's not to say that Honda didn't ever visit a wind tunnel. Many trips were made. It's one thing to have decided to make the fairing as helpful as possible to manoeuvring, and it's entirely another not to make the best use of what you have left.

YAMAHA

It's never been easy for Yamaha to keep their bike cool. An across-the-frame four-cylinder blocks off the airflow through the bike, so any modification that makes the situation worse really does complicate matters. In Yamaha's case they had mounted the engine at the cylinder head, leaving lots of room for a pair of air ducts

to the slipper clutch, a component that can get quite a lot of work at this very stop-start track.

TEAM ROBERTS

The same basic fairing design has served Kenny Roberts's team well for nearly four years, with three different power plants and innumerable different chassis setups.

The old five-cylinder engine wasn't the most powerful in the paddock but, with a lot of internal friction, it did manage to create a lot of heat. Even in cold weather the team had problems cooling the bike down. In Qatar and Malaysia, they were on their limit.

In 2005 they had the opposite situation – the KTM engine is so efficient it needs very little cooling at all. At the start of the year the bike even had its cooling ducts covered over. By the early summer meeting at Mugello the temperatures required a little more airflow.

The 2006 use of a Honda engine told a similar story – very little cooling required at low temperatures and more as the weather warmed. Roberts's unique use of adjustable-size radiator exhaust ducts makes this easy to see, but there must be a question as to whether this design allows enough air through the radiator to minimise lift with the higher top speeds produced by the Honda engine.

SUZUKI AND KAWASAKI

The two smaller Japanese factories share the honours for waiting the longest to get serious about the benefits of aerodynamics. Both factories had made basic overtures with logical improvements made to their bikes over several years. It wasn't until late 2005 and early 2006, respectively, that fairings looking like they had spent some time in a wind tunnel were used.

Both companies went for a similar solution (straight line efficiency and air intakes located right in the centre of the high pressure zone at the tip of the nose fairing) and they did so probably because they both had the same problem – lack of sufficient power on the straights. The large central intakes would make a difference, but these benefits have to be kept in perspective. High-speed air pressure alone might add 2bhp to 3bhp to an engine's output (worth having, yet nothing to write home about), but the correct design of the inlet duct, typically a divergent cone, could make a bigger difference as it slows the intake flows and converts the high-speed air to a slow-speed high-pressure flow.

Both companies also concentrated on smoothing their bikes' air penetration with new cowlings over the rider, and revised side fairing and radiators.

LEFT: Rossi's crew noticed from the datalogging that the wind at nearly 200mph was pushing on the lever and putting the brakes on – not good if top speed is your aim. This cutaway lever was introduced and quickly copied all through the pit lane.

BELOW: Suzuki's 2006 bike was new, but the fairings and air inlet positions had been trialled in the latter days of the 2005 season.

BOTTOM: Kawasaki brought new fairings for the ultra high speed straight of Mugello in 2006, the new bodywork was slimmer and slipperier; the new cowl had a bigger inlet and the side panels bigger radiator exhaust ducts.

ACKNOWLEDGEMENTS

Dedication

For Mum

I wouldn't have been in a MotoGP pit lane without the priceless education in motorcycle sport I have received over the years from a whole bunch of people.

In rough order of appearance then:

The editors of the now defunct *Cycle* magazine, who first added the 'why' question to my motorcycling vocabulary.

Gary Pinchin and Alan Cathcart. When I asked Gary, then editor of *RPM*, to write something about the Supermono class he didn't just say no; he told me to get on and write it myself. Alan, possibly after he had assessed my riding ability, helped me to organise a Supermono Cup series to support the World Superbike meetings held in Europe.

I met Charlie Hennekam and Steve Whitelock at the first Supermono Cup meeting. They brought with them a massive reservoir of organisational and technical knowledge; together we even ended up writing a 'rule book without any rules' for the free-thinking Supermonos.

By 1998 Supermono needed additional bikes and something newsworthy. I decided to race a rare Ducati Supermono with a selection of riders via my own race organisation Sigma Performance. Jonathan 'Corndog' Cornwell was the first rider. He was then Carl Fogarty's Ohlins engineer and also a multiple Canadian 250 and Dirt Track champion. He won at Daytona and my education in suspension was on its way.

Bruce Maus, an ex GP crewchief and mechanic (and as a rider a US national 250 race winner) came on board for the next race at Donington, and race team organisation, racecraft, tuning and setup from the pit lane standpoint went onto the curriculum. That year we had five different riders, and each one brought new challenges. Bruce runs Sigma's workshop still.

Over the next few years, as Sigma raced a selection of increasingly expensive Ducati's up to and including British Supersport, Duane Mitchell of Ultimap in Australia patiently answered every question I had on Ducati engine and fuel injection setup.

Once the racing was done, it was time to look at the underlying design of the bikes. I had met Pierre Terblanche of Ducati at an early Supermono Cup meeting. A shared interest in fast, light and slightly unconventional motorcycles meant that our paths crossed again. We have now been to, and critiqued, the contents of most of the decent Motorcycle museums in Europe. I guess we will have to start on the rest of the world soon, and I still haven't won a discussion!

And then I went to have a look at MotoGP. The sheer enthusiasm and professionalism of everyone in the paddock was stunning. It has been an absolute joy to watch the development of an entire class of bikes from their unruly beginnings through to the technically superb machines of 2006.

In particular I would like to thank Masao Furusawa of Yamaha, Satoru Horiike of Honda, Claudio Domenicali of Ducati, Ichiro Yoda of Kawasaki, Masahito Imada of Suzuki, Kenny Roberts of Team Roberts, Luigi Dall'Igna of Aprilia, Peter Clifford of WCM and Heinz Payreder of KTM for all their help in putting this book together.

This book would have also been impossible without Jerry Burgess and his crew, Pete Benson and the Louth brigade, Alan Jenkins, Beefy Bourguignon, Tom O'Kane, Stuart Shenton and last but definitely not least Chuck Aksland, Tom Jojic and Warren Willing. And then there is the rest of the MotoGP paddock...

To all of you, thank you.